CLANDESTINAS

CLANDE

CLANDESTINAS

WOMEN IN THE CUBAN REVOLUTIONARY UNDERGROUND, 1955–1959

CAROLLEE BENGELSDORF

With photographs curated by Susan Meiselas

DUKE UNIVERSITY PRESS / DURHAM AND LONDON / 2025

Printed in the United States of America on acid-free paper ∞
Project Editor: Liz Smith
Designed by Matthew Tauch
Typeset in Warnock Pro and Saira by Westchester Publishing Services

Library of Congress Cataloging-in-Publication Data
Names: Bengelsdorf, Carollee, author. | Meiselas, Susan, photographer.
Title: Clandestinas : women in the Cuban revolutionary underground,
1955–1959 / Carollee Bengelsdorf ; visual essay by Susan Meiselas.
Description: Durham : Duke University Press, 2025. | Includes
bibliographical references and index.
Identifiers: LCCN 2024060607 (print)
LCCN 2024060608 (ebook)
ISBN 9781478032199 (paperback)
ISBN 9781478028970 (hardcover)
ISBN 9781478061168 (ebook)
Subjects: LCSH: Women—Political activity—Cuba—History—
20th century. | Women revolutionaries—Cuba. | Cuba—History—
Revolution, 1959—Underground movements—Participation, Female.
Classification: LCC F1788 .B385 2025 (print) | LCC F1788 (ebook)
LC record available at https://lccn.loc.gov/2024060607
LC ebook record available at https://lccn.loc.gov/2024060608

Cover art: Clandestinas detained at the Cárcel de Mantilla.

FOR MIRTA, NILDA, AND CARMEN, for their belief in possibility and their courage in always striving to realize this.

AND FOR ROBERTO, for almost everything.

CONTENTS

ABBREVIATIONS

AAA/TRIPLE A	Auténtico Party Armed Action (Acción Armada Auténtica)
ACRC	Association of Combatants of the Cuban Revolution (Asociación de Combatientes de la Revolución Cubana)
ANR	National Revolutionary Action (Acción Nacional Revolucionaria)
ARG	Guiteras Revolutionary Action (Acción Revolucionaria Guiteras)
ARO	Orient Revolutionary Action (Acción Revolucionaria Oriental)
BRAC	Bureau for the Repression of Communist Activities (Buró para la Represión de Actividades Comunistas)
OCCC	Zero Cabaret, Zero Cinema, Zero Shopping (Cero Cabaret, Cero Cine, Cero Compra)
CIA	Central Intelligence Agency
DEU	Directorate of University Students (Directorio Estudiantil Universitario)
DR	Revolutionary Directorate (Directorio Revolucionario)
FCMM	José Martí Women's Civic Front (Frente Cívico de Mujeres Martianas)
FDMC	Democratic Federation of Cuban Women (Federación Democrática de Mujeres Cubanas)
FEN	National Students' Front (Frente Estudiantil Nacional)
FEU	Federation of University Students (Federación Estudiantil Universitaria)
FMC	Federation of Cuban Women (Federacion de Mujeres Cubanas)
FMLN	Farabundo Martí National Liberation Front (Frente Nacional de Liberación Farabundo Martí)
FON	National Workers Front (Frente Obrero Nacional)
FSLN	Sandista National Liberation Front (Frente Sandinista de Liberación Nacional)

ICAP	Cuban Institute for Friendship with the Peoples (Instituto Cubano de Amistad con los Pueblos)
ICRT	Institute of Cuban Television and Radio (Instituto Cubano de Radio y Televisión)
INAV	National Institute of Savings and Housing (Instituto Nacional de Ahorro y Vivienda)
MNR	National Civic Resistance Movement (Movimiento Nacional de Resistencia Cívica)
MOU	Opposition Women United (Mujeres Oposicionistas Unidas)
MRC	Movement of Civic Resistance (Movimiento de Resistencia Cívica)
OA	Authentic Organization (Organización Auténtica)
ORI	Integrated Revolutionary Organization (Organización Revolucionaria Integrada)
OSPAAL	Organization of Solidarity with the Peoples of Asia, Africa and Latin America (Organización de Solidaridad con los Pueblos de Asia, África y América Latina)
PSP	Popular Socialist Party (Partido Socialista Popular), formerly Cuban Communist Party
SIM	Military Intelligence Service (Servicio de Inteligencia Militar)
SIN	Naval Intelligence Service (Servicio de Inteligencia Naval)

ACKNOWLEDGMENTS

I first went to Cuba in June 1969 with the Committee of Returned Volunteers, former Peace Corps members who opposed the war in Vietnam. At the Cuban Mission to the United Nations (UN) in New York, we had been told that we would travel through Mexico City and, after six weeks on the island, return via Algiers. This seemed something of a strange itinerary but then Cuban relations with the world at large were equally weird. In Havana the Cuban officials who greeted us on our arrival literally guffawed when we mentioned planes to Algiers. This was not apparently in our future after all. Rather, we would wait for a boat to Canada. And wait we did: for three and a half months. First we spent two weeks traveling around the island doing harm to various crops (I am from the Bronx, which is not known for the agricultural prowess of its inhabitants). Then we spent a third week on the Isle of Pines (renamed the Isle of Youth in 1976) living in a campamento with a group of very engaging and friendly teenagers, who we had been told were juvenile delinquents. The grapefruit we planted together blew away in a hurricane the next month. When we returned to Havana our Cuban guardians, seemingly bored with us, left us free to do whatever and go wherever we wished to, which we did. It was a time of crisis in Cuba, although the word may seem somewhat overused in the context of the island. The Cuban leadership had launched the country's heresy, challenging the established orthodox path to the "achievement of socialism and communism." Posters across the island stated "We will create wealth with consciousness and not consciousness with wealth," which no one seemed to understand, but the effects became all too clear. In 1968 whatever remained of private enterprise down to the small corner stores was nationalized, but by all appearances no one seemed to have given much thought to alternate means of distribution. And this was accompanied in 1969–70 by a year-long effort involving the entire population in producing ten million tons of sugar, a goal that everyone who was familiar with sugar production knew was impossible. Except Fidel. He was wrong as it turned out.

The last thing Cubans whom we met while wandering the streets of Havana guessed was that we were from the United States. We were strange animals who had not been around for quite a while. But that did not stop them and indeed actually encouraged them in typical Cuban fashion to invite us into their homes for coffee, although since there was no coffee this was usually an odd mixture of ground chicharos (yellow peas) and a grain or two of the real stuff. In the course of these visits, I began to fixate on the manner in which women moved through their environments and to hypothesize about the ways in which the revolution had changed or not changed this. And I decided that hypothesizing would not do: It required that I investigate.

But life, as is its wont, got in my way. Over the years I scribbled a few articles dealing with Cuban women and produced a book, *The Problem of Democracy in Cuba: Between Vision and Reality*, but I got drawn into other endeavors. But the project of coming to understand women's positioning in the wake of the revolution and exploring the degree to which the insurrection itself impacted this positioning found a place in my mind and refused for decades to slink off silently.

I once observed in an article I wrote years ago that Havana was a city governed by rumors, almost all of which were true. Although *rumor* is not quite the right word here. Just as I was beginning to undertake fieldwork, proceeding methodologically with what one Cuban friend once labeled my "investigaciones de esquina," I received a call from two women who had fought as teenagers in the underground movement in Havana in the 1950s insurrection. They asked me to come talk with them. Mirta Rodríguez Calderón was nineteen when she was caught by Batista's police trying to set off fósforo vivo in the fur department of the upscale department store El Encanto. (Fósforo vivo is a paste of dynamite powder or any other type of explosive, which, when combined with a capsule of acid, produces an explosion.) Many years later, she became the organizer of MAGÍN. Nilda Ravelo, who joined with Mirta in speaking with me, had the distinction of being one of the first women to be held in Mantilla, the women's holding prison, where she served a total of sixteen months for her involvement in multiple insurgent activities. I explained my reasons for undertaking my investigation and my intention to carry it out drawing entirely on the lives and experiences of women who are either absent from or pictured as peripheral in the narratives of the underground movement in Havana. In response they proposed that they would assist me in whatever they could. For reasons I did not understand at the time, Mirta said that they themselves would not do such a study. But she emphasized that the last thing either of them wanted was for me to be their mouthpiece. Whatever I wrote, whatever I argued, whatever I concluded was mine alone. Rather, they would help to put me in contact with other women like them, who as teenagers had been part of the clandestinidad.

As it turned out, their help went immeasurably beyond this. While I carried out virtually all my interviews on my own, each was preceded by a call from Mirta, paving my way. The circles of former clandestinas have grown ever smaller with the passage of time, but there remains a network of women who knew and know about one another. And among these women Mirta's introductions carried great weight: Her personal intervention meant that my initial approach to the women I interviewed had a certain openness, almost familiarity. As a result, these interviews tended to go beyond simple recitations of facts to provide more nuanced, complex, and, on occasion, deeply personal and conflictive accounts of each woman's time as a clandestina. These first interviews were sometimes followed by second and even third sessions, which allowed me to clarify and delve more deeply into what had emerged in earlier meetings. Further, on several occasions and after I had pestered them endlessly with queries, a small group of former clandestinas organized themselves into gatherings to speak collectively about what they had lived through. These sessions were orchestrated by Sonnia Moro and Pilar Sa, and included Mirta, Mariíta Trasancos, Hidelisa Esperón, Digna Abreu, and Consuelo Elba. At times their accounts built on each other; at other moments, in timely ways, they reflected subtle or not-so-subtle differences in interpretation and perspective.

Nilda took a somewhat different approach to helping me. As I will elaborate, Nilda still lived in the clandestinidad, and in her mind she harbored an encyclopedia concerning it. She spoke about the insurrection with no one except trusted others, one of whom was Mirta. I believe that this was why I was so immensely fortunate as an outsider that she came to give me her trust, at first within some limits. Nilda would sit on my porch without notice, telling no one why she was there and simply waiting until I appeared. And then she took me to meet and interview people I am sure I would have otherwise had no access to: Sor Acela, who had been closest to Pastorita Núñez during her years at the Santovenia retreat; Carlos Enrique Pelayo, the son of Aida Pelayo; Dianita Ramonín Domitro, the only child of América Domitro; José (Pepito) Robustillo, the son of Ibia Robustillo and the godson of Pastorita Núñez (the three lived together). And I was able to interview Ángel Fernández Vila (Horacio), who had driven the car in which 26th of July insurgents kidnapped the Argentine race-car driver Juan Manuel Fangio for two days. Horacio in turn took me to interview Agnes de los Ángeles Afón, one of the two daughters in the house in which Fangio was sequestered, who had been most involved in caring for him. Nor did we miss the wakes and the funerals and memorials in the Colon cemetery for former insurgents trusted and therefore most dear to her.

My imposition on people in Havana did not end here. I dragooned a small crew to read and critique various drafts of chapters. The first of these readers was Mirta, who sat me down beside her and literally read every line of a number of draft chapters in a language that was not her own. She challenged none of the arguments that I was trying to make. Rather, she identified factual errors, elaborated on actions in which she had participated, and sent me to meet others who might provide me with further accounts of these actions. The sociologist/historian Juan Valdés Paz, who passed away several years ago, leaving virtually the entire Cuban academic world and others in perpetual mourning, would appear on my porch to complain vociferously in his booming voice as I handed him a revised draft of the same chapter he had just read and had come to discuss. This did not stop him from giving me hours-long accounts of Cuban history in the last half of the twentieth century, complete with his characterizations of the individuals who inhabited the period. During Sunday evening chats, the Dra. Graziella Pogolotti described to me what it was like to live in Havana as the times grew darker after 1957. And she regaled me with tales of characters she knew well who would play a central role in my text: in particular Aida Pelayo, Marta Frayde, and other founders of the Frente Cívico de Mujeres Martianas. Julio Dámaso, who during the insurrection was a captain in the 26th of July Movement in Havana and is now historian of the Asociación de Combatientes de la Revolución Cubana, spent hours with me going through the piles of papers and old books and magazines in his office in search of any material dealing with the women who were in the clandestine movement in Havana. Certainly foolishly on his part, he generously responded at any time of the day to the barrage of questions that I pelted him with in my efforts to fill both major and minor lacunae. Consuelo Elba, who was in the process of making her film *Mujeres de la clandestinidad*, invited me to tag along—which I did.

My coven of friends and colleagues at Hampshire College, who regularly read and comment on one another's work, reviewed drafts of chapters in different incarnations and then used various chapters in courses, providing me with both their own feedback and that of their students. Margaret Cerullo and Lynne Hanley in particular read the entire manuscript in its unfinished and finished forms, and as a result they offered a steady stream of suggestions about what needed elaboration and what needed to be irrevocably disappeared. And Carmen Diana Deere, who escaped our coven some years ago by moving on to the University of Florida, Gainesville, has over the years subjected herself to reviewing the entire scant body of my academic production. Masked by her gentle manner, Carmen has always been merciless in her reading of my work and thereby supremely helpful. Only one of her strenuous efforts with regard to what I write has failed completely: her futile efforts to keep me from spending the equivalent of a lifetime on each of my projects.

And then there is Susan Meiselas, who conceived and realized the photographic essay that concludes the book. Susan is, of course, among the finest documentary photographers anywhere in the world: This is a given. For decades she has provided us with the visual language to grasp the toll that crises and conflicts in the world have taken on the lives of peoples and communities; to recover and bring into the light the stories of these peoples who have been confined to oblivion, erased from history or on the precipice of being erased.

On a far smaller scale and in a very different context than *Kurdistan*, her magistral book, Susan followed the same pattern in constructing the visual essay she made for this book. With the images she gathered from former clandestinas and their families, and with the help of her assistant Kristina Sumfleth, who played a critical role in the organization and production of the visual essay, Susan surfaces a powerful story about the presence and the involvement of women in the clandestine movement. For me, this narrative in images underscores what I sought to do in words in the text itself. It was pure pleasure to work with her and to watch her work.

Now to the actual production of the book itself: It is a bit embarrassing to say how many people were involved or to note the geography of this involvement. First, of course, my editors at Duke University Press, initially Gisela Fosado and for the long haul Alejandra Mejia. Ale managed to overcome my stubborn tendencies with unfailing grace combined with firmness. In this same spirit she dealt with the multiple if varied concerns that Susan and I had, and throughout she maintained amazing patience. Liz Smith ushered the production process through brilliantly. The readers to whom the manuscript was sent for review did remarkably close readings of it, providing detailed critiques that helped me enormously in clarifying arguments and revising the manuscript.

But my debts extend far beyond this, to individuals on a couple of continents and a handful of countries. In Havana, Emilio Heredia and his 1984 Moskvitch, given to him forty years earlier as the first trumpetist of the National Symphony Orchestra, were my chariot and chariot driver for the interviews I did. While he never intervened in the interviews themselves, Emilio is constitutionally unable not to be interested in everything. As a result he is in the midst of his own inquiry into the clandestine movement and has become a loyal friend and helpmate to some of the women he met. And each night when I came home to the wonderful and genealogically complex house in which I lived, its regular inhabitants, Silvia and her sons Max and Ale, were waiting for me in the kitchen, ready to regale me with their version of the day's events in that dry, rapid-fire, distinctly Cuban humor. Loren González, with occasional input from her brother David, produced transcripts of my interviews almost before I gave them to her. Nury Acosta labored over her computer trying to make sense of my mixed-up ordering of paragraphs and sentences. When she truly despaired in doing this, she consulted with a favorite former student of mine, Alana de Hinojosa, who after years of working with me knew my ways. Linda Rock dealt with my life while Kate McGregor dealt patiently with my minute-by-minute computer tragedies. Indeed after a while it seemed a good idea to simply set up a bed for Kate in my home. And Linda Thompson, with endless cheer, became my eyes in making her way through days of work on the entire edited manuscript.

However, this rainbow of support does not begin to come anywhere near matching what it was that I subjected my great friend Roberto García to. I dragooned Roberto over many a year into truly unreasonably demanding and equally unreasonable intensive work on almost every aspect of the book, with the exception of its writing. His microscopic vision never missed an out-of-place comma and certainly not a repeated phrase or a missing endnote. Far more enjoyably for him, he worked closely with Susan in tracking down and identifying photographs for possible use in the visual essay. Given all this, and given the fact that I may not be the easiest person with whom to work, Roberto has clearly earned the right to do me bodily harm. But he has promised not to do this as long as I promise never to write another book.

INTRODUCTION

Flores y palabras lindas han recibido . . .
[Flowers and pretty words they have been given . . .]

MIRTA RODRÍGUEZ CALDERÓN / "MUCHACHAS EN EL CLANDESTINAJE"

There can never be a single story. There are only ways of seeing. So when I tell a story, I tell it not as an ideologue who wants to pit one absolutist ideology against another, but as a storyteller who wants to share her way of seeing.

ARUNDHATI ROY / "COME SEPTEMBER"

The Cuban revolution as it burst onto the world stage in the 1950s seemed a most extraordinary, almost impossible happening. And what was perhaps most extraordinary about it was the ages of those who fought to bring it about: Fidel Castro, thirty-three, was among the oldest insurgents. With this, a legend was born of a revolution made by a group of young bearded men in the Sierra Maestra mountains in eastern Cuba fighting an improbable battle against equally improbable odds to successfully overthrow a dictatorship. And they accomplished this in two short years. This legend has managed to prevail, has seemingly indelibly embedded itself as actual historical fact both on the island and in the world at large.

But in truth it is a misrepresentation of historical fact. In its telling of what is at best a partial story, it occludes far more complex, messy realities. Above all, these complex, messy realities rotate around the critical, indeed perhaps even the central, role in overthrowing the Batista regime played by the insurgency fought not in the sierra but in Cuba's cities—the llano.[1]

And because it was in the llano where the overwhelming numbers of female insurgents actively fought, the occlusion of the story of the llano further underpins a tale that with few exceptions focuses exclusively on the centrality of men in the making of the Cuban revolution.

The youths who brought down the Batista regime in both the sierra and the llano are, of course, no longer youths. Many, including Fidel himself, have died; those still alive are in their late seventies or eighties. But the legend somehow lives on as the official story of the revolution, taught in schools, reproduced in television documentaries and in frequent re-creations of events, and given concrete form in monuments.

There have been efforts on the island, particularly recently, in Kristin Ross's apt phrase, to "emancipate" this history,[2] in part by surfacing the story of the llano. But this has happened in a disjointed fashion, largely in autobiographical and testimonial form (both oral and written) and therefore accessible only to limited audiences. Among the most recent and perhaps most promising of these is the Club Martiano de Herencia Rebelde, formed by the children of those youths who decades ago made a revolution. These children are themselves no longer children: They are middle-aged, and most are women. Their goal is to preserve, really to bring alive once more, the memory of what their parents did in the underground movement in Cuba's cities to bring down the dictatorship. They are intent on building a museum in Havana on the former site of the Bureau for the Repression of Communist Activities, a center of imprisonment and torture during the dictatorship. The building housing the Bureau had been torn down on Che Guevara's orders, given what it symbolized. This museum would make available to the public the many unpublished personal documents and letters written or given to them by their parents concerning the insurrection, which remain in their possession. That is, it would be a physical site of remembrance.

But more immediately, they seek to tell the story of the insurrection in which their own parents took part in effect by re-creating it with children in primary and secondary schools. And they do this by actually taking these children to the places in the neighborhoods in which they live that during the insurrection were active sites of insurgents' actions, or houses in which they took refuge, or even places where they were killed. Their purpose is to bring alive the clandestine struggle for these children. The visual material that the group uses in talking to children is a chart composed of a mixture of the faces of the heroes, mainly of the insurrection, in Cuban history. Each face is used to represent a distinct neighborhood in the city. Among these faces none is of a woman.[3] In effect then, in the very act of trying to bring to life the experiences of the clandestinidad in Havana, they are inscribing on a new generation a clear definition of who were and who were not the insurrection's protagonists.

My intention in what follows is to interrupt this story, to excavate an alternative reading of women's positioning in the narrative of the nation by reinterpreting the manner in which they lived their lives in the underground movement. And thereby to situate them not simply as protagonists in the male construct of the nation but implicitly or explicitly as transgressors upon this construct.

This re-reading asks of us a prior interrogation: to address yet again the question that has been the central concern of countless books, novels, and essays dealing with Cuban history—the question of national identity. In the pages that follow I argue that national identity in Cuba from the time of the wars of independence and for the century following them has been a male construct, excluding women as active subjects. And the manner in which the story of the insurgency against Batista has been told and retold has reproduced and further embedded this construct.

The issue of national identity is, of course, everywhere fraught and in every case necessarily fragile and constantly the subject of reinterpretation, re-creation, and reconceptualization: Nations are, after all, the products of both history and the myths in which that history is entangled. The parameters of the nation are never fixed and always subject to multiple contestations. Given this, the idea of the nation seems always to require the assertion or rather the myth of unity, a coalescing around a single dominant historical narrative which, in its need for unity, must exclude constructions that potentially pose threats to it. The Cuban sociologist Juan Valdés Paz has aptly observed that history is the enemy of unity.[4] But perhaps better said, histories are unity's most dangerous adversaries. In the name of the nation, unity seems always to demand the channeling, erasure, retelling, and even suppression of other histories.

For Cubans, history and myth are woven together in a particular way. The long wars of independence in the nineteenth century had not produced independence. Rather, as the historian Louis Pérez Jr. has written, they left "a brooding sense of a history gone awry . . . of an unfinished history, of an incomplete nation."[5] What they had produced, however, was a vision of the nation and a cast of characters who were understood as embodying this vision, giving form to the yet-to-be-realized idea of the patria. They served as the touchstones on which the story of the nation has been told and retold for a century and a half in a narrative whose theme was constantly evoked, exactly because its aspirations remained unfulfilled. The 1950s revolutionary leaders understood this and declared themselves the inheritors of one hundred years of struggle for the country's liberation, thereby embedding themselves and the revolution they made in this constancy. The nineteenth-century wars of independence, in the course of which the idea of the Cuban nation coalesced, are largely the story of the male heroes who led these wars: Carlos Manuel de Céspedes, José Martí, Antonio Maceo, Maximo Gómez.[6] And in like fashion, the story of the making of the 1952–59 revolution focuses almost entirely on the male guerrilla leaders in the Sierra Maestra and, above all others, Fidel Castro, Che Guevara, and Camilo Cienfuegos.

My agenda is to challenge this story by surfacing one of its exclusions at one of its most decisive moments: the overthrow of the Batista regime during the 1950s. And I interrogate the narrative of his overthrow from the perspective of this exclusion: specifically, the manner in which the narrative of the Cuban insurrection positions the girls and young women who fought in the underground movement in Havana to rid the island of Batista. Although it is beyond the subject at hand here, it can be argued that this construction affected concretely their positioning in the years after 1959. Subverting the dominant narrative requires resignifying its terms to fundamentally understand the girls and women who fought against Batista not as subordinate to the main, almost always male, actors, but rather as among its protagonists.

But to do this, first another buried story must be surfaced: the role played by the llano in ridding Cuba of Batista. The overwhelming majority of the girls and young women who risked their lives to overthrow the dictatorship were concentrated in the cities: Without excavating this prior story we cannot begin to discuss the positionality of women in the 1950s insurgency. Therefore, another layer needs to be peeled back: Even when the story of the llano is told, it too is almost always a tale of male heroes and martyrs to the nation. Thus, if we are to challenge this portrayal, the story of the llano itself must be interrogated.

This undertaking requires first a brief accounting of the manner in which the idea or ideas of "cubanidad" began to take form. The complexity of the issue of national identity in Cuba, of coming to terms with what and who is Cuban, was made historically almost irresolvable due to slavery in all of its ramifications. In the mid-nineteenth century those classified as slaves or free people of color composed 53 percent of the Cuban population.[7] As so many have written, the abolition or continuation of slavery fractured or at least exacerbated the deep divisions of nineteenth-century Cuban society along every line, between slaves and free people of color, between africanos de nación and Cuban-born (criollo) slaves, between blacks and whites, between peninsulares and white criollos (both groups deeply invested in their own divergent interests), between different regions of the not-yet-coalesced nation, between the dramatically contrasting social and economic structures of life in eastern and western Cuba, and related to this, among the white population itself divided by legal, social, political and economic statuses.[8] These fragments, all of them inextricably wound into each other and unable to find common ground, prevented Cubans in contrast to much of the rest of Latin America from fighting for a Cuban nation until the last half of the nineteenth century.

The seemingly unresolvable, fractious nature of mid-nineteenth-century Cuban society reflected life on the island. And it found expression in cultural production: thus, for instance, Cuba's "foundational fiction," to use Doris Sommer's classical term.[9] The foundational novel of virtually every Latin American country always seems to reach for some sort of melding, or a path to the consolidation of the imagined nation. Cuba's "foundational fiction," the novel *Cecilia Valdés* by Cirilo Villaverde, centers on incest and ends in assassination, murder, and lunacy.

The dominant discourse in the first half of the nineteenth century concerning "what is to be done" about forging or not forging the Cuban nation, was carried out largely by white male intellectuals living in exile or by choice abroad in Europe and, as the century proceeded, increasingly in the United States. And the acknowledged or unacknowledged heart of this discourse had to do with the black population. Solutions ranged, complicated in no small measure by geography. Until late in the century the owners of the large plantations in western Cuba saw slaves as vital while in eastern Cuba sugar was not as central an economic concern. The solutions proposed by these white intellectuals were conflictive and contested; none resolved the conundrum. Meanwhile, Spanish rule, odious and restrictive, continued.

It was José Martí who, in his untiring work to forge unity among the disparate and conflicting interests and beliefs of Cubans both in exile and on the island, articulated most clearly another vision of the nation-to-be: Martí's Cuba would be at its heart a nonracial society. To be Cuban, he declared, was to be more than white, more than black. Martí's elaboration on this vision was essentially performative. He was not redeeming the Cuban patria, but building on the Ten Years' War (1868–78), he was constructing it (hacer patria). He was, in short, defining cubanidad.

Martí spoke of the Ten Years' War as a "conflagración purificada necesaria" (a purifying and necessary conflagration). Ada Ferrer writes that, for Martí, the Ten Years' War "had resolved materially and morally the dilemma of slavery and nationality."[10] The coming of a second war of independence, for Martí, would continue this process and see its culmination: By shedding blood together, black men and white men would dissolve the chasm between the races that had so impeded the possibility of realizing it; "Barefoot all and naked all, blacks and whites became equal." This embrace, he wrote, conquered death itself: "The souls of whites and blacks [rose] together through the skies."[11]

Ferrer notes that the embrace Martí evoked was transcendentally fraternal, always between men and at its core productive of a community that was inherently masculine.[12] Or, as Vera Kutzinski concludes from her reading of nineteenth- and twentieth-century Cuban literature and cultural artifacts, the construction of this true and pure independent Cuban nation was a male homosocial project which in Martí's vision, was forged by black men and white men of all classes.[13]

It can surely be argued that every national project in the modern era could be described as a male homosocial construct. I do not point to the Cuban national project as unique in this regard, but rather I account for the matter in which the specificities of this construction are melded in the Cuban context. The first of these specificities takes us once again to slavery, formally abolished on the island only in 1886, thereby excluding black voices in the construction of the nation-to-be and in its aftermath.

The realities of the independence wars revealed the underside of Martí's vision: Unity was not so easily forged. Years before Martí articulated his vision of a nonracial Cuba, at the very onset of the Ten Years' War the terms were set. The 1869 Asamblea Constituyente de Guáimaro (Constituent Assembly of Guáimaro), which declared Cuban independence, was an elite, white, male-only gathering. These men in doing so positioned themselves as the trustees of the nation-to-be, the sole arbiters of its structures and its laws, and, by their absence in the documents, determined its exclusions: Women, writes Ada Ferrer, were "excluded . . . from the symbolic birth of the nation."[14] These upper-class white men understood their roles in combat as further confirming their right to define the nation-to-be. Almost a century later, in the wake of the victorious 1952–59 revolution, the reconstruction of the nation with few exceptions would once more be the domain of white leaders who understood themselves and would largely be understood to have the inherent right to frame and to determine the future of the nation.

A second specificity concerns the extreme evocation, celebration, and glorification of martyrdom and death, virtually without exception of men, which are embedded in the narratives of the nineteenth-century wars and recapitulated in the 1950s revolution.[15] In *Cuban Memory Wars*, Michael J. Bustamante cites "spectacles of historic righteousness" in a February 1959 commemoration overseen by Fidel Castro and the short-lived president Manuel Urrutia in which the bodies of the men who died in the *Granma* landing, and in the skirmishes with Batista's air force directly after, were put on display in the Capitolio in Havana for public viewing.[16]

The physical display of these corpses explicitly fed the myth of the *Granma*'s landing and its aftermath, in which the story tells us dedicated revolutionaries sacrificed their lives for the nation. Fidel, in placing these bodies at the very seat of the deposed government, underscored the unchallengeable right of the revolution under his command to determine the form and content of the nation and its reconstruction.

These specificities bring us back to a further consideration of the moment at which the nation-to-be was proclaimed. Blacks were not alone in their exclusion from the symbolic birth of the nation. As I noted, the 1869 Constituent Assembly of Guáimaro was a men's-only affair. The single woman in attendance, Ana Betancourt, was representing her sick husband Ignacio Mora. But Betancourt is remembered above all for her declaration at the Assembly. The undercurrent during the debate at the Assembly rotated around deciding on the definition of who was Cuban. Betancourt, intervening, raised the issue of those who were excluded from the debate, who were therefore in effect condemned to be nonmembers of the new nation, non-Cubans: slaves and women. She drew the parallels between these noncitizens: "Citizens: The Cuban woman, in the dark and still corner of her household waited patiently and with resignation for this beautiful hour when a new revolution would break her free from her yoke and release her wings. Citizens: in Cuba everything was enslaved: cradle, color and sex. You wanted to destroy the slavery of color, emancipating the slave. The moment has come to liberate women."[17]

Nydia Sarabia writes that when Betancourt spoke these words, Clara Zetkin, who would become a leading feminist voice in the socialist movement in Germany, was twelve years old, and movements for women's rights in Europe and North America were just beginning. Sarabia postulates that there might have been concrete links between Betancourt's call for the rights of women and slaves and demands being made by women in the 1848 revolutions in Europe.[18] The content and phrasing of Betancourt's intervention seems to evidence as well her familiarity with both Sojourner Truth's "Ain't I a Woman?" declaration at the 1851 Women's Rights Convention in Akron, Ohio, and the contemporary writings of Harriet and John Stuart Mill.

Betancourt's intervention has been absorbed into the lore of the Cuban revolutionary narrative. Her interjection into the debate, with some notable exceptions, served a specific purpose in the way in which history has recorded the Assembly. Its male delegates, hearing but not acting on her declaration, along with the majority of those who have celebrated Guáimaro's progressive nature in their writings, used it as an indicator of the enlightened bent of those males who were beginning to constitute the patria. Indeed, her very presence at the Assembly served and serves to underscore this image. But Betancourt, at the moment when the story of the nation took form, became a footnote. As Elda Cento writes, at Guáimaro her words "remained floating in the wind."[19] Her bold attempt to make visible both slaves and women had no concrete resonance. The potential challenge it represented to the homosocial framework within which the nation to be was shaped went unheeded. Only later, in the twentieth century, when her remains were returned to the island, was she formally celebrated as a prescient forerunner of women's rights in Cuba.

The exclusion of women's voices from a role in determining a national project was hardly unique to Cuba, and certainly prevailing patriarchal societal structures on the island were central to the seemingly unquestioned and unquestionable assumptions inherent in a male homosocial construct. But almost a century later, on a vastly different terrain and despite the evolution over decades of societal norms with relation to women, visible threads still wove together the positioning of women in the insurrections. Constructs by their very nature are fraught and thereby permeable; their borders require policing, sometimes explicit, sometimes unspoken. For women the most fundamental and enduring effect of this policing in both the nineteenth-century wars and the 1950s revolution was to confine and define what they could do and thereby what they could not do. The male leadership were the sole active subjects: They did the fighting.[20] Women were almost always cast in the role of enablers for these men, and if what this involved clearly differed, given the dramatically different circumstances of these insurrections, by definition women were therefore secondary; they were not those who would determine the wars' direction. Their positioning as secondary served to naturalize and thereby legitimate their exclusion from a role in framing the nation.

Further, the permeable borders of the male construct of the nation made indispensable varying forms of policing around female sexuality. In the narratives of both the nineteenth-century wars and the 1950s insurrection, the desexualization of women fed into defining the degree of their adherence to the project of the nation. And this required policing. During the Ten Years' War this policing was filtered through the myth of the eternally faithful wife. Unlike the male mambises, whose commitment to the nation-to-be was inherent in their combat with the Spaniards, the narratives of the war make clear that a woman's positionality in the nation-to-be was mediated through her undying faithfulness to her mambí husband, even after his death. Her loyalty to the nation was therefore entirely determined by and measured through her loyalty to him.[21]

In the 1950s insurrection, young clandestinas' commitment to the battle to overthrow the dictatorship was of course not mediated through men. Nonetheless, a violation of sexual abstinence was seen as a betrayal of the insurrection itself, as a deviation from commitment to the struggle to rid the island of Batista. The narrative of desexualized relationships in the devotion to a purified nation would surface once again, this time, particularly in the stories of the men and women who lived together in close contact.[22] When a woman in the insurrection engaged openly in a sexual relationship, knowledge of this was passed among the close-knit rebel groupings and policing was expressed in various ways: verbal denigration, suspicion, indignation, condemnation. That is, a woman's sexual involvement colored negatively her very presence in the underground movement. On the other hand, the men in these relationships suffered no such consequences. Their status and position in the hierarchy of the movement were never challenged; the power they exercised never diminished. The most well-known of these sexual relationships involved Norma Porras and Ángel Ameijeiras (Machaco), head of Action and Sabotage in Havana from March 1958 until his assassination in November of that year.

I discuss this relationship and the controversies around Porras herself in greater depth in chapter 4.

———

In what follows in this book I have attempted, however inadequately, to meld together a variety of different types of sources—historical texts, oral histories, interviews, and testimonies—to frame and then analyze the positionality of women, and specifically the girls and women in the urban underground arena in Havanna, the clandestinas, in the battle to overthrow the Batista regime. First, I must add a caveat: I did not intend to write nor have I written a history of the Cuban insurrection. Rather, what I seek to do is employ a thematic lens through which to view this history by what I argue is one of its most profoundly consequential silences. This is intended as a work of excavation, of surfacing another story about the making of the revolution.

First, as Michelle Chase and Lorraine Bayard de Volo have so cogently shown, in the years following Batista's coup and prior to the onset of the guerrilla war, women played a most critical role, taking upon themselves in multiple contexts the mantle of the nation's "moral authority."[23] In doing so, they effectively denied the Batista regime any possible path to legitimacy, thereby undermining it in a manner in which it would never recover.

In chapter 2 I turn to an in-depth discussion of one of the first among the oppositional groupings, made entirely of women. The women who formed the core of the Frente Cívico de Mujeres Martianas (the José Martí Women's Civic Front, FCMM), or the Martianas, began organizing in the days following Batista's seizure of power. Although the Frente has been reconsidered in greater depth in recent studies,[24] it is generally referred to as one of a number of civic organizations, in this case made up of mainly middle-aged women, who provided support for the insurgent movements and engaged mainly in more public actions.[25] I argue to the contrary that while the group undertook and joined in public demonstrations of various stripes, the core members were integral to the underground struggle and must be understood as such. My reasons for discussing the FCMM early in this study and prior to the later chapters on women in the clandestine movements is first to underscore that women had begun to organize themselves into anti-Batista fronts before the later male-dominated groups (in particular, the Directorio Revolucionario and the 26th of July Movement). Second, the Martianas, as I understand them, served as one of the indispensable spines of the insurgency in Havana. That is, in themselves they represent a fundamental challenge to the very roots of the official narrative of the making of the revolution.

If a nation is always in the process of rewriting itself, reinscription implies an original inscription. In the wars of independence, this original inscription with the passage of time and the absence of women's voices has meant that a great deal of their history is forever lost. In the case of the 1950s revolution, however, a number of the young girls and women who over a half century ago actively participated in its making are still living and able to provide their own accounts, perhaps clouded or perhaps clarified (or both) by memory. I will turn to what these women related to me about their experiences in the clandestinidad in chapters 3–7.

In chapter 8, I seek to get at complex questions of memory and of inheritance by listening to the voices of the children, mainly the daughters, of these same insurrectas. What did they know or understand about their mothers' actions and lives in the urban insurrection? How did they fit this into the narrative that surrounded them everywhere as they were growing up: a tale, again, of a revolution made by young bearded men coming down from the mountains?

In the course of my work on this project I spoke with thirty-one women, twenty-two of whom were teenagers during the years of the insurrection. Twenty were in the 26th of July Movement; seven were in the Directorio Revolucionario; one claimed militancy in both the Directorio and the 26th of July Movement; three were members of the Juventud (the youth branch of the Partido Socialista Popular), and one of these three said she worked with both the Juventud and the 26th of July Movement.[26] I focus my text overwhelmingly on the triumphant 26th of July Movement because most clandestinas were insurgents in that movement. But I do this somewhat reluctantly, particularly because with the exception of the Directorio's March 13, 1957, attack on the Presidential Palace and its tragic immediate aftermath, the official narrative of the revolution has virtually erased the actions of the Directorio. Further, although I bring into my discussion women involved in the insurgency on a range of fronts, my focus in these chapters is almost entirely on the young girls and women, ages thirteen to twenty-five, who were engaged in various ways in Action and Sabotage. And another qualification: The women with whom I spoke were not involved in mobilizations or actions in factories or trade unions.

In undertaking work with and about these women, I relied primarily on multiple in-depth interviews with individual clandestinas, which led fairly regularly to very personal reflections on their lives in the underground movement, as well as extended conversations between and among clandestinas, to explore collective memory. I drew on existing published interviews and accounts written by women on the island and elsewhere and on unpublished interviews and correspondence that the women with whom I spoke so generously shared with me. In the case of seven women I discuss who have died (five of whom were the founders of the FCMM), I depended on the reminiscences of their closest friends and their families, unpublished letters, and brief published accounts of their lives. Although I certainly drew from these sources, my intention is not to provide life histories: This to some degree has been done, albeit in abbreviated form, both on the island and by scholars elsewhere.[27] Given my purposes in undertaking this study, I very specifically sought out women not among the handful of those whose names are engraved in the official narrative of the revolution.

A further note concerning the manner in which I approached the women interviewed. My intent was not simply to gather accounts of what they did in the underground movement but to anchor these accounts in a discussion of their lives. These were young girls who chose to radically transgress the norms of the societies into which they had been born, to risk their lives by doing this, and in the course of their actions to suffer consequences, for some physical and for others long-term trauma. What was it that motivated them to make the choices they made? My intent was to capture their lives in a manner that would allow them to be seen as persons. I sought thereby to anchor their time in the clandestinidad in multiple dimensions in order to underscore their physical presence in the uprising and the critical role they played in it.

What I attempted to convey in the text with words, the documentary photographer Susan Meiselas achieves with perhaps far greater impact in her visual essay that concludes this book. Meiselas developed this photographic narrative by engaging with former clandestinas and their families, gathering and compiling photographs of them at various moments of their lives. Various former clandestinas returned with her for the first time to the sites that profoundly resonated in their memories of their time in the insurrection. She melded her photographs of these reencounters with her narrative. She drew from diverse materials she found in various archives in Havana, as well as from distinct personal and public collections that were often disorganized and poorly preserved. Through this research, Susan Meiselas molded a photographic narrative that is intended to breathe life into the stories of these women and make visible their presence as rebels in the uprising that brought down the Batista dictatorship.

In an investigation such as this, one must inevitably confront the problematic of memory and subjectivity. What can we understand about these years now more than six decades later, relying in the main on the insurrection's participants? Elizabeth Jelin, in her discussion of women's representation in history, argues that given the faint traces of this representation, the reconstruction of history through personal testimony must be prioritized.[28] But memory is always a site of ongoing construction; it is never static or fixed. As Alessandro Portelli observes, it cannot be taken as a "passive depository of fact but must be understood as an active process of the creation of meanings."[29] How then does one distinguish between memory and representation and the manifold and multiple layers of subsequent representation in which they have been inevitably enveloped?

In the case of Cuba this is made all the more complex by the ways in which the story of the llano has been suppressed in favor of the "official truth." The problematic, then, as Kristin Ross writes, is to account for how the "official story" came to claim for itself alone the mantel of the "official truth."[30] And then, how to dismantle this? In her analysis of the manner in which the "official story" of the May 1968 events in France came to be constructed, Ross chose to rely not on interviews with participants but on accounts published in the aftermath of the events. Given what she calls the problematic of social memory and amnesia, "what possible controls could govern [her] selection of the testimony of participants in a mass movement that extended throughout France?" Rather, she chose to set against one another multiple competing analyses claiming to tell the story of the May events, and she traces the manner in which the "official story" emerged from these analyses.[31]

The problem with applying Ross's methodology to the Cuban revolution is that on the island itself there existed no competing narratives. The official story of the revolution is not solely the product of its aftermath, and it did not emerge from competing narratives. It began to form during the initial episodes of the very making of the revolution. Michelle Chase, examining clandestine ephemera produced during the insurrection, argues that the icon of the guerrilla as the sole representation of the insurrection consolidated late in 1958, specifically in the wake of the failed general strike in the cities in April of that year. She points to the disappearance in insurgent propaganda portraying images of urban insurgents and women.[32] While this may be true, in fact the symbol of the Cuban guerrilla revolutionary gained a kind of dominance both on the island and in the world generally even at what was perhaps its weakest moment. Two months after the disastrous landing of the *Granma*, it was given distinct form and a specific point of reference in February 1957 when *New York Times* reporter Herbert Mathews visited the rebel camp and published an account of his interview as well as photographs of himself with Fidel in the camp itself. Wrapped in the imagery of romance and desire, the legend of the young bearded guerrillas in the mountains led by the increasingly legendary figure of Fidel and beside him Che Guevara and Camilo Cienfuegos, only gained further authority in the "afterlife" of the insurrection itself.[33] In the year after the taking of power, on the island itself all possible competing narratives were either erased or subordinated to a single tale.

The disputes between different sectors of the insurgent forces both within and without the 26th of July Movement which followed the taking of power were largely overwhelmed by denunciations. Accounts by those who left Cuba carried little weight on the island. Even decades later, few published accounts by those who fought in the llano, supplemented by collections of brief testimonies of participants, exist to provide any degree of alternative reading of the official story. This story of course is told by those who have been and remain in power on the island who came quickly and decisively to control its telling. And in this telling it fits precisely into the historical narrative of the construction of the nation. For all of these reasons, I did not have the option of pursuing the course charted by Ross. In order to surface an alternative narrative of women in the making of the Cuban revolution, I would have needed to carry out a significant number of interviews with those women who were actively a part of it but had left the island in the years following 1959.

Ross's critique of the temporal and geographic reductions that had come to bound the events in France to a single month and a single city resonates in the official tale of the Cuban revolution. Time is bounded by *Granma*'s return to Cuba in December 1956 and the arrival of the guerrilla columns in Havana on January 8, 1959. Place is circumscribed by the Sierra Maestra mountains and by the procession of the Caravan of Liberty across the island following the collapse of the dictatorship.[34]

But drawing on the testimony of participants about events that took place almost sixty years ago presents a land mine of problems for obvious reasons. My subjects are now decades older, with all that this might imply. How does one measure the effects of events and relationships on the discursive memories told sixty years after the fact? Memories have inevitably been colored and reshaped by years of personal experiences intertwined with rapid and radical changes that have characterized the complex and crisis-filled history of the island after 1959, and by the very dominance itself of the official narrative concerning the insurrection. Forgetting is sometimes as powerful as remembering. In some cases, personal or political antagonisms still hold, seemingly unabated. Some of these antagonisms are present in early collections of testimonies in which the names of those who subsequently left the island are often followed by the word *traitor* (added apparently by the editors). Needless to say, directly following the taking of power, innumerable Cubans for innumerable reasons falsely claimed involvement in the insurrection. Among the women with whom I spoke, when I could identify an account that was largely fictional, it might have been rooted in an explicit desire to enhance what they actually did or they might simply have repeated an episode so frequently that with the passage of time it had become fiction.[35] All this is made more complex since by definition, those in the underground movement could not and did not operate as a collective community.

I tried wherever I could to sort this out by repeating interviews with the same woman in an effort to trace possible variations or for that matter the absence of variations in her story. Further, I sought to clarify accounts by bringing together small numbers of clandestinas in informal settings to discuss actions in which they were jointly involved; by speaking separately with those involved in these same actions; and by reading whatever I could find about these actions. But obviously this process of sifting has its limits. I have sought in what I have written here to take these into account.

My decision to focus this study with some exceptions on women insurrectionaries in Havana and my use of terminology require elaboration. First, my choice to center my inquiry on Havana. If the clandestinidad everywhere on the island was, as Frank País, the national coordinator of the 26th of July Movement until his assassination in July 1957, described it in a letter to América Domitro, like living in a "ratonera" (mousetrap) the realities in Havana proved particularly difficult.[36] It was in the capital that the full weight of Batista's repressive apparatus was concentrated. And, as I will elaborate in chapter 3, Havana's size, geographic location, social and kinship networks, heterogeneous class structure, the existence of multiple oppositional movements, and even its architecture, by comparison for instance to Santiago, Cuba's second and easternmost largest city, profoundly complicated the daily threats faced by the insurgents in Havana. Santiago, from the time of the nineteenth-century wars of independence, is celebrated in Cuban lore always as "la ciudad héroe" (heroic city), the cuna (cradle) of Cuban revolutions.[37] If Santiago is the site of revolutionary impulse and success, Havana is the "difficult" or "problematic" city, the site of impediments to revolution and of their fracasos (failures). This was never more so than in the verdict drawn by the 26th of July Movement leadership in the sierra about the failure in Havana of the critical April 9, 1958, strike, which was to finally end the Batista regime. The diminution and at moments even the dismissal of the centrality of the revolutionary movement in Havana in bringing down the Batista dictatorship must inevitably have the effect of making even less visible the roles played by clandestinas in Havana during the years of the insurgency. Here too these implications in the official narrative need to be interrogated.

Second, the terms *clandestina/o* and *clandestinidad* in the literature about the llano and even more so in accounts of individual insurgents' involvement in the urban insurrectionary movement are confused and confusing. They are sometimes used to designate all those involved in the struggle, and sometimes to describe those who are forced to leave their homes because word had come that they were specifically being hunted by Batista's various esbirros (henchmen). At times the designation *clandestina* is applied only to those women involved in action and sabotage, and other times it designates those living in safe houses as the fictive wives in order to mask the identity of males in the leadership.

Indeed, this is one of the definitional confusions that led Julio César Rosabal García, in his authoritative 2013 doctoral dissertation specifically concerning the operations of the 26th of July Movement in Havana, to replace the term clandestina/o entirely and to use instead geographically determined descriptions of the movement to bring down the Batista regime: urban insurgents, sierra insurgents, and insurgents operating outside Cuba to garner money, arms, and international publicity for the struggle on the island.[38]

Despite the slippery definitional edges, I found it hard to abandon *clandestina/o* and *clandestinidad* given that the words capture an imaginary that seems to me missing in collapsing the struggle in the llano, the sierra, and the exterior into three geographically based categories. And even more, those who fought in the insurrection in the llano refer to themselves and to each other as clandestinas/os. With only a few exceptions, most of the women on whose experiences I primarily draw led in some form or other and at great cost to themselves underground lives in their struggle to put an end to Batista's dictatorship. I therefore continue to refer to them as *clandestinas* while at moments using the designation *insurgentas* as synonymous. I do this although personally I reject for instance the distinction drawn between collaborators and clandestinas exactly because the phrasing itself diminishes the critical role played by numberless anonymous women and almost always women in families who took on the very dangerous responsibility of giving shelter to insurgents in their homes, thereby risking not only themselves but even their children. In my definition, every one of these women was involved directly in the underground movement. Therefore, I understand all of them as clandestinas. But given my focus in this study, I examine in chapter 3 in detail the actions of only one such woman.

Third, further clarifications regarding terminology: Throughout this study I use the phrase *the official story/narrative/account/telling of the making of the revolution.* By this, I am using a shorthand to refer to a generally projected narrative that centers the insurgency against the Batista dictatorship almost exclusively around the rebels who fought in the Sierra Maestra mountains and particularly around the figure of Fidel Castro.

Finally, a caveat or, perhaps better said, an unconvincing excuse. Julia Sweig, in her study of the the final year of the 1950s insurrection, underscores what she sees as a central problem in writings about this period: the myth in which the year 1959 is wrapped. She points out, in particular, that any account of this period must recognize the multiple influences and effects that the 1930 revolution had on the 1950s insurgency and insurgents.[39] This is most certainly a primary deficiency of my study as well. Cuban historians have written and have continued to write extensively about the 1930 revolution.[40] But what is absent from these writings is any substantive consideration, or any consideration at all, of the women who were a part of that revolution. This is problematic in multiple contexts. As the historian Gladys Marel García Pérez adamantly asserts, it is impossible to fully grasp women's involvement in the 1950s revolution without grasping the nature of women's presence and participation in insurgencies dating from the nineteenth century. The women who took part in the 1950s revolution, as she says, did not just fall from the sky.[41] Nor, I might add, were they awakened from a deep sleep by Fidel. Bayard de Volo, heeding García Pérez's caution, devotes a section of her study of women in the Cuban revolution to those she notes were veterans of the 1930 insurrection, with brief paragraphs highlighting what they did in the 1950s.[42] But for the purpose of this study there is yet another problematic. What for me is critical is to get a concrete sense of what it was that women in the 1930 revolution brought from it to their involvement in the insurgency twenty years later. That is, how they understood the situation on the ground and how they formulated what was to be done in terms of the strategies and tactics they would bring to bear. At least for the insurgency in Havana, only the women who formed the core of the Frente Martiano begin to provide us partial answers. I will explore these in chapter 2.

—————

This book is about a specific revolution in a specific country, made by the people of that country, and it focuses on a very specific time period. But my impetus in undertaking this project went beyond the bounds of what is here: that is, beyond my desire or my need to try to illuminate certain silences surrounding the Cuban revolution and to reconsider it using other lenses. I spend no time exploring these other dimensions, but let me at least mention them here because I believe there have been and are real-life consequences born of the story of the Cuban revolution as it has been told, not just for and on the island itself.

The first of these involves the generalized idea that the 1950s revolution was made in the countryside, in the mountains, by a small band of guerrillas. This version of the making of the revolution, the foco theory as it came to be called, affected a generation of Cubans and indelibly reverberated in the ways in which others sought to copy it. Or, better said, the effect of its lessons in the third world, particularly in Latin America, was nothing short of tragic. The exaltation of the role of the sierra, and within this the focus on the role of the peasantry, was adopted elsewhere and not just by Che Guevara in Bolivia, establishing for decades a profoundly misleading blueprint for revolutionary change.[43]

The second consequence involves the positioning of women in the historical tales of revolutionary situations. While the Cuban formulation of this has, of course, distinct roots in terms of its expression, it is true that in their telling no modern revolution or really any revolution has ever portrayed women as anything but at best secondary actors: Men have always been the protagonists, in both physical and ideological terms. Feminists, in early attempts to challenge this, searched with utmost diligence through dusty tomes and dustier archives to rescue the names of individual women who played key roles in assorted revolutions. But the problem here is twofold. First, in too many cases, these individual women were then celebrated for having taken on in their actions what were regarded as men's roles. Second, this work of excavation of the examples and names of individual women too often resulted in making invisible the actions and lives of the masses of women who must inevitably be involved in a societal upheaval as profound as a revolution. While this work of unearthing was certainly valuable, its unintended side effect has been to further the job of reducing these other women to oblivion. In more recent books, Bayard de Volo and Chase have approached the study of women in the Cuban insurrection by drawing on feminist literature to contextualize their studies in a more analytical, incisive, and critical fashion.[44] In doing so, they reveal how much more there is to be done in the case of Cuba.

Several years ago I asked my bright and studious Cuban goddaughter, then eleven, to tell me what she knew about various Cuban revolutionaries: Martí, Maceo, Fidel, Che, and so on. When I got to Haydée Santamaría, this was her response: "Haydée Santamaría was a very brave woman. She fought for our liberty when all the other women stayed in their houses doing nothing." At first I was flabbergasted: Where had she learned this? Certainly not from her family. Quickly, I realized that she had simply extrapolated this from what she had learned in school and from the television: the narrative of a revolution that was made by young bearded men fighting Batista's forces in the Sierra Maestra and then across the island, finally arriving triumphantly in Havana. Haydée's role in Moncada and her successes in gathering and delivering arms and munitions to the sierra during the period of the insurrection positioned her as playing a role in this version of the making of the revolution. This book is an attempt to speak, among others, to my goddaughter.

BATISTA'S QUEST FOR LEGITIMACY

Fulgencio Batista seized power in Cuba in a coup d'état on March 10, 1952. At midnight on December 31, 1958, he and various of his cohorts boarded a helicopter and fled the island. How do we explain the brief duration of his regime? Michelle Chase notes that other contemporary Caribbean dictators, Rafael Trujillo in the Dominican Republic and Anastasio Somoza and the Somoza family in Nicaragua who had risen to power in the 1930s, held on to their dictatorships for decades.[1] To understand Batista's rapid demise, we would do well to reexamine the explanation for it that is given in the official story of the insurrection: Much becomes clear in the way in which this story is framed in terms of what is included and what is consequently excluded. First, the official narrative is built around a clear and seemingly uncomplicated timeline. In this narrative the insurgency against Batista began on July 26, 1953, when Fidel Castro led an attack on the Moncada fortress in Santiago. Then Fidel, released from prison in 1955 in part due to a national campaign, went to Mexico, where he organized the group of male rebels who would return with him to the island in December 1956 and make their way to the Sierra Maestra mountains in eastern Cuba to wage a guerrilla war that would bringdown the dictatorship. This timeline ends with the arrival of Fidel in the Caravan of Liberty in Havana on January 8, 1959.

The end of the Batista regime in this story is an entirely male affair. Fidel and the men around him are the sole occupants of the stage for the duration of the drama. The destruction of the dictatorship is the work of a single entity: the 26th of July Movement guerrilla fighters who, led by Fidel Castro, bonded during their time in the sierra. Told in this manner, the official story affirms the indisputable right of this group of men and specifically their leaders to be the architects of the reborn nation. Indeed the seeds of this are sown in the immediate aftermath of the attack on Moncada, the story's opening act. It is articulated by Fidel in "History Will Absolve Me," his denunciation of the dictatorship given as his defense at his trial following the attack. The denunciation, in its description of the tortured bodies of the rebels murdered in the attack's aftermath, would begin to lay the foundation for the claim by what would become the 26th of July Movement to be sole protagonists in the insurrection to overthrow the Batista regime.

The official story leaves little space for accounts of what happened on the island between Fidel's imprisonment after the Moncada attack and his return on December 2, 1956, to begin armed struggle. Yet Chase notes that if we are to understand the rise and the success of the armed insurgency, we must first study these underexamined years, the period that Lorraine Bayard de Volo characterizes as "time in abeyance."[2] I might add that there is a further question to be explored: why this period is underexamined in the official history of the making of the revolution. I argue that the official account of the taking of power implicitly required only passing reference to much of what happened in these years. The diminution of this time in favor of time marked by guerrilla struggle has had the effect of separating out certain women's undertakings and thereby masking the centrality of the role played by women during the "time in abeyance" in opposition to the regime. It relocates the actions they undertook to a disparate landscape as background to what would be the real struggle to bring down the dictatorship. As Chase argues, anti-Batista women employing what she describes as a "creative repertoire of dissent" were indispensable in preparing the terrain on which the dictatorship would be defeated.[3]

THE COUP AND CIVIL SOCIETY

Batista's problems with Cuban civil society were multiple. Given the limits of support for his coup, he had to manage at a minimum to ensure the passivity of substantial sectors within it. Unlike the despots in Nicaragua or El Salvador during this period, who exercised virtually absolute power in countries in which any sort of civil society was negligible, Cuban civil society was substantial, rooted, and understood itself in European and particularly American terms. That Cubans and Cuba belonged to this world was perhaps particularly true of the middle class or aspiring middle class in Havana. Havana had for decades looked north rather than to the rest of Latin America or the Caribbean to take measure of itself. The coup violated these Cubans' beliefs about themselves and their country. The seizure of power by Batista was experienced by Cubans in a range of ways not necessarily in contradiction with one another. Cuba's very progressive 1940 constitution, which if not realized, had been a source of enormous pride for Cubans even in the face of the blatantly corrupt governments elected both before and after its enactment. Immediately after seizing power, Batista suspended the 1940 constitution and voided the presidential election that was to have been held in June 1952. The very fact that there had been elections from the end of the American occupation in 1902, however corrupt in their staging and their aftermath, made Batista's military coup even more of an outrage. His enactment of the Estatutos Constitucionales, which he substituted for the 1940 constitution to give his presidency a veneer of legitimacy, fooled no one.

For a majority of the middle and lower middle classes, disproportionately concentrated in Havana, who had already witnessed their city progressively degraded by the outside world and labeled the fleshpot of the Caribbean, this was yet another insult.[4] The island would now be seen by that world as little more than another banana republic, with Havana as its Tegucigalpa. As the columnist Eduardo Ardura noted, for Cubans of every social class, "there is something of a sensation of shipwreck."[5] The decades-long unrealized dream of the moral republic articulated for all Cubans by José Martí and central to Cubans' self-conception had yet again been shattered. The frustrated and frustrating years of politiquería (dirty political maneuvering) under successively more corrupt governments had for some reached another breaking point. And all this was the work of the very man who first came to de facto power in 1934 with the direct complicity of the United States in its efforts to put an end to the 1930 revolution.

But the coup was greeted as well with resignation and a sense of impotence. In the days immediately following it there was little noticeable disruption of daily life in Havana. The most visible exceptions to this were the students and those who joined them at the university. The university as it had in the 1930 revolution served as a magnet for those protesting the coup and the site for angry protests against it. And it would be the point from which young people in particular would later go out onto the streets in defiance of the regime. In the days immediately following the coup students both at the university and in pre-universities wore armbands to signify mourning. On the steps of the university students carried and symbolically buried a coffin containing the 1940 constitution.[6] And in January 1953 in a demonstration protesting the tarring of the bust of Julio Antonio Mella on the university campus, Ruben Batista, an architecture student, became the first person killed by the police.[7] His death evoked a massive protest: His funeral cortege was followed by a huge number of people.[8]

Yet many of the parents of these young people saw the coup as another version of what they had been witnessing for years. Some of this older generation had been directly involved in or sympathetic to the frustrated 1930 revolution. And Cubans across the island who had listened intently every Sunday night to the charismatic Eduardo Chibás's denunciations during his radio broadcasts of the corrupt political class had their hopes dashed once again when in 1951 Chibás committed suicide while on the air.[9] Parents cautioned their children against any sort of involvement in anti-Batista activities. It wasn't worth it; it would end the same, they concluded. Sonnia Moro, who would join the insurrection some five years after the 1952 coup, relates that her father on multiple occasions cautioned her not to "meterte en esto" (get mixed up in this).[10]

This then was the context in which women opposed to Batista collectively formulated, organized, and staged a panoply of protests that, Chase observes, redefined how public protest might be imagined. She enumerates in detail the range of these reimaginings, among them the ways in which women "repurposed traditional female spaces": Churches served as sites for planning and passing on plans to other women. When women followed the coffins of murdered insurgents, this form of protest used cemeteries as places for the performance of grief and loss laced with implicit denunciations of the regime. Knowledge about different protests passed through telephone chains and rumor networks (in a country where rumors are a central source of communication).[11]

Mothers' marches, organized by and consisting entirely of women, served as the most publicly visible denunciations of the regime. These marches were double forms of resistance given that demonstrations were banned by the regime and often ended in physical confrontations with the police. In Santiago, in the wake of the torture and murder of youths connected with the 26th of July Movement, processions centered the mothers of those killed by agents of the regime.[12] Surrounded by and leading an assemblage of other mothers and fictive mothers, they wove their mourning for their dead children into public protest, accusing the dictatorship of assassinating their sons.[13] These public performances of motherhood underscored in visual terms their denunciation of the Batista regime as immoral, brutal, criminal, and illegitimate. Chase notes that "protests and denunciations of state violence were instrumental in establishing a narrative that depicted the insurrection as a moral struggle against a violent dictatorial state, a narrative that helped delegitimate and destabilize Batista's rule."[14]

BATISTA, THE POLITICAL CLASS, AND THE "CIVIC DIALOGUE"

Batista understood public actions by women as secondary. Given that his major concerns centered on maintaining his rule, his focus was elsewhere. While he used his police force to shut down women's demonstrations, his major strategy for securing his position involved gaining the acquiescence of the traditional male-dominated Cuban political class. To accomplish this, he sought to reprise the strategy he had successfully employed in the 1930s during his de facto first round as dictator through a combination of graft, allocation of positions, and fostering the expectation among the political class that the dictatorship would in the short run end.[15]

But Batista's efforts to reenact this after 1952 were unsuccessful. In the immediate aftermath of the coup, the two major political parties, the Ortodoxos and the Auténticos, split internally. Initially, in both parties, those who rejected any idea of compromise with Batista—a "civic dialogue" in favor of armed revolt—were a small minority. But various factors undermined Batista's support among the political class who had initially sought this "dialogue" with him and discredited those who had opted for it. First, Batista's role in fostering and benefiting from the enormous and obscene escalation of graft and corruption that was already an endemic feature of Cuban political life. Batista's drive to accumulate massive personal wealth opened the door for the US mafia at a level of venality that promised almost to put the island up for sale to it and, most critically, irrevocably tied him to it. The promise of a seemingly open-ended confiscation of the island by the mafia threatened the position of the political class.

Second, this same political class was misled by the expectation that Batista would reprise the action he took in the 1940s and accede to free elections in 1954. Seeing the writing all too clearly on the wall, the Auténtico Party candidate, Grau San Martín, was alone in contesting Batista in the 1954 presidential election but withdrew his candidacy the day before the election was held.

By 1955, then, the notion of a "civic dialogue" had proven bankrupt. The older generation of established politicians had been in effect made obsolete, had lost any claim to whatever moral and political authority it had possessed. In a matter of a few years "civic dialogue" gave way to the alternative of armed struggle and the hegemony of a new political subject: the youth. Parties split horizontally along lines of age. The collapse of the civic dialogue and with it the loss of legitimacy among those politicians who had earlier rejected armed struggle was the death knell for the two parties. The path for armed struggle was now open. At this point, the seeds planted at the moment of "History Will Absolve Me" began to be harvested. The scenario embedded in the official narrative of the revolution took form as a battle between two groups of men: Batista and his men who sought by ever more violent means to shut down the insurgency, and the armed guerrilla forces in the sierra who sought to overthrow his dictatorship. What drops out of this story of a contest between men is the indispensable work done by women in denying Batista any moral authority and in transferring this authority to the righteous cause of the rebels. As any possible base within Cuban society in which Batista might stake a claim to legitimate rule dried up, the insurgents' claim to rightfully rebel against him gained strength.

Failing to legitimate himself as president of Cuba, and in the face of the growing insurgency, Batista resorted increasingly to "demonstrative violence" and then, in the final years of his rule, a crescendo in the use of terror. By April 1958, in the wake of the failure of the strike initiated by the 26th of July Movement, insurgents in Havana and other cities experienced what some describe as a virtual reign of terror.[16] While the official narrative of the revolution during this period of the insurgency focuses virtually entirely on the failure of Batista's May 1958 summer offensive, an all-out attack on the sierra, the llano bore the overwhelming brunt of the dictator's final onslaught. From March to December 1958 the number of assassinated insurgents increased dramatically, their tortured bodies often left on public display on street corners.

It was not insurgents alone who were impacted by this. The population in general began gradually to experience it in their daily lives. The literary critic Graziella Pogolotti describes walking on the streets of Havana: "I recall that this happened to me myself, when I was walking down a sidewalk with a male friend. . . . A police car came, and . . . it began to move alongside us, at our same pace, and you had to act as normal as possible, to keep on walking as if nothing happened. Nevertheless, if you had the luck of finding a cafeteria on the way, then you went inside to drink whatever, to conceal your concern and see if they decided to keep going. But in everyday life in this environment a very abnormal, tense situation brewed."[17] And the writer Margarita Mateo, then a child of seven, remembers: "Each time I saw one of Batista's patrol cars go by I was terrified. We were all afraid of them, all we kids were afraid of police cars. There was a very strong atmosphere of panic, of terror in the city."[18]

In his resort to violence, Batista could not even rely on the military. Perhaps the most stunning result of the summer offensive against the sierra was the speed with which his army melted away. Desertions and surrenders were so numerous that the rebels, unable to deal with this, turned their prisoners over to the Red Cross. Batista's hold on the military had always been tenuous. Military dictatorship of any sort flew in the face of military traditions or rather the lack thereof in Cuba. In countries such as Argentina or Chile, which later in the century would suffer years of brutal military dictatorship supported by a substantial proportion of these countries' people, there was a long tradition of military service among the elite and powerful sectors of society. The military profession was passed proudly from one generation to the next. Succeeding generations of sons and grandsons carried the credentials and the social status of their forebears. In contrast, Cuba had no such tradition. The rebel armies of the nineteenth century, by the end of the 1895–98 war of independence and hardly drawn from Cuba's elite, had been delegitimized, disregarded, and disbanded by the United States occupation force. Indeed, Cuba effectively had no military in the period after independence until Batista's rise to power in what was his de facto military coup in 1933.[19]

Further, most of the men known to be responsible for the torture and murder of young people in the llano came from the higher ranks of this military. As I have written, even the military itself was not a reliable constituency for Batista. His hold on it, unlike Pinochet's in Chile and Videla's in Argentina, and its loyalty to him were far from assured. Gladys Marel García Pérez argues that Batista's actions after seizing power decisively undermined his hold on the military.[20] He sought to secure his power by calling out of retirement and into the highest positions in the military various of his cronies from the 1930s: the "lumpen proletariat in uniform," as Louis Pérez Jr. labeled them.[21]

The diminished treatment in the literature of other anti-Batista movements during the "time in abeyance" is made to further confirm the singular role of the sierra guerrillas in overthrowing the dictatorship. However, other groups did in fact organize and undertake actions during the years that Fidel was in Mexico. The most important of these were the Acción Revolucionaria Oriental and the Directorio Revolucionario.

The Acción Revolucionaria Oriental coalesced in 1953 around the figure of Frank País. In 1954–55 the ARO was established nationally as the Acción Nacional Revolucionaria (ANR). País was a widely known and beloved figure in Santiago and a brilliant organizer. By 1955, as Lillian Guerra notes, he had forged a network of revolutionary cells that were "disciplined, loyal, and armed."[22] These proved critical to the survival of the straggling band of men who with Fidel managed to make it to the Sierra Maestra mountains after the landing of the *Granma*. In 1955, after meeting with Fidel in Mexico, País dissolved the ANR into the 26th of July Movement and become its national coordinator. At the point of this merger with the 26th of July Movement, País enters as a protagonist in the story of the revolution. The story, the scope, and the import of the ARN and its predecessor, the ARO, fade from history.

In Havana, students at the university, led by José Antonio Echeverría, the president of the Federación de Estudiantes Universitarios (FEU; Federation of University Students), would, between 1955 and 1956, organize what became the Directorio Revolucionario (DR), whose leadership was at first entirely drawn from the student body. The Directorio, in its very name, sought to take on the mantel of the 1930s Directorio Estudiantil Universitario. Echeverría was a natural leader, widely respected, and always on the front lines of student demonstrations. Prior to his death in 1957 he was probably the best-known and most-respected anti-Batista leader in Havana. In 1955 in the name of the Federacion Estudiantil Universitaria and the Directorio, Echeverría signed with the then-exiled Fidel Castro the Carta de México committing all three movements to the path of armed struggle to bring down the dictatorship.[23] But the Directorio would enter into the official story of the revolution, memorialized only on the anniversary of its failed attack on the Presidential Palace in March 1957, and represented only by the figure of Echeverría, who died in that attack.

—————

It was women, the core of them veterans of the 1930s struggles, who constituted one of the first organized groups aimed at ridding the island of Batista. As I will argue in the next chapter, their organization, the Frente Cívico de Mujeres Martianas (FCMM), in the actions they undertook and the roles they played in the insurrection constituted a critical force in the urban underground in Havana. For this reason, I turn next to a discussion of the FCMM.

DISRUPTING THE NARRATIVE
THE FRENTE CÍVICO DE MUJERES MARTIANAS

In March 1952, in the days immediately following the coup, Aida Pelayo, Carmen Castro Porta, Pastorita Núñez, and Marta Frayde began to discuss forming an all-women's organization to fight the Batista dictatorship. Three of these women had been active as students in the 1930s anti-Machado rebellion and following the fall of the one hundred days government in 1934, in actions against Batista's de facto rule. During the years of the Spanish Civil War and its aftermath both Pelayo and Castro Porta worked in organizations focused on Cuban combatants in that war.[1] These initial discussions were rooted in their lived experiences over decades and drawn from the strategies and organizational forms employed by women in the Spanish Civil War. They fed into the formation of Frente Civico de Mujeres Martianas (the Jose Marti Woman's Civic Front; FCMM), the all-women's organization that served as the site and the framework for the actions they would take during the insurrection against Batista. The Frente was formally constituted in November 1952, in the Salón de los Mártires at the University of Havana.[2]

The official narrative of the triumphant 26th of July Movement concerning the making of the revolution tends to position the FCMM as a "civic sustenance organization."[3] Its role was to perform tasks at the edges of the critical arenas of the struggle against the Batista dictatorship. This portrait of the FCMM as simply another civic organization is challenged by Lorraine Bayard de Volo and in particular by Michelle Chase, who both paint a far more in-depth picture of the role of the Frente.[4]

In fact, if we examine the politics and personal histories of those who conceived of the Frente as well as the actions in which it was involved or which it initiated in the period from 1953 to 1958, what emerges is a portrait of a group of women whose key members understood themselves as revolutionaries, as protagonists in the struggle to rid Cuba of Batista, and who acted strategically and tactically as such.

The name they gave to the Frente evidences with absolute clarity their understanding of what was to be done during the insurrection and its aftermath. Each of them spoke about the importance of Jose Martí in their lives and as a motivating force in what they would do. Pastorita Núñez recalled: "I discovered Martí through my father. Martí shaped my ideas and sent them into flight. I was in love forever with the gigantic, exceptional person that he was. From that moment on my entire life was defined."[5] Both Carmen Castro and Pastorita Núñez had been followers of Eduardo Chibás and were active members of the party he founded. Carmen led the Women's Front of Chibás' Ortodoxo Party; both she and Pastorita served on its national executive committee.

The Martianas, as the women of the Frente were known, define the organization as a collective—this, they asserted, was their first principle—with Aida Pelayo as general coordinator and Carmen as coordinator of organization and propaganda. Decisions about and plans for actions were always preceded by discussions among this collective. And the Frente made it their single objective to overthrow the Batista dictatorship—the "desgobierno," as Pelayo described it—and establish a government "in accordance with the aspirations and sovereign will of the Cuban people."[6] Given this single objective they cooperated with all groups and movements they deemed to share it. Pelayo remembers that among the twenty-two women present at the assembly that formally constituted the Frente were women affiliated with a range of different political groups as well as women with no affiliation (but, she adds, "certainly not anyone from the ranks of the political sellouts or collaborators").[7]

The Frente met with and in effect interviewed leaders of the various organizations to identify these "sellouts." Pelayo's characterization of Prío (the president deposed by Batista) as "a political cadaver" indicates some of their conclusions.[8] But they continued with their round of assessments. Carmen Castro's description of Acción Armada Auténtica (AAA) leader Aureliano Sánchez Arango bears noting.[9] He met with Carmen, Pastorita, and Maruja Iglesias dressed as a cowboy: "We made an effort to recognize the person who had just appeared at the door. In an instant, we remembered our childhood watching American westerns and its characters: William Hart, Tom Mix and 'Perico Metralla' . . . but this time it was the very same Aureliano in person. Our eyes fell upon the pistol tucked in his belt, the grenades hanging from the front of his pants, and the medallion hanging on a little chain. He was Christ crowned with thorns. There were assorted machine guns placed on the table in front of us. The atmosphere felt bellicose and he declared his opposition to the course we had chosen and in a most macabre voice he predicted: 'Recovering freedom will cost a great deal of blood.'"[10]

And so it went. With García Bárcena, who was adamant that the solution was a coup from above; with the old mambí Don Cosme de la Torriente Brau, who was calling for a "civic dialogue."[11] But Carmen Castro saves her best adjectives for the Martianas' encounter with the ex-president of Cuba, Grau San Martín, the "old zorro," as she labels him.[12] Here is Carmen's definition of a "zorro" (and therefore of Grau):

It is an animal whose malice compensates its lack of strength. It has long feet, a pointed snout and sharp teeth; it is, by nature, the thief of poultry coops throughout the world. This description is applicable to a mammal of the hound family and to the personality of former President Ramón Grau San Martín. A lean figure with long legs and arms, big hands with overly long, slippery and malignant fingers which are experienced in grabbing (i.e., stealing) and lazy in giving and long, and sharp teeth. He compensates for his feeble constitution with a malevolent sharpness that flows from his dynamic gray cells. He used the Public Treasury as his own back yard, to replenish his private coffers through constant robberies.[13]

Carmen is writing from long experience of Grau, summarizing his exceptionally corrupt turn as Cuban president from 1944 to 1948. When she was being a bit less vivid, Carmen dismissed Grau with the epithet "el cantinfleo," a reference to Cantinflas, the comic character in contemporary Mexican cinema who speaks but says nothing.[14] As can be imagined, these were not the men or the organizations with which the FCMM would deal. Although, as we shall see, the old guard of the FCMM, Aida and Carmen, had no problem using them or anyone else when they were deemed useful for specific ends.

Thus for instance the meeting scheduled to be held in October 1955 in the Plaza de los Desamparados in Old Havana, planned by Carlos Prío (who had returned to Cuba) and the leaders of various opposition parties who sought to encourage the "civic dialogue" and a peaceful solution to the "Cuban problem." The FCMM received an invitation to participate. Having decided collectively that the meeting might be turned to other purposes, they sent Aida to the planning session, which was to decide who would speak about what. At this session, Aida was allotted the theme of the family and peace. They then determined the order of the speakers. Aida's mind wandered: "As the discussion went on she absentmindedly contemplated the theme of peace . . . , but the sort of peace enforced with other things starting with a 'p': like a 'p' as in palo [stick] to hit one with, or 'p,' as in plomo (bullet) or again, 'p' as in 'palmacristi' [a strong laxative used by esbirros in the 1930s to torture jailed militants by forcing it down their throats with a funnel]."[15]

But she came back to earth in time to hear that her talk would warm up the crowd for Prío. It probably does not need to be said that once in the Plaza she chose an entirely different theme and did indeed warm up the crowd: It responded to her words with calls for revolución and shouts of "¡Batista Asesino!" (Batista, Assassin!) and "Abajo los traidores!" (Down with the traitors!). Prío ended the meeting, telling Aida, "Chica, you forced me to change my closing address." To which Aida responded, "I forced you to put on your pants" (i.e., act like a man).[16]

The Frente worked most closely in its early years with the Federation of University Students and in particular with its president, José Antonio Echeverría (later the head of the Directorio), with the Directorio militant Joey Westbrook, and with Fernando Alfonso Torices (or Morúa, his name in the clandestinidad), of the 26th of July Movement, who had met Aida when both were militants in the Acción Revolucionaria Guiteras (ARG).[17] Through Westbrook and Morúa in particular, the Frente came to know a younger generation of women and girls at various levels of schooling. Although Aida, Carmen, Pastorita, and other Martianas had long-standing personal relationships with the top leaders of the various clandestine movements, the Frente concerned itself not so much with and among this leadership as with medium-level cadres and militants of the various clandestine movements in the cities. Carmen makes clear their reasoning: "We wished to be wherever the greatest potential for combativeness and for attacks against the enemy were concentrated, and where the consequences of repression were most intense and brutal; where detentions, torture and disappearances and casualties were most numerous."[18]

As Cuba became a battlefield against Batista, the Frente came to encompass, according to Pelayo, thousands of women across the island in some form.[19] The primarily older generations of women who formed its original core were joined by a younger generation, mostly students from pre-universities, and in particular the Instituto de La Habana and the Escuela de Comercio de La Habana, both of which were hotbeds of resistance to the dictatorship. The degree to which the Frente's strategy of constituting a union of women whose single goal was to rid Cuba of Batista becomes clear: Most of the women and girls who participated in the actions of the Frente were also in a range of distinct movements, particularly the 26th of July Movement and the Directorio; others identified themselves as Frente members independent of these movements.

The unity achieved formally only at the August 1958 meeting in the sierra between the 26th of July Movement and other opposition groups characterized the Frente from its beginning and throughout its existence. The Frente's inclusiveness was hardly accidental; rather, it was both a political and strategic statement. The women who formed it sought to embody in it the possibility and the means for unified action among what were disparate and fractionalized groups seeking to depose the dictatorship. Thus their response when in 1955 Fidel Castro, in a letter written from Mexico to his "much admired" old friend Carmen Castro, expressed his desire "to continue the contacts I started with you before my departure [to Mexico after he was released from prison in 1955]. From the very beginning, I said that the collaboration of the Frente Cívico de Mujeres Martianas [with the 26th of July Movement] is critical. Due to our ideological affinity and our similar history of struggle and sacrifice without hesitation or rest, we are called upon to closely unite our efforts."[20] He then proposed that the FCMM "be joined by every woman who agrees with our cause and transformed into the Women's Branch of the 26th of July Movement. You can play an important role in every aspect of the Movement, above all in the workers' sector and in the area of ideology and revolutionary propaganda in general. And you would also have, of course, a corresponding representation in the National Leadership. I already spoke to you about this once."[21]

There is no record of Carmen's answer to Fidel's letter. In 1991, in private correspondence, Faustino Pérez, the head of the 26th of July Movement in Havana until May 1958 and a close friend of Carmen's, tried his best to explain that no response was really necessary: "Both entities—the Movement and the Martianas—always sought the same goal, identifying with and supporting each other. . . . This explains why they never felt the need or urgency of a formal or structural merger, because the essentials of the spirit of what Fidel discussed in his important letter to Carmen Castro was fulfilled."[22]

The problem with this explanation is that it explains nothing. Rather, it raises the question of why Fidel made his proposal in the first place. There would seem to be a logical answer to why, as far as anyone knows, Carmen did not respond to Fidel's request: Given the Frente's firmly stated, steadfastly held goal of overthrowing the Batista dictatorship, and its strategic understanding that inclusiveness was key to achieving this goal, formal affiliation with any one organization would have been unacceptable.

But tellingly, at least in terms of who these women were, how they related to each other, and how they were seen by the male leadership of the 26th of July Movement, there is another story to recount concerning Fidel's suggestion. Soon after Fidel and the survivors of the *Granma* landing reached the sierra, he sent Carmen Castro another message, this time a verbal one, delivered by Armando Hart and Faustino Pérez, proposing once more that the FCMM become the women's front of the 26th of July Movement.[23] But Hart set a condition: If the FCMM agreed to this, Aida could not be the Martiana in the national directorate of the 26th of July Movement. Carmen cut off the conversation: "'Hasta aquí, no más' [No more discussion]. . . . That was not what Fidel and I talked about."[24] And she said nothing to Aida about the message.

Why did the 26th of July Movement in the person of Hart and Pérez qualify its proposal in this way? Fidel had known Aida well and for a very long time: Indeed, he was her defense lawyer in a 1951 trial. As I will discuss later in this chapter, Aida was a defendant with him at the 1953 trial of the Moncada assailants, even though she was on the other side of the island in Havana at the moment of the assault. And Aida and the Frente had organized the national campaign for amnesty for Fidel and those imprisoned with him in the wake of the Moncada attack. Rosa Mier's unabashed exaltation of Aida hints at the problem: "A woman with the personality of Aida Pelayo, a leader at the national level, one of those Martianas with such strength and so much prestige, acknowledged by all the prisoners, the revolutionaries, the combatants."[25]

But Aida's personality and her political history were apparently exactly the problem for the 26th of July Movement leadership: The lesson Aida had taken from her years in the 1930 revolution was that the only way to rid the island of its avaricious political class and at last realize the nation imagined by Martí was with arms. When the AR Guiteras dissolved into the gangster wars of the 1940s, rumor had it that Aida was part of that.[26] Apparently the 26th of July Movement did not see this as a fitting profile for the head of its women's front, to say nothing about as a member of its national directorate.[27]

Carlos Enrique Pelayo relates that after the triumph, on the day that he arrived in Havana, Fidel spoke with Carmen in the Havana Libre Hotel in which he had established his temporary headquarters and asked her why she never replied to the message he sent her. Carmen told him, "We will talk about it one day." But they never did.[28]

As history has proven, the FCMM's strategy of unity around a single goal had profound consequences in practice for the insurrectionary movement as a whole in the llano. In the entire body of what has been written by or about them, mostly in brief testimonial form, a large number of clandestinas, whether 26th of July Movement or the Directorio Revolucionario, identify as having taken part in actions by or with the FCMM as well. In opening this space defined only by a common goal, the FCMM was central in drawing young women into the resistance and in promoting, facilitating, and coordinating joint actions on the ground by different groups.

The fact that older members of the FCMM knew each other well and had worked together politically over decades allowed them both personally and strategically to make quick collective decisions: This manifested in multiple ways during the insurrection. The existing networks connecting the Martianas among themselves enabled the speed with which news circulated about the arrests of insurgents and, with that, life-saving information concerning to which police station they had been taken. As we shall see, this was critical. Word traveled along these same personal networks when safe houses were about to be raided so that those living in them could make a quick exit and/or destroy incriminating material.

The information thus provided meant that witnesses could be contacted to make public the fact that those taken by the esbirros were alive at the time of their arrest. This made it difficult for them to be disappeared or murdered once imprisoned. When the surge of brutality in the last months of the dictatorship essentially disarticulated contact within and between insurgent groups and individual clandestinas/os, it was probably the Frente networks alone that continued to operate. Individual Martianas became virtually the only possible contact point for insurgents seeking even the most temporary of refuges.

Something fundamental was at work in all of this. The women at the center of organizing the FCMM were really among the only people who, on March 10, 1952, had the experience of actively fighting dictatorships in Cuba. Aida and Carmen had been on the front lines of the student movement in the 1930 revolution against the Machado dictatorship and against the first de facto Batista coup in 1934. For their actions, they had served time in jail. They knew what they faced: This was, after all, their second time fighting against Batista and others among his retinue. They understood the need for multifaceted strategies and they had the experience to formulate them. And they put these strategies into action as no other oppositional group or organization initially did. These groups, including most of the insurgents in the 26th of July Movement, had, as it were, to learn on the job. It is no accident that in the months directly following the coup, youths from the FEU, many of whom would form the Directorio and the 26th of July Movement, among them Fidel Castro, were nightly visitors in Carmen Castro's living room. We can assume that given his wont Fidel probably talked a good deal during these visits, but Pelayo reported that he also listened. These were women from whom he could learn. In the years preceding the coup, as he made a name for himself as a lawyer and an Ortodoxo Party candidate for a seat in the Senate, Fidel at times asked Carmen to read and edit speeches he was to give.[29] When he was released from prison in 1955, before leaving the island for Mexico, one of the first things he did was to ask to see Carmen Castro, Aida Pelayo, and Pastorita Núñez.

In a 1992 interview Aida lays out what she calls the "two different methods of operation of the Frente": "We led two sorts of lives: the legal one, that we conquered ourselves just because we felt like it, without asking anyone's permission, and the illegal one. We made constant denunciations of human rights violations. Long before people began caring about that, we already did."[30]

The first "life" that Aida mentions, the Frente's public face, is what is generally associated with it in existing literature: that among other groups (the Civic Resistance Movement [MRC], etc.) it provided support of various sorts for insurgents. As it is presented in *La lección del Maestro* these included "propaganda oriented at awakening consciences; love for the patria, impetus to act against the dictatorship, utilizing radio and the press, making and distributing fliers and leaflets; organizing public rallies; exposing the sell-out and conciliatory politics of the opposition political parties which advocate a 'civic dialogue' with the dictatorship; providing legal, moral and material assistance to political prisoners and to combatants' families; denouncing all violations of human rights; giving different types of support to other groups involved in the struggle." The second, insurrectional tactics, included all kinds of violent actions; sabotage, transfer of weapons, street rallies; attacks against esbirros; prisoners' escapes; providing refuge for those being persecuted; extending medical assistance for those wounded in action; identifying the bodies of murdered combatants, providing free funeral services for fallen fighters."[31]

Even in their own terms the line between what Pelayo calls the Frente's "two lives," as they are laid out above, is slippery. For instance, as we shall see in chapter 5, food was only one of the items delivered by girls and women in visits to prisoners. These visits were also a way to deliver messages between imprisoned insurgents and those on the outside, and they enabled identification of informants among the prisoners. We can perhaps re-read or reconfigure even the public, supposedly legal face of the Frente to paint another story, unraveling the distinction that Pelayo herself makes above between legal and clandestine actions to understand both as evidence of the degree of their protagonism in the struggle against Batista. This other story is molded by the Frente's clear tactical sensibilities, which in its "legal" actions both reflected and employed tropes drawn from the historical framing, for over a century and a half, of the patria.

Certain postures taken by it underscore this tactical sensibility. Thus, for instance, nowhere in the Frente's literature is there any denunciation of the United States for the role it had played in Cuba from the time of its entry into the War of Independence through its recognition and provision of arms to the Batista regime. Indeed, in a leaflet distributed by the Frente, Carmen praised the United States as "a country of liberties and democracy."[32] Given their political histories and the times through which the organizers of the Frente had lived, they were, of course, painfully aware of a very different United States. And in later interviews they leave no doubt about this. Their silence concerning the United States during the years of the insurrection echoed Fidel's silence about the United States in "History Will Absolve Me." In this case we are surely looking at a tactical decision. Thus as well the Frente's employment and performance of the trope of motherhood and widowhood in different contexts and settings.

As Michelle Chase writes, this performance is implicit in the roles that they assumed as "defenders of home, family and morality"; in their consistent presence in public milieux (funerals, churches, demonstrations); in their daily visits to insurgents imprisoned in Mantilla, the women's holding prison, and El Príncipe, the male holding prison, purportedly to bring food and so on; in their efforts to recover and identify the bodies of assassinated insurrectionaries to bring them back to their mothers or wives; in their continuing financial and emotional support for these families; in the black clothes they donned for any form of public demonstration (marches, funerals); in their use in Frente literature of the familiar and deeply rooted tropes of the abnegada mother whose steadfast commitment to the patria is above all embodied in her production of the sons and husbands who will fight in its name; and in the moral force of their commitment to the patria, expressed always in urging these sons to action.[33] Thus, the Frente's 1956 "Message to Cuban Women" could easily have served as a plea to mothers and wives during the wars of the nineteenth century:

> We should not stir hatred or resentment. Nor should we, as hyenas, do, voice a desire for bloodshed out of a barbarian delight or a desire for revenge. But neither should we resign ourselves to the sacrifice of the blood running through our own veins, when, to cure a shameful ulcer we are called upon to cut our veins open. Cuban mother, do not reproach your rebel son's patriotic rapture. Do not turn your offspring—out of your loving affection—into an indifferent person vis-a-vis the pains the patria is suffering. Merge his longings with your own. If you have a soldier son, instill in him firmness in the fulfilment of his duties as a son of the people, to whose ranks he belongs. In the case of your husband, whom you love, encourage him, uniting his longings with your own. If your brother embraces the ideal of freedom, imitate him, dignifying your blood ties in the most vigorous understanding possible. Cuban woman,

honor your glorious forefathers. . . . "Tombs"—said the Apostle—"cry out for their seeds, as do furrows. Let us water the furrows with love and sacrifice."[34]

But while the Frente used the trope of motherhood, it was neither conceived nor organized around the identity of motherhood. Rather, its core members' commitment was to armed struggle to bring down the regime and its closest ties were to the insurgents in the two movements, the Directorio and the 26th of July, whose commitment likewise was to armed struggle.

It will suffice here to examine the manner in which they led or participated even in major open-street demonstrations in Havana. These revolved not around protest, but around militancy and action. Passive witness, employed for instance by the Madres de la Plaza de Mayo in Argentina (claiming motherhood to legitimize their protest), was rarely chosen as a message by the Frente or indeed as a part of their tactics and actions. While their banners might read "peace," their actions—putting their bodies on the line and physically fighting back against the esbirros and the police who habitually used force in reaction to their demonstrations—were always intended to show that no peace was possible as long as Batista was in power.

The Frente always staged the demonstrations it organized in Havana (demonstrations were in themselves illegal acts, as they had been banned by Batista) along Galiano, the main shopping street at the center of commercial Havana, during shopping hours. Their target audience was clearly female. These demonstrations, witnessed by residents and by the women who worked or were browsing in the shops and department stores along Galiano, ended with very unfeminine pitched, if uneven, physical battles between the police and the Martianas. And the Frente choreographed these demonstrations with great care to maximize in every way they could the widest possible public audience.

On December 5, 1955, the Frente organized a reprisal of a 1930s demonstration in protest against the Machado dictatorship, which had been led by members of the 1930s Directorate of University Students (DEU). Those students' objective then, as it supposedly was for the Martianas twenty-odd years later, had been to reach the home of the old mambí Cosme de la Torriente to stir him into action. But in 1955 the Frente had more than this in mind. Following the plan elaborated down to the minute by Carmen Castro and orchestrated by her to garner widescale exposure in the media, Martianas carefully positioned themselves in stores and cafés that lined Galiano. At exactly six o'clock in a matter of seconds, a large contingent of women in organized formation moved from the sidewalks on both sides of the street to occupy the middle of the street. At the same moment a Martiana stationed in a drugstore next to the CMQ radio station received the call to proceed to the station with a prepared note: "A group of unidentified women has just left the corner of Galiano and San Rafael streets. They seem to be heading out to the law firm of Dr. Cosme de la Torriente, the old mambí soldier in Old Havana." Carmen Castro, reflecting on the Martianas' strategy here, comments: "It was a clever move to give those initiating the march the advantage over the forces of repression."

They positioned themselves with carefully planned precision. Carmen Castro led the march with two other Martianas. "When the police [tried] to block us, saying: 'you have to break up. This is illegal,'" Carmen, invoking the right to peaceful reunion guaranteed by the 1940 constitution (which Batista had revoked), turned and walked past them, saying, "Let's march." The demonstration became a compact mass of women. Pastorita Núñez and Olga Román followed Carmen with a banner reading "We want peace, not blood. Freedom is the essence of life" (this last phrase a quotation from José Martí). When a policeman tried to rip the banner from them, Pastorita fought energetically; the policeman reacted violently, dislocating her wrist and fracturing her little finger. Relates Carmen: "The banner gets ripped but Pastorita doesn't let go of it." Olga, trying to protect Pastorita and the banner, grabbed the policeman by the throat and, with a strong arm firmly wrapped around his neck, dragged him a few yards. The demonstration halted. A large group of women and some policemen surrounded Olga and the policeman. But Olga was not ready to let go of the policeman, who seemed to be at the point of suffocating. His eyes were glassy. Olga continued to squeeze his throat. Aida intervened. She made room through the crowd and a policeman hit her. Aida bit his arm. Aida realized that the policeman in Olga's hold could hardly breathe. She yelled at Olga: "Let go of him, you are killing him." Olga finally released him and the policeman fell to the ground.

Aida, not to be outdone, went for the testicles of Tatica Hernández, the captain of the Third Police Station, who had just knocked her down and was trying to force her into a patrol car. Carmen continues: "Meanwhile [a group of thirty] women and policemen are engaged in a hand-to-hand fight. The policemen raise their clubs and the women grab them . . . fighting boldly against the police."

People on balconies and on sidewalks, watching this theater staged by the Martianas, applauded and protested the police actions. "The shouting and jubilation are intense. Photographers and filmmakers are shooting the unequal fight. From the balconies people are shouting: 'abusers'; 'down with the dictatorship!'"

As all this was going on, a second note was delivered to Radio Reloj, which immediately broadcast it: "The demonstration that kicked off from Galiano and San Rafael a few minutes ago is made up of Mujeres Martianas and other revolutionary women."[35] Individuals sympathetic to the insurgent movements at both of these radio stations made sure that the demonstration received significant coverage.

With their acute sensibility about the strategic use of the media in confrontational acts and demonstrations, and with the same careful planning, the Martianas maximized effects in the actions they took around the July 1957 hunger strike in El Príncipe. This time one generation of Martianas passed off lessons in planning and strategy to the next. Now it was not the "mothers" on the front lines of the demonstration; this time it was a performance led by the "sisters" and the "novias." With the same intent and the same strategy and tactics for achieving this goal, "lucha en la calle," young Frente members led the demonstration in support of the hunger strikers, who were demanding the removal of the particularly vicious and bloody Ugalde Carrillo, who had charge of the men's prison on the Isle of Pines. A small group of teenagers—including Anolan López, age fifteen; Maríta Trasancos, age sixteen; and Norma Porras—in consultation with Carmen Castro laid out the plan for the march. As in the 1955 demonstration, they proceeded once more to Galiano. They chose a Saturday at three o'clock, when they would have the greatest public and specifically female audience. They had gone several blocks down Galiano when the police confronted them. Anolan López reports:

> Because our demands were written on posters that we had tied around our bodies, many of us were thrown to the ground [by the police] to tear them off, and they dragged us over the pavement. At the same time, those beasts flogged us with their bicho 'e buey and we fought back with our finger nails and teeth.[36] I, at least, know that I left a good dental imprint on one of them. Nevertheless, we collected the remains of our placards, regrouped and retook the streets. Although our goal was to stage the protest in order to get reports of it in the news, we did not know any reporters, so some of us headed to the main offices of the daily

newspaper *El Mundo* to denounce the beatings the women were enduring. We arrived there running, with our hair in a mess, and then ran back to Galiano Street, where the rest of our compañeras were still resisting. We were relieved to see that the press was already reporting the big row the demonstration had turned into.[37]

When some of the demonstrators managed to move the melee in front of the site where the Habana Hilton (renamed the Habana Libre after January 8, 1959) was being built, the construction workers rained bricks and whatever else was on hand down on the police.[38]

The use of media in every context they could characterized all the actions undertaken by the Martianas. During the February 1958 hunger strike in the women's prison at Mantilla, Mirta Rodríguez Calderón, one of the strikers, writes, "Without them, the hunger strike to protest the abuses taking place at the Isle of Pines penitentiary would have gone without any echo or the widely spreading impact that it did have. It would have been impossible, if the Martianas had not been the solid supporting column that they were, for the news of the sacrifice of the El Príncipe and Mantilla prisoners to spread through the streets and to flood the media."[39]

The Frente combined the efforts of the generations that composed it in other contexts as well. Concha Cheda, thirty years old and a social worker in the nearby Calixto García Hospital, systematized visits, particularly by younger girls, to prisoners in El Príncipe, keeping a record of what was needed by prisoners in terms of medicine and food. She used the fact that she was a social worker to mask the frequent entries and exits of young women to and from the hospital, supposedly seeking her counsel but actually getting the goods to be delivered to the prisoners. This experience of acting as messengers to and from El Príncipe was one of the main avenues by which young women entered the fight against the dictatorship. Concha Cheda was arrested six times during 1958.

The Frente's performance of the roles inhabited by women—motherhood, daughterhood, noviahood—extended as well to widowhood. They became, when they thought it effective, the twentieth-century equivalents of the abnegada viudas of the wars of independence. This, an extension of the trope of motherhood, effectively erased the boundaries of legal versus illegal. They dressed for the part. The older generation of the Martianas were popularly known as the "moñudas": In public actions and depending on the demonstration, they wore only black and pulled their hair severely back into buns. On occasions thus attired, they frequented (that is, infiltrated) church services, unfurling banners calling for the end to the dictatorship, always combined with a quotation from Martí. They attended funerals of slain insurgents, very effectively shaming guards at cemeteries, who were often instructed to block the entrance even of the widows of these insurgents, with references to the guards' own mothers. These internments were of young men whose bodies had been brutally savaged. They were terrible and tragic occasions. And by necessity, the funeral cortegas were almost always composed of women and mostly women in the Frente. But funerals also served as yet another venue for passing on messages and critically important information.

With some exceptions, for instance, Aida and Carmen themselves, Martianas of various generations were insurgents as well in different clandestine movements. At times the Frente planned and/or participated in actions in the early years of the dictatorship mainly in coordination with the FEU but later with these different movements. In practice the fact that many FCMM members were involved with these other insurrectionary movements facilitated their active participation in actions organized and executed by a range of distinct groups.

Who then were these women who chose to organize an all-women's resistance group as their first course of action against Batista? Their personal and political histories in their own accounts of their lives mark them explicitly as feminists and revolutionaries and as transgressors of the male construct of the nation. Aida spent a good deal of her life in and out of prisons for her political activities. In the years after the 1952 coup she seemed to be in a constantly revolving door between jail and the outside world: During these years she was arrested seventeen times. Indeed, she estimated that she probably spent more time in jail and in hiding than she did organizing on the streets. (Here she underestimates her presence and her impact in the street protests.) By all accounts Pelayo was a powerful speaker, an agitator by nature, the "oradora de barricada" (orator on the barricades), as she is remembered by everyone who knew her, and she used this talent most effectively in mobilizing people to act. Although in Havana at the time of the Moncada attack in Santiago, Batista's forces swept her up into prison in its immediate aftermath: "They came for me at 7:00 a.m., on the 27th. That was an odyssey! From my home I was taken to the Military Intelligence Service [SIM]: from there to the Bureau for the Repression of Communist Activities [BRAC], and then from BRAC back to SIM; from there, to the Guanabacoa jail and then to Guanajay, the women's penitentiary. From Guanajay, they took me to Santiago de Cuba, until the end of the Moncada trial. At all times, I was in the custody of the Army General Staff."[40]

Pelayo was put on trial as a supposed participant in planning the attack on Moncada, together with those who had been captured in its aftermath. When the other defendants were asked at their trials about Pelayo's involvement in Moncada, Fidel Castro responded: "Why is Aida Pelayo here? Every time a gunshot goes off in this country, the police accuse Aida Pelayo."[41]

In Santiago on January 28, 1956, the 103rd anniversary of José Martí's birth, a group of Martianas including Pelayo, all of them dressed in black with white roses pinned to their chests, attempted to enter the Santa Ifigenia cemetery where Martí was interred to place a wreath made of white roses.[42] The police blocked their entrance and hauled them off to prison. At their hearing two days later, they were absolved of any guilt. But Aida was banned from ever returning to the city.[43]

In her characteristically off-color account of her life, Pelayo situates the inevitability of the paths she would choose in her life to the Cuba that greeted her at birth: "I was born during one of Menocal's presidential election campaign celebrations, on the eve of October 10—only ten minutes before midnight. It was all hooting, rattles, gunshots, sirens, cannon shots, so I was born in the midst of all that uproar. So, I had to be a revolutionary or I should perhaps say a lunatic."[44] Pelayo grew up mainly in a single-parent, female-headed household (her parents had separated) and she re-created this household in her adult life. She had a son but never married.[45] Rather, she embedded herself as a mother and her son in a fictive kinship network. Carlos Enrique, Aida's son, relates: "Carmen Castro was my godmother; and my mother's female friends were my aunts."[46] He grew up in a kind of geographically extended female commune: He lived as much, or more, in Carmen Castro's home as in his mother's. Carmen, he recalls, always wanted to have a child and he became that child. This network extended beyond Aida's coconspirators in the Frente. Carlos Enrique relates that when he was living with his mother in the popular barrio of Colón in Central Havana, the neighborhood's prostitutes would come running to tell him to hide, because the police were in the area.[47]

Years after the triumph of the revolution, Carmen, whose entire family had left Cuba, sick, moved in with Aida and her son. Rosa Mier, who was among the founding members of the FCMM, remembers her first meeting with Aida:

> I went to Aida Pelayo's home because I wanted to meet her. Oscar Cabrera took me there. . . . She was a teacher, living on Industria St., number 260. It was a very modest apartment, hardly big enough for its four occupants. It had only one room, where her invalid grandmother, a sister, and her eleven-year-old son lived. Aida arrived and, as soon as we were introduced, she said, "Wait a second, I just have one pair of stockings, so the first thing I do when I get home from school is wash them and hang them to dry." Yet, this was such a famous woman, who was a revolutionary since the times of Guiteras, an incorruptible, transparent woman, one of the greatest women this country has produced. Shortly afterward, she returned and began to ask me what I wanted. Conversations always spun around how to unseat Batista. Because Carmen [Castro] and Aida were familiar with Batista from the times of his other dictatorship, they knew that he could only be overthrown by the force of weapons; from the very beginning, they knew he had to be ousted through armed struggle.[48]

Pelayo's serious and sustained political involvement began during the demonstrations against the Machado dictatorship when she was sixteen and a student in the Escuela Normal de Maestros (a teachers' training school) with the Ala Libertadora Estudiantil (a student left-wing organization), a split-off from the Student Directorio at University of Havana, which she joined while still a secondary school student.[49]

Daily demonstrations continued after Machado was forced from office, intended to push Grau San Martín's One Hundred Days government, which followed the Machadato, to undertake more radical reforms. In the course of these struggles Pelayo began to practice the tactics that two decades later she, and with her the Frente, could employ in helping to bring down the Batista dictatorship. Reflecting on what she calls the "war of the '30s," Pelayo concludes, "We learned a great deal. We learned where we were wrong, where we were confused."[50] We can assume that these lessons weighed heavily on the women who shaped the Frente in the weeks following the 1952 coup.

Aida's friendship with Carmen, with whom she would organize the FCMM decades later, began when both worked on multiple fronts related to the Republican cause during the Spanish Civil War and its aftermath, the Cuban branch of the International Red Cross and the Committee for Repatriation of Cuban prisoners of war, and in amnesty campaigns for those arrested during the Machado regime and its aftermath and in various Latin American countries under dictatorial rule.[51] She served as a delegate to the 1939 Women's Congress, which militated for equal rights for women in the 1940 constitution. But she qualifies her participation: "We did, of course, and still do consider ourselves feminists but our struggle was also a revolutionary, political struggle for the full participation of women and the underprivileged in all levels of society, including politics."[52]

In 1940 the Cuban Communist Party, on orders from Josef Stalin to all communist parties to form united fronts against the Nazis, entered into the political process and, legalized by Batista, assumed posts in his government as ministers without portfolio. The two who did so were Juan Marinello and Carlos Rafael Rodríguez. Pelayo then quit the party and refused subsequently to join any party. She explains:

> An electoral political party has its characteristics: it has to steal votes, it has to adulterate the census, it has to buy votes, it has to reward people with posts. That is the truth underlying an electoral party, and if you are well disposed to this, you must accept all these consequences. It is not a revolutionary party. And it has to play the game. If a worker wants to join a strike, you cannot let him. "No, mi vida," it has to be like that, because if you are in the opposition, it is okay but if you are in the government, no. That is how I understood it, and I did not like it, so I never again joined any party.[53]

For this same reason Eduardo Chibás, years later, approached her to join the Ortodoxo Party he was then forming and to stand for the Senate as a member of this party, particularly because both were fiery orators. Chibás told her, "Imagine you and I speaking in the Senate. They will kill us both." She refused. For Pelayo, a political party that participated in elections could not be a revolutionary organization. Rather, she says, "I was always fighting in favor of something. I can't say I remained quiet or placid, because that's not in my spirit. I spent many years of my life making revolution."[54]

Chibás was only one of those who recognized her impact as a fiery speaker. Nilda Ravelo, a 26th of July Movement militant and later a close friend of Aida, recalls: "The sound of her voice still rings in my ears. Before personally meeting her, I heard her speak in Parque Central. We were talking of the time of Batista's [first] dictatorship, and there was a political rally going on there; it seems that Aida was not scheduled to speak, but at a given moment someone told her 'You should talk, to liven this rally up.' So, Aida takes the floor, and in that very rally, she denounced the assassin of Jorge Agostini."[55]

Among the various and sundry charges leveled against her in her multiple arrests, Aida was accused of "disrespect for authority," and as one charging document phrased it, "it is a well-known fact that the above-mentioned Pelayo is in the habit of opposing 'revolutionary governments,' as she had done between 1930 and 1933."[56]

If Aida was the "oradora de barricadas" of the FCMM, Carmen (or Neneína as she was called by everyone) is remembered by all those who knew her as its "cerebro" (its brain). She was its strategist, the authoress of all of its public documents, whether signed or anonymous, and the recorder of its deeds and history. Recalls Rosa Mier: "Aida never wrote nor sent any document, ever. That was the role of Neneína, a journalist, an intellectual, immensely learned, and a very brave woman. There was such a mutual understanding between Aida and Neneína that divergences never emerged between them, because each of them knew what their role was."[57]

Angela Alonso, a 26th of July Movement clandestina, explaining a friendship that she says "defied storms and survived extremely convulsed historical circumstances," observed: "Carmen required Aida's vitality to channel her own determination to struggle. Like the phenomenon of opposing poles explained by Chinese philosophy. Yet I believe that, above all, Carmen's nature as a unifying person allowed her to develop a mutual understanding with others and to get along with everyone."[58] Aida's son, Carlos Enrique, remembers: "Carmen was a teacher of youths. It must have been very difficult to have a pupil such as Joey Westbrook.[59] Cubans have no idea about the number of people who visited Carmen's home."[60]

Among these visitors were many girls, mostly in upper secondary schools or pre-universities, who would join both the FCMM and one of the clandestine movements. And by all accounts there was probably hardly a single member of either the Directorio or the 26th of July Movement who did not spend some time in Carmen's living room. This becomes poignantly clear in what she wrote late in her life, looking back on these nights in conversation with young insurgents:

Sometimes my mind overflows with memories. I see Joey Westbrook arriving, dressed immaculately; sitting down in the rocking chair in front of me, crossing his legs and beginning to inquire about past struggles. Juanito Borrell, sorting out tasks—sabotage to be taken by the militias; helping to organize the night of one hundred bombs: the assassination of the chief of the regime's chivatos. He had been full of merriment and affection, passing an olive green lighter when he was released from jail. I see Armando with his affectionate, smiling eyes, revealing his very white teeth that contrasted against his smooth black skin, telling a spicy anecdote. And Tirso Urdanivia coming in happily asking: "Are the philosophers coming tonight?" And Mario Reguera, with his bullfighter gait, arriving and going straight to the rocking chair to tell me about his clandestine activities, and most of all, that foggy night when Mario talked about how much he would like to tell his grandsons about the struggles they were waging against the tyranny. "Do you believe that I might be able to?" [he asked. I replied,] "Why not, Mario?" Months later, when I went to the morgue to see Reguerita one last time, he was completely naked and his head was leaning to one side. He looked like a bronze statue into which his intrepidness had been sculpted, together with the whisper of his secrets and longings. I gazed at him with infinite sorrow and even greater indignation, thinking that the wild beasts unleashed by the tyranny had cut short, once and for all, his big dream of telling his grandsons the epic of the struggle against the tyranny.[61]

Carmen was born in 1908 into a family that espoused liberal politics. Her father's medical career was at moments interrupted by his public oppositional stances. Carmen's active entry into the world of political agitation and journalism began substantively in 1925 at the age of sixteen when, as a student in the Instituto de Segunda Enseñanza de Matanzas, she joined hundreds demonstrating in support of the jailed revolutionary student leader Julio Antonio Mella, who was in the midst of a hunger strike. Of this demonstration she recalls, "That was the spark, or better, the detonator that awakened in me my first revolutionary unrest."[62] Three and a half years later the assassination of Mella in Mexico would shake the souls of Neneína and her contemporaries. It was there that her career as a radical journalist took root. The return of Mella's ashes for burial in Havana in 1933 further heightened Carmen's commitment to revolutionary change.

Mirta Rodríguez Calderón notes in her article about Carmen, "A Woman Against Three Dictatorships," that by the age of twenty-five she had joined in actions alongside the Directorio Estudiantil Universitario, in dozens of street clashes with the police in the struggles to overthrow Machado, and had begun her career as a radical journalist with articles in the newspapers *Alma Mater* and *Mella*. She was arrested for the first time in 1930 and briefly detained, first in El Castillo de El Príncipe and then in the women's prison in Guanabacoa, along with a group of women who tried to accompany the mother of an assassinated student on the first anniversary of his murder to the cemetery where he was buried.

In 1932 Carmen was again arrested with twelve other young women and imprisoned on false charges of involvement in an attempt to explode an automobile bomb in front of the house where leading members of Machado's police were meeting. She was made to serve almost a year in the Presidio Modelo in Gerona, the capital of the Isle of Pines, where some twenty-one years later Fidel and the survivors of the attack on Moncada would be sent. These thirteen are the only women in the history of Cuba ever to be imprisoned in the Presidio Modelo. It was not an easy place: Its distance from the mainland meant virtual isolation from family and friends. The diary of reflections she wrote during her time in the prison gives texture to the complex weaving of thoughts and feelings in which she wrapped herself during that year: melancholy, even despair, boredom, discomfort, conviction. Here are excerpts of these reflections:

"The First Night":
We gathered in the spacious back yard on a clear night. I will never forget those faces, bathed in a glowing blue light, with their expressions of eternity. Everything was immobile: the pallor of the lifeless; the quietness of dreams; the coldness of the rigid. . . . We spoke, and our voices were like distant echoes. The static eyes, the moon standing still, the untwinkling stars, the dormant vine on the gray wall, the serene environment. The wind had suspended its caresses. The voices ceased. Everything was engulfed in a quiet, intrepid silence. It was like the complete collapse of all movement. It was then that we had the feeling of something unending, infinite.

And "Free Ideas":
Who puts barriers on thought? Who can stop the brain, preventing it from freely functioning? Who could be capable of jailing ideas? Despots, tyrants have yet to invent that prison.

And "Escape":

To get out of jail and travel far away, you must close your eyes and not see dark prison blocks, rusty gates, old walls, black bars or small windows. Nothing, nothing that prevents you from fleeing far, far away from the horrible reality of the ergastulum.[63]

The solitude of her life was broken by the books she requested her brother-in-law to send her, notably the poems of Rabindranath Tagore and Oscar Wilde and *The Prison Letters of Rosa Luxembourg*. This last book accompanied her throughout her life and it was among her personal effects at her death.[64] It is doubtful that in Cuba in 1931, or for that matter in 1931 anywhere in the world, many people were reading Rosa Luxembourg.

Following her release from the Presidio Modelo, she participated in organizations formed to confront immediate political concerns: amnesty for those arrested after the fall of the One Hundred Days government; opposition to the fascist "black shirts" then seeking a base on the island; work with committees to repatriate Cubans in prison in Spain in the aftermath of the Spanish Civil War and with the International Red Cross. At that point Carmen met Aida. They worked together in various different capacities through the end of the 1930s and into the 1940s and 1950s when they founded the FCMM. Carmen was arrested six times during the insurrection against Batista, charged with terrorism, and like Aida, among other charges accused of "disrespect for authority."[65]

Olga Román, although not one of the four who generated the idea for the FCMM, was central to it. Olga, younger than Carmen and Aida, first encountered Aida as a militant in the Gutierrez Revolutionary Action (Acción Revolucionaria Gutiérrez). Born in Guantanamo, Olga came to Havana in 1952 and moved right into Aida's extended household. Her path and Aida's crossed at every point in the fight against Batista: She was Aida's constant "companion in crime" as it were. While Aida who, given her reputation, was awarded the title "la incendiaria" (the incendiary) by Havana insurgents in the aftermath of another in the FCMM's constant efforts to disrupt the normal state of things, Aida herself reported that was actually Olga who really had earned the name. Together with Aida she had attempted to set fire to a float, which was part of a beauty pageant parade on the Malecón and sponsored by Wrigley's chewing gum. It didn't work; rather, one of the other floats caught fire. No one was hurt. As Aida relates: "By the time they got to the Wrigley's float, the Malecón was already empty. In the meantime, we had received the order to do nothing because there was no public, nothing. But she [Olga] made a movement with the hand [Aida imitates the movement], and with this she set off the ball of flames and the float caught fire. It looked really pretty, with sparks flying everywhere and women jumping off it."[66]

By every report of those who fought with them, Olga and Aida shadowed each other in every action, public or clandestine, that the FCMM took against the dictatorship. Carlos Enrique comments, "Olga was the violent one and my mother . . . my mother was a very ordinary person. She was a people's person, and so was Olga."[67]

And they were fearless: Aida relates one such action. On January 28, 1955, the anniversary of Martí's birth, Batista, the newly elected president in an electoral masquerade and seeking to legitimate himself, was about to formally present his new legislature. Aida relates:

> Our work in the clandestinidad did not contemplate terrorism, but we resorted to it whenever the situation demanded and at the time it was necessary. Olga and I left with the package, heading for Galiano Street in Central Havana. We went round and round, we took a bus, waiting for the sun to set a bit and for shops to close in order to avoid accidents. No one would suspect two women strolling with a bomb through the streets. We got off at Galiano and San Miguel and lit some cigarettes. When we got to San Miguel and Campanario we saw a group of young men involved in a lively chat. Among them was a very ugly short man who was the most agitated of them all. When we were passing them, they gallantly moved to give us room and we heard one of them say, "I'll take the blonde" [Olga]. And the short one said, "I'll take the brunette" [Aida]. . . . I could not allow it. I suddenly stopped, took the package and began to open it. Olga, very alarmed, asked me, "What are you doing?" I replied, "Wait just a second, I am going to blow up that very fresh guy." You can just imagine how Olga tried to convince me of the fact that "it was a question of taste and bad luck."[68]

They finally placed the bomb on the latch of the door of the shoe shop across the street from La Época department store. Pelayo concludes: "Once again, Martí had his honor restored."[69] Olga would be arrested eleven times during the years of the Batista dictatorship. Like Aida and Carmen, among the various charges leveled at her, she was always accused of "disrespect for authority."

Pastorita Núñez, the third woman who met at Aida's house that night in March 1952 when the seeds of the FCMM were planted, was born into a poor family and raised by a single parent, her father. Like Carmen she never had a child but considered her godchild, José (Pepito) Robustillo, as her own son and raised him with his mother, Ibia Robustillo. Like Aida she was an "oradora de barricada," a fiery speaker. And like Olga, although closest to the older generation of Martianas personally and politically, she was too young to have participated in the 1930s insurgency. But she remembers well how it affected her: "When Machado was overthrown the first victim from my hometown was my cousin Hortensia, murdered in the rally we were attending. Like me, she was ten years old. Her burial was tremendous: the body was covered with a flag and transported on people's shoulders. That was the first major impact I experienced. A path of struggle was forever traced for me."[70]

Pastorita had been a close personal friend of Chibás and one of his most ardent and articulate supporters. She was among the last people to see him on the day he committed suicide. Along with Carmen, she served in the national directorate of the Ortodoxo Party. Following Batista's coup Pastorita fought to get the party to take a stand in favor of armed revolution but failed. The Ortodoxos, as I noted in chapter 1, split into two wings, one of which espoused negotiating with Batista and the other, led among others by Pastorita, called for armed struggle.

Pastorita is best characterized by her unflinching commitment to what she believed in: This was as true of her commitment to the ideas of Martí as it was of her adherence to Chibás and to the Ortodoxo Party and, until her death in 2010, to Fidel Castro. Unlike Aida, Carmen, and Olga, but like so many of the younger girls and women who would join the FCMM, Pastorita was a militant in both the Martianas and the 26th of July Movement. Her ardent belief in Fidel and the revolution never flagged, despite her personal disappointments in the years following the triumph. I deal with these in chapter 7.

Margot Aniceto, a lawyer whose name appears over and over again in the testimonies of clandestinas/os, played a key role in the insurgency. As a lawyer, Aniceto seemed to arrive at the police stations to which arrested clandestinas/os were taken almost before they did or to be able to tell their families where they were. Witnessing that one's child was alive after being arrested meant that it would be very difficult for the esbirros to subsequently murder or disappear her. Given the closely interwoven and informal nature of family and social life characteristic of Cuban society, Aniceto's rapid discoveries of where those arrested had been taken meant that families could begin to seek out friends or relatives or friends of relatives or godmothers and fathers or employers or other people at work who had connections with someone in the carceral world into which their children had been taken and could be used to try to get them out. And in some cases these contacts did release their children. For instance, when Margot discovered through her own channels that Pilar Sa, a young clandestina, had been taken to the Fifth Police Station she informed Pilar's mother, which then set the wheels in motion. Her mother contacted her son's godmother who was a friend of Mirabel, one of the esbirros at the station. The godmother then went to the bar next to the station, which she knew was frequented by the station's police, where she spoke with Mirabel about Pilar. Pilar's mother was thus allowed to visit her daughter. This meant that, having been seen alive, Pilar was most likely safe.[71]

Margot could do this largely by the force of her personality, operating within the multiple networks through which she moved. She was, as Mariíta Trasancos, a young clandestina, notes, "en la eschucha" (in the know).[72] She lived her entire life in her mother's house in Old Havana, a barrio in which multiple clandestine groups, mainly of young men adhering to the 26th of July Movement, formed during the early days of the insurrection. These were the children of the neighbors she had known for decades; they naturally came to her when their children fell into the hands of the police. Like the older generation of the FCMM, Aniceto had built up a lifetime's worth of contacts on all sides of the political spectrum. She had been, among other things, a member of the Auténtico Party and in 1948 had been elected a city counselor. And she had no qualms about using these contacts no matter who they were, including, as we shall see, even those responsible for the worst torture, to save lives of insurgents.

Nor did she stint on making full use of what was a typically Cuban informal, porous, and rumor-laden legal milieu inhabited by other lawyers, judges, informers, and even some of the regular police who, along with judges themselves, were often anti-Batista. In her role as a lawyer, Aniceto moved constantly within this milieu. She went daily before the tribunales de urgencia where she argued endlessly for the enforcement of the laws concerning the constitutionally guaranteed time limit (one hundred days) that prisoners could be held before being brought to trial, and about restrictions on the imprisonment of minors.[73] Her successes were central to making Batista's jails seem at moments to have revolving doors. In the police stations she frequented she became well acquainted with and often befriended police guards who were also not necessarily pro-Batista and in many cases were even anti-Batista. She was so ubiquitous around these police stations and the women's prison in Mantilla that guards on occasion mistook her for one of the prisoners. The girls and young women in Mantilla joked that "Margot is such a good lawyer that if she can't get us out of prison, she joins us in it."[74]

The wide range of contacts and networks she drew on and cultivated gave her access to all sorts of invaluable information, not just about arrests but even about houses in which clandestinos were living or meeting that were about to be raided by Batista's esbirros. And through the FCMM, whose members constituted perhaps the insurgency's most efficient and organized network of contacts, she was able to channel this vital information to the endangered insurgents.[75] Further, her ongoing relationships with the families of individuals whom she had represented provided her with deep pockets in terms of homes in which a clandestina/o being hunted could find temporary refuge: She was perhaps the greatest and most consistent resource in finding families willing to take in hunted insurgents in Havana.

Aniceto was born into a middle-class family, and her parents were professionals. She was of the generation of Aida and Carmen and, like them, had been actively involved as a student in the 1930 revolution in which her only sister was killed. Like Pastorita and Carmen, she never married or had children. Pilar Sa, with whom Margot was in close contact throughout the years of the insurgency and who, with her daughters, remained very close to Margot until her death, described her as "a man trapped in a women's body."[76] Although with the exception of Pilar this was and is not spoken about or acknowledged even by those who knew her well, she did not keep it a secret. But given the times and the place, she did not live this life openly. Following January 1, 1959, and for the remainder of her life she lived as she always had, in her parents' house in Old Havana.

Margot was arrested twice. In her first arrest the charges included the accusation that she "was known for her defense of the 26th of July conspirators." And like Aida, Carmen, and Olga, she "regularly disregards or disrespects authority." The second time she was arrested she was charged with insulting Evangelina de la Llera, a minister in Batista's government who had a hand in the murder of the Giralt sisters.[77]

On January 28, 1959, the anniversary of Martí's birth, in front of his tomb in the Santa Ifigenia cemetery in Santiago, the FCMM dissolved itself. Aida gave what in essence was its eulogy: "Maestro, as you taught us, we have fulfilled our duty, simply and naturally. We did so during the war and will continue to do so in peacetime."[78]

In terms of the manner in which the Martianas had defined themselves, the dissolution of the Frente was consistent with both their goal and their methods. Their goal had been to rid Cuba of the Batista regime: That had been accomplished. Their methods, forging unity among the forces working to do this, led them logically to the conclusion that their task as Cubans was now to integrate themselves as individuals into the revolution and work in unity with others in its project.

But given what would follow January 1, 1959, in terms of organizing and representing women, not a few of those who had been involved in the insurgency came to see their dissolution as an error.

MALE BONDING
THE SIERRA VERSUS THE LLANO

I begin this chapter with an anecdote drawn from my several years of fieldwork among the clandestinas. I went with the two now-grown daughters of a clandestina who had been arrested and tortured there, to what had been the Fifth Police Station in Central Havana. It is now a school. A young man, a twenty-four-year-old from Santiago, was standing in the doorway. He explained to us that he began teaching at the school when he was sixteen and was now its vice director. When we told him why we had come, he took us on a tour of the school, explaining what had happened to the girls and women brought there during the insurrection. He assured us that everyone in the school—the administrators, the teachers, the students—had to know in detail its history and what had transpired within its walls. Wanting to know how he integrated this knowledge with what he himself had been taught concerning how the revolution was made, I asked him to give us his account of this. He began with the attack on the Moncada fortress, then to Mexico with Fidel Castro, then to Fidel's return to Cuba on the *Granma*, and then to Fidel and Che Guevara in the Sierra Maestra mountains. His only mention of a city was his description of Che's arrival in Santa Clara in December 1958.[1] In essence then, even for this serious young man who had lived eight years of his life around or in the Fifth Police Station, there was no melding, no integration, no cognizance of the critical role played by the llano and, within this, the centrality of clandestinas in the making of the revolution.

The story told to us by this young teacher is surely a measure of the success of the official narrative of the guerrillas and the revolution in invisibilizing the role played by the llano: That is, portraying it as peripheral to and primarily supportive of the real struggle in the sierra. As I have written, this invisibilization has had profound and direct consequences for a further invisibilization: the story of women in the llano. And given that the vast majority of female insurgents fought in the llano, this underscores their exclusion from the tale of the making of the revolution as a whole. Therefore, any discussion of the manner in which women have been positioned in the official narrative makes it incumbent upon us to come to terms with this young teacher's account. That is, we must interrogate the sources of the suppression of this story to deconstruct the gendered conditions, assumptions, and circumstances by which the llano, and with it the majority of female insurgents, was peripheralized.

Che Guevara's *Episodes of the Revolutionary War* was the earliest and perhaps still the most widely circulated, although extremely sketchy, account of the making of the Cuban revolution. It is doubtful that Che envisioned or intended *Episodes* to be understood in this fashion; rather, as was his habit, it was a diary much like the one he would later keep in Bolivia, comprising a series of notes in which he recorded what he experienced or witnessed. Nonetheless, what emerges from its pages is the tale of a group of young men who struggle to survive together, who live together, who do battle and shed blood together in the wilds of the eastern mountains of the island, bound by a common goal and by a common understanding of how they would achieve that goal. In short, Che's narrative, which provides the underpinnings of the official story of the 1950s insurrection, is framed by that same male homosocial construct within which the nineteenth-century mambí armies fought in birthing the Cuban nation. Che's unifocal account of the sierra may have had something to do with the fact that until the last months of 1958, Che had no experience with the geography of Cuba except for the Sierra Maestra mountains. Indeed, among the first shipments of arms from Santiago were a short book on Cuban history and a map of the island, which Che had requested.[2] His wanderings around Latin America had not included any of the islands of the Caribbean. He touched Cuban soil only after landing on the *Granma* and then, along with the men who survived this landing and its immediate aftermath, straggled up to the sierra where he remained until the end of August 1958, when the column he led left the sierra on its march across the island.

But with this aside, *Episodes* is a tale of transformation. Organically woven into this tale and subsequent reminiscences by Che and others in the guerrilla is the myth of a kind of rebirth, a purification in the sierra experienced by the men among the rebel army. This "purity" forged in the sierra was set up against the corrupt and sullied city, in particular Havana. It is rooted in what is an almost romantic idyll with the peasantry, who are portrayed as the untainted and uncorrupted Cubans. In its telling in the official story, the romance begins with the disastrous landing of the *Granma* (Che called it "not a landing but a shipwreck") and its immediate aftermath, which resulted in the straggling arrival in the Sierra Maestra mountains of at most twenty-two of its eighty-two-man expeditionary force.[3] In the highly unlikely story told about this arrival, the peasantry, perennially accustomed to nothing but exploitation from outsiders, greet without hostility or even suspicion a strange group of raggedly dressed men carrying whatever arms they had managed to salvage from the *Granma*'s landing. In truth, however, these strangers' very physical survival immediately after they made it to the Sierra Maestra mountains was the work of the llano, and specifically Celia Sánchez. Sánchez's father, a doctor in Manzanillo, had taken her with him as she was growing up on his visits to provide medical care to campesinos in the nearby mountains.[4] As a result, she knew the region of the sierra nearest to the city; with some of its inhabitants she had organized a network of peasant support for the *Granma* rebels who were to land near Manzanillo. It is certain that without this support, and shortly thereafter without the additional men, armaments, and supplies sent by Frank País from the urban underground in Santiago, the guerrillas who managed to make it to the Sierra Maestra would have had the shortest of physical existences, to say nothing of any kind of engagement in armed struggle.

This idyll of bonding between the male peasantry and the male guerrillas was underscored by silence about sexual relations in guerrilla-controlled zones in the sierra, further evoking the aura of purity. We are told that among the guerrilla the rape of a peasant woman was a crime punishable by execution. Female insurgents in the sierra campamentos say that consensual heterosexual relationships were acceptable and that marriages were performed.[5] And we know the rapidity with which guerrilla leaders, for instance Raúl Castro and Vilma Espín, married in the immediate aftermath of the taking of power. But there is a kind of implicitly accepted omission of any discussion of these relations in the narrative.

This male homosocial construction of the story of the sierra guerrillas, as in the nineteenth century, required that the women (who among the guerrillas in the sierra numbered, at given points, some three hundred) be in essence absented or moved to the margins, where their presence could not challenge it.[6] In *Episodes*, Che mentions only three women, Haydée Santamaría, Celia Sánchez, and Vilma Espín, by name.[7] And in recounting the guerrillas' interactions with peasants, he refers only to the unnamed women who brought their children to him for medical care.[8]

Che's conception of women's place in the sierra insurgency is revealing. In *Guerrilla Warfare* he writes, "Because they do not possess the indispensable physical characteristics . . . naturally the combatant women are a minority."[9] That is, biology itself removes women to the margins of the guerrilla groupings, depriving them of a key requisite to any claim to the title of a guerrilla combatant: the direct involvement in struggles with the enemy and with this, logically, the right to carry and employ arms. Che notes that women are well attuned to carrying messages, objects, money, and so forth, because as women their movements were bound to be less subject to suspicion. And if captured, their treatment was far less brutal than for men. But he elaborates at greatest length on their natural role as cooks. In *Guerrilla Warfare* he notes:

> When the internal front is being consolidated . . . a woman can perform her habitual tasks of peacetime: it is very pleasing to a soldier subjected to the extremely hard conditions of this life to be able to look forward to a seasoned meal which tastes like something. . . . The woman as cook can greatly improve the diet and furthermore, it is easier to keep her in domestic tasks; one of the problems in guerrilla bands is that all works of a civilian character are scorned by those who perform them; they are constantly trying to get out of these tasks in order to enter into forces that are actively in combat.[10]

It is, then, the male guerrilla, forged in the purity of the sierra, in possession of and innately able to employ arms, and free of urban corruption, particularly of Havana, who comes down from the mountains to sweep the cities into revolt. This image of the guerrilla has been made to resurface every January 1 to January 8, when Cuban television rebroadcasts footage of the vehicles in the Caravan of Liberty as it weaves its way across the island to Havana. In this footage the caravan is largely a male domain; women appear as participants most usually among the cheering crowds, or when they jump onto one of the vehicles in the caravan as it proceeds on its victory march to Havana. Perhaps even more important, each year during this celebration, children in each province (girls and boys) dressed as guerrilla fighters reenact the caravan's movement. The official story of the victory as made by the revolutionary forces in the mountains has thus been embedded in the childhood of successive generations.

Not only does Che tell the tale of the revolution in terms of the heroic male guerrilla, but he himself with his death in Bolivia has become the physical embodiment of the heroic guerrilla. It is a label that has become synonymous with him in Cuba, repeated after every official invocation of his name. Children in circulos infantiles begin each day with a reinforcement of this. In reciting as a chorus "We shall be like Che," they imbibe this official narrative and perhaps most importantly the images it carries. And those are male images. These young boys and girls are not being asked to be like the Che who as minister of industry feverishly studied economics (not well, as it turned out) all night so as to be able to make critical decisions about the direction of the Cuban economy. They are not being asked to understand the Che who engaged in endless debates with economists and theorists within and without Cuba about the law of value and whether it applied in socialism. They are not being reminded of his wry sense of humor. They are being asked to emulate Che the guerrilla who fought, along with other men, armed battles against dictatorships in both Cuba and Bolivia. This is very specifically a male image.

The effect of this official narrative and this bonding of the men in the sierra, sealed by their control of arms, is to deny any measure of centrality to the llano. Only those (men) who were a part of the homosocial construct forged in the mountains were to be trusted. The othering of the llano manifested itself in multiple ways in the early years after the revolution took power. First, only one of the 26th of July Movement combatants in the llano, Faustino Pérez, and he only briefly, was among the inner circle of those who would make the critical decisions in the weeks and years immediately following the triumph.[11] The core of the tightly knit circle mainly comprised those who had fought in the sierra.

If this othering of the llano was critical to the official story of the war, it was facilitated by a level of disdain, distrust, and hostility directed toward it on the part of key figures in the sierra. This disdain would be articulated most openly by Raúl Castro and Che Guevara; Fidel remained largely neutral or even silent. This drumbeat of criticism of the llano leadership grew ever more dismissive as the years went on. It was clearest, as we shall see, in the aftermath of the disastrous 26th of July Movement's April 9, 1958, national strike. But it was vocal and at moments virulent even before April 9th. Che, forgetting perhaps his own background, anchored his distrust of llano insurgents in his view of them as bourgeois and as not fulfilling what he saw as their primary task: arming the sierra. In this and other regards he suspected them of having the secret intention of bringing on a US intervention.[12]

Multiple ironies are embedded in this disdain. First, as Julia Sweig concludes in her masterful study of the relationship between the leadership in the sierra and the leadership in the llano, "had it not been for the work of the 26th of July Movement outside of the Sierra Maestra during the first seventeen months of the insurgency, from November 1956 until April 1958, the final period when the anti-dictatorial struggle gained unstoppable military and political momentum would simply have not been possible."[13] Second, buried in the official narrative is another irony. Sweig meticulously documents the fact that prior to the May 1958 meeting of llano and sierra leaders at Altos de Mompié, "the lion's share of decisions regarding tactics; strategy; resource allocation; political ties with opposition groups; Cuban exiles, and clandestine adversaries; and relations with the United States (in Havana and in Washington) were made by lesser known individuals from the urban underground—not Che Guevara, Fidel Castro or his brother Raúl."[14]

Sweig's purpose is to focus entirely on contact and conflict between leadership cadres in the llano and the sierra; she does not intend or attempt to get down to the street level of the insurgency. Given this focus, it is logical but revealing that, with three exceptions, Sweig does not refer to women insurgents in her discussion. Since the national leadership cadre during the insurrection was virtually exclusively male, her efforts to correct the imbalance between the llano and the sierra in the story of how the Cuban revolution was made logically excludes the critical role played by women. Besides Haydée, Vilma, and Celia, Sweig includes in her book a mention of América Domitro, whom she refers to as Taras Domitro's sister and Frank País's girlfriend. I will discuss América Domitro in more detail later in this book.

This brings us to a third consideration: In his singular focus on the sierra, Che blinds himself altogether to the terrible reality that life in the sierra for female as well as male insurgents was something of a cake walk by comparison to the daily realities of life in the insurgency on the ground in Cuba's cities. The degree of this blindness and of his scorn for the llano and its leaders, and by inference for all urban insurgents, male and female, is startling and remained constant even after he left the sierra on his march to Havana. When Che, with his column of rebels, arrived in Las Villas in December 1958, Enrique Oltuski, who was head of the 26th of July Movement in Las Villas, went to talk with him in the mountains of the Escambray. It was a nasty conversation. At its end and in the midst of a torrential rain, Che informed Oltuski, "I'm sorry but tonight you will not be able to sleep in your bed with its white sheets. Here you will have to sleep in a hammock, under the rain and the mosquitoes." To which Oltuski replied, "Yes, that is true, but at least I will be able to sleep here, because in my bed at home with its white sheets, the danger that follows us every minute is so great that I can never sleep well. Here at least I feel safe."[15]

For the clandestinas in the llano this was equally their reality. Without exception, the women with whom I spoke, some of whom were insurgents both in the cities and the sierra, testify to this: To be a clandestina in the llano was to live in what Frank País described as a "ratonera." Graciela Aguiar, who fought both in Santiago and in Havana, and later, quemada (a target for esbirros) in both cities, made her way to the guerrilla front headed by Raúl Castro in the Sierra Maestra mountains:

> In the liberated territory [in the sierra] you felt protected . . . [and] although there was always the danger of attacks by army aircraft, you were among your people. There are those who live off the legend, who have invented their legend; well, let them be content [with that]. However, if you declare that you felt happy [in the clandestinidad], you are lying. The clandestinidad was destructive, terrible. If you were walking down the street and saw the same person twice, [you wondered] "What if I am being followed to check if I were carrying a gun?" So, you ask yourself, "What should I do?" Because, if you go home, "What if they then raid the house?" Or you are inside a house which is not your home and you hear a noise, you see some kind of motion and you think it is a police car; you see someone behaving in a strange way and you think that "they are

going to raid your house, that they are after us." That is something hard. The hardest thing for a revolutionary person to experience is being in the clandestinidad. It is a life-or-death test and you are always jumpy. If you are being followed, if you are being hunted down, if they knock [on your door] at night, if they stop you, if you are accompanied by a comrade whom they are trying to capture . . . this is the clandestinidad.[16]

Consuelo Elba, who like Graciela was an insurgent in both the llano and the sierra, recalls that "being in the guerrilla [in the sierra] felt as if it were paradise. You had the enemy right in front of you."[17] And Natalia Bolívar, a Directorio Revolucionario clandestina, remembers the manner in which its members spoke about the two sites of combat against the dictatorship: "Go to the sierra so you can rest. I will tell you this in plain language. The struggle, particularly in Havana, was a fight to the death. They killed you first and asked questions later."[18]

Women who were quemada in the llano, and not just those in Santiago where there was far easier access to the sierra, were faced with limited choices. They could either go into exile or could seek refuge—and it was seen as refuge, as relative security—in the sierra. For instance, Conchita Fernández, who had been Eduardo Chibás's secretary. When she was threatened during the intense repression in Havana that followed the Directorio Revolucionario's failed March 13, 1957, attack on the Presidential Palace, Fidel himself acknowledged how much more dangerous life was in the llano. He sent her a note telling her to make her way to the Sierra Maestra: "Come here, where you will be safer even behind a tree."[19]

But getting to the Sierra Maestra mountains from Havana was at best perilous because of distance, and the roads going out of Havana in particular were patrolled by the Guardia Rural. The writer Margarita Mateo, then seven years old, recalls a trip from Santa Clara to Havana with her parents, who were sympathizers but in no way active participants in the insurrection: "I remember that my father had packed our clothes in a large olive-green suitcase of his, unrelated [to the use of that color for guerrilla items]. But they [the police] were conducting searches on the road, so I remember that, because it was olive green, when they opened the trunk of the car in their search, they began to run up and down, all around the car, whistling signals to each other. It was horrendous. The police made us panic."[20]

Many of those women who were quemada in Havana had little choice but to go into exile where they joined forces with 26th of July Movement clubs particularly in Mexico and in the United States. Mirta Rodríguez

Calderón, after her release from her second imprisonment and unable to return to her parents' home because it had been ransacked in the course of a police search, was sent into exile in Mexico by the 26th of July Movement leadership in Havana.[21] Elvira Díaz Vallina, coordinator of a cell in the Movement of Civic Resistance, was informed by the 26th of July Movement leadership in Havana that should she be caught again after two imprisonments, she and those with her would be killed.[22] She left Cuba to attend a Latin American student conference, planning to use this as a roundabout route to the sierra. Batista fled the island before this last leg of her trip).[23]

Some simply refused to leave the insurrection in the llano, understanding it to be both the center of the rebellion against the dictatorship and its most difficult front. Nilda Ravelo was the first woman in the 26th of July Movement to be imprisoned in Havana. Nilda would spend a total of sixteen months in Mantilla, the women's holding prison, during 1957 and 1958. When informed by her lawyer during her second imprisonment that she could be released with some money under the table and an agreement to go immediately into exile, Nilda adamantly turned down the offer, stating that she had no intention of seeking safety by going into external or internal exile. By internal exile she meant the sierra. She remained in Mantilla until January 1, 1959.[24]

While these are anecdotal stories, they give flavor to the degree of danger compared to the sierra that female as well as male insurgents faced in the llano, particularly in Havana. The clandestinas with whom I spoke some sixty years after the events could still with startling currency point out the locales of safe houses and the exact locations where compañeros were captured or where their bodies were found. But while they seem to know the story of every clandestina/o, by contrast, the same organic bonding true in the sierra was far more difficult to achieve in the llano. By its very nature the llano was a dispersed terrain in which people acted within small groups rather than as any kind of unified community. And the effect of Batista's strategy in pinpointing for assassination the leadership (men) meant that any kind of organization in the llano was in a state of permanent reconstruction. In the remembrances of those insurgents who were imprisoned, the only site of bonding on any scale or across different movements that was possible in the llano was prison itself.

This dispersal of forces was certainly more true of Havana, the major object of Guevara's disdain, than of Santiago, Cuba's second city. Havana was (and is) far larger than Santiago. In Santiago, people were far more likely to know one another or to know someone who knew someone, and families were often intertwined. This kind of familiarity might have existed in different barrios in Havana but could not have characterized the city as a whole. The anonymity of the much larger city made it more difficult to locate houses in which insurgents could with confidence meet or be sheltered. Further, Havana was characterized by a diverse economic and social structure: It was here that the wealth and the wealthy of the country were concentrated. This meant that among those actively engaged in the insurgency there was a greater range of responses to it, from active support to passive support, from active opposition to apathy. As we shall see in chapter 6, Havana housed the whole range and variety of the regime's repressive forces. Even the architecture of Santiago, with its single- and double-storied homes often on narrow streets, afforded greater safety. Vilma Espín tells of eluding a police raid by jumping from one roof to another. In Havana, where multistory apartment buildings dominated the landscape in central areas of the city, this was impossible. Further, given the proximity of the sierra, clandestinas/os quemada in Santiago had a kind of safety net that was infinitely less available to insurgents in Havana. The 26th of July Movement in Santiago had virtually no competition from other anti-Batista forces, and had far more uniform popular support. By contrast, Havana was home to multiple competing or potentially competing civil and political organizations and movements. Among these were the remaining, although much-discredited, Ortodoxo and Auténtico politicians, the underground Organización Auténtica, the Triple A, and, most important, the Partido Socialista Popular (PSP) and the Directorio Revolucionario.[25]

This complexity of potentially competing movements in Havana and in particular the relationship between the PSP and the two major clandestine movements has a great deal to do with the diminution in the official narrative of the llano. Once more, Che best elucidated this in his disdain for the llano. Among the leadership in the sierra, Che's opinions about the llano and not simply about its leadership carried particular weight. Che's critics argue that his attitude toward what he considered the "bourgeois" llano indicated his communist leanings. But the evidence of this is at best unclear. What is certainly true was his generally favorable view of the PSP. His distrust of the llano underscored his naiveté about the PSP. Che's ideas about revolutions and their failure began to coalesce during his sojourn in Arbenz's Guatemala in 1953–54.

The lessons he drew from Guatemala were twofold: the impossibility of any kind of peaceful transition to a just society in Latin America and therefore the necessity of armed struggle; and, reinforcing this, the need for armed revolution to prevent the otherwise inevitable US intervention. Prior to the April 1958 strike, in a private communication, the PSP informed Fidel that "the militarization of the strike plans was the result of a secret plot within the 26th leadership in the llano to rid Cuba of Batista by means of an American intervention." Writes Sweig, "Che Guevara agreed. He believed that the FON [National Workers Front of the 26th of July Movement] and the National Directorate were unwilling to work with the PSP because of the underground's antipathy toward communism and toward genuine social revolution, as well as its inherent deference to the United States."[26] Che attributed the antipathy toward the PSP he saw evident in the 26th of July Movement militants in Havana as the sure sign of their anticommunist bent. But this attribution to those insurgents on the streets, at least in Havana, needs to be interrogated.

Certainly, in Cuba as in the United States in the 1950s, anticommunism was in the air one breathed. For a very considerable number of those who had joined in the effort to rid Cuba of Batista, their opposition to communism or indeed anything that smacked of socialism would become clear in what would follow in the early years after the triumph, in their departure from the island. And this exodus, which included a significant number of those who had been llano insurgents or sympathizers, logically heightened the need to invisibilize it in the story of the revolution.

But what has been written on both sides of the controversy surrounding the relationship between the PSP and the 26th of July Movement urban insurgents in the lliano tends to focus entirely on attitudes among their national leadership. Among the llano insurgents I spoke with, whether male or female, all of whom had remained on the island, the issue was not anticommunism. During the insurrection only a very few had the least idea what communism was. Rather, their antipathy toward the PSP and its youth branch (the Juventud Socialista) was based on their experiences with them on the ground in the course of insurrection. Until March 1958, when the PSP's *Carta Semanal* published an article officially stating its support of the guerrilla struggle in the Sierra Maestra, it officially opposed the strategy of armed insurrection and had publicly denounced both Fidel's assault on Moncada and the Directorio's

March 1957 attack on the Presidential Palace as "putschist."[27] But nothing had changed on the ground in the llano; rather, while it now supported the sierra guerrillas, the PSP had not altered its critique of the clandestine movement in the llano. Its own strategy, in keeping with communist parties worldwide, was focused on the workplace, where it held that workers' grievances and actions about these grievances in unions would eventually yield a general strike that would bring down the dictatorship. The Democratic Federation of Cuban Women (FDMC), the PSP's women's front, espoused this same strategy, proscribing its members from participating in the armed insurgency in the llano. Michelle Chase cites an unsigned flyer entitled "Open Letter to the Cuban People on Mother's Day," later revealed to be written by Mirta Aguirre, a prominent PSP member. This flyer, Chase writes, "dovetailed" with the party's strategy of portraying women as "aggrieved mothers and homemakers" and assumed women's immediate demands would focus on housing and food prices.[28]

In PSP rhetoric llano insurgents were "terroristas" and "dinamiteros."[29] Although there were members of the Juventud who broke discipline to participate as individuals in 26th of July Movement actions, throughout the years of the insurrection they remained formally subject to immediate expulsion for doing so.[30] In Havana, bitterness toward the PSP among the 26th of July and Directorio insurgents ran deep. And it was not resolved either before or after January 1959. As I have written, in the barrios and the schools where they were concentrated, communism was not the issue for young clandestinas/os. Rather, their one steadfast and single-minded goal was to overthrow Batista. Few had given a thought to what might be beyond this. While most would probably have adhered, had they read it, to the general vision of social justice in Cuba as outlined by Fidel in "History Will Absolve Me," what would follow after Batista's demise was not in any way their central concern. As Juan Valdés Paz wryly observes, on January 1, 1959, at the moment of Batista's flight, for these young people "the Moncada Program might as well have been written in hieroglyphics on papyrus."[31] Indeed, virtually none of the clandestinas with whom I spoke had any notion, during their years in the insurrection, of what communism was. Pilar Sa, nineteen years old and in Action and Sabotage, recalls that until 1961, when she went to study in the Soviet Union on a scholarship, she had not the least idea who Lenin or Stalin were.[32] What these young insurrectionaries, both men and women, did know in practice were PSP and in particular

Juventud members at the base level. And these Juventud members were disdained for their refusal to support, and at moments their opposition to, the actions that the Directorio and 26th of July Movement militants fervently believed would bring down the regime they deplored. The clandestinas with whom I spoke remembered with continuing resentment the role played by the PSP during the insurrection. They regularly referred to PSP and Juventud members as comuñangas (a derogatory word for communists) or as los viejos pericos (old parrots).[33] Their only contribution, said the 26th of July Movement clandestina Hidelisa Esperón, was "blah, blah, blah. That's all they did. They distributed their own publication, *Carta Semanal*, and nothing more."[34] By contrast, Directorio and 26th of July Movement clandestinas distributing anti-Batista literature, pamphlets, and leaflets did not discriminate between who or what was producing this literature. Natalia Bolívar, a Directorio insurgent, relates that when she was arrested in 1958 Batista's esbirros found all sorts of papers hidden in her house: *Carta Semanal*, as well as bonos (coupons) from the 26th of July Movement.[35] And Sonnia Moro, a 26th of July Movement member, reports that she handed out virtually anything that denounced Batista, including *Carta Semanal*. This distrust of PSP and Juventud members went even farther. Pilar Sa recalls: "When you were in jail and a new woman inmate arrived, you had to make sure she was not a chivata or in some way related to the PSP. It was the same in El Príncipe. Whenever PSP members were taken there—by the way, very few of them were jailed—in those cases, we were warned because [they] could alert their party and thereby frustrate whatever task we were carrying out."[36]

For the older generation of women in the movement, some of whom had been members of the Communist Party before its 1940 alliance with Batista, distrust of its members and particularly its leaders had deeper roots. The position taken by the PSP in 1940 (and at other moments) reflected above all its steadfast allegiance to Stalin and to a Stalinist version of "socialism." In the years leading up to and during World War II, in the face of the Nazi threat, Stalin had directed communist parties everywhere to pursue "popular fronts" with other political parties.

The anger against and distrust of the PSP, remembered and shared by almost all of the clandestinas with whom I spoke, was captured by Pastorita Núñez, as I have written, both a 26th of July Movement militant and a founding member of the Martianas. After she was called to the Sierra Maestra by Fidel in May 1958, he assigned Pastorita to collect taxes from the US companies doing business in the areas controlled by the rebels.

In August 1958, in the course of collecting these taxes, she encountered Carlos Rafael Rodríguez, a PSP leader, as he came to meet with Fidel in his camp in the sierra: "This path is not for you," she told him. "This path is for revolutionaries."[37] As we shall see, she would later pay dearly for this remark.

Relations between Directorio and 26th of July Movement insurgents were markedly different. At the leadership level they were complex and at key moments conflictive. In 1955 in Mexico, the top leadership of the two organizations had jointly committed themselves to armed struggle as the means of ridding Cuba of Batista. But the Directorio's understanding of what was to be done differed markedly from that of the 26th of July Movement. The Directorio drew explicitly on the tradition of student urban struggle centered in Havana and at the university. It focused its actions specifically on selected ajusticiamientos (executions) of Batista's esbirros, on sabotage, and on capturing control of key sites of power: what Julio César Guanche describes as "golpear arriba" (to strike at the top), which would decapitate the regime. This was to be the clarion call for a general insurrection that would bring down the dictatorship.[38]

But on the ground in Havana the stories told by insurgents give evidence of regular interactions between the two groups. What allowed this cooperation, particularly among the male llano leadership who were students at the University of Havana, was a level of trust rooted in friendship and familiarity and, most particularly, by periods of imprisonment. But above all, both male and female insurgents in the two movements were joined by a single, shared goal: the determination to rid Cuba of Batista through armed struggle.

On March 13, 1957, the Directorio leadership, all male, attacked the Presidential Palace in a bold but failed and tragic attempt to realize their strategy of golpear arriba by killing Batista. In the wake of the attack and the brutal repression that followed, the Directorio was decimated. If it was arguably the most visible insurrectionary force in Havana prior to March 13th, the debacle of the attack reduced both its leadership and the base from which it drew the majority of its members. In the official narrative of the revolution, the story of the Directorio Revolucionario begins and ends on March 13, 1957. It has been in effect erased. And this has served to further invisibilize the insurgency in the llano.

In fact, the Directorio, while much reduced in numbers, did not disappear in the city after March 13. Insurgents in Havana in the 26th of July Movement and the Directorio, both male and female, tell a different story about what happened on the ground in the wake of the failed attack. What was left of the Directorio leadership departed the island to plan and organize a second front in the Escambray mountains in central Cuba. And the regime launched a wave of terror unmatched to this point, targeting the Directorio militants who remained in Havana.[39] But the male Directorio militants with whom I spoke understand March 13 as the point at which they and the 26th of July Movement insurgents drew closely together. Héctor Terry asserts that after the attack on the Palace, "without a leadership in the Directorio which was a students' movement, and since what we wanted was to fight against Batista, we began having contacts with compañeros from the 26th of July Movement."[40] Guillermo Jiménez, like Terry a Directorio clandestino and member of the executive committee after the March 13 debacle, similarly asserts that, "after the March 1957 attack, this collaboration was mutual, continuous, constant. . . . [T]here came a point when we were all the same."[41] Thus, for instance, Jiménez was key in finding a way to get the then-sixteen-year-old 26th of July Movement clandestina Mariíta Trasancos out of Havana and to Santa Clara after her second arrest made it clear she would not live through a third one.[42]

But in their accounts of what they did, female clandestinas from both movements make no such distinction between the periods before and after March 13. Among the written and oral testimonies of female insurgents, the number of women who understood themselves as militants in or collaborators with both movements is notable. In José Bell Lara's 2012 study of clandestinas in the llano, five of ten women giving testimonies identify themselves as members of the 26th of July Movement and collaborators with the Directorio; three as Directorio and collaborators with the Movement of Civic Resistance; and two describe themselves as members of both insurgent movements.[43] As Magaly Martínez, who considered herself a militant in the 26th of July Movement, the Directorio, and the Frente Cívico de Mujeres Martianas, said, "There weren't any membership cards."[44]

The texts and subtexts of accounts given by or about female insurgents evidence the critical role that women played as bridges between militants in the 26th of July Movement and the Directorio. The women who formed the Frente, in particular Carmen Castro and Aida Pelayo, had deep, sustained ties to insurgents in both movements, which allowed them to provide a common ground for communication, coordination, and mediation. Guillermo Jiménez asserts that the Directorio was literally founded in Carmen's living room.[45] This common ground was further amplified by the fact that the Frente itself purposefully united female insurgents from both movements in its membership ranks.

Anecdotes of various younger female militants further evidence the degree to which women in both the 26th of July Movement and the Directorio provided the infrastructure between militants without distinguishing between the two groups. Laura Fernández Rueda, a 26th of July Movement clandestina in Pinar del Río, recalls: "The struggle was complicated. Sometimes I was with the University [referring to the Directorio] and at other times I was with the 26th of July Movement. . . . I can't separate one from the other, it was all mixed. . . . José Antonio Echeverría [head of the Directorio] stayed in my house on many occasions, coming in and out, secretly . . . and he and Pepín Naranjo [a 26th of July Movement militant] met frequently in my house."[46]

This extended to actions that included sabotage jointly undertaken by female insurgents from the two movements. Talía Laucirica Gallardo, who identified herself as a member of the Directorio and a collaborator with the 26th of July Movement, describes working with Verena Pino and other 26th of July Movement insurgents in Santa Clara: "We carried out all kinds of jobs: propaganda, selling bonos, transporting dynamite or weapons; we did all that needed to be done. And how did we do it? In a very coordinated and interconnected way. Because I must say that, at the base level, we never had any differences; when the Directorio and the 26th [of July Movement] worked together, we never had differences."[47]

But the role played by the Directorio and its female insurgents in the making of the revolution was further invisibilized in the immediate aftermath of Batista's exit from the island. Before Fidel's January 8th arrival in Havana, DR members, following the organization's unrealized plans for March 13, 1957, sought to occupy the university and the Presidential Palace and to seize weapons from various police stations and the Cuartel de San Antonio. Fidel's instructions to 26th of July Movement militants in Havana clearly conflicted with these actions. He had no intention of sharing power. After Che took Santa Clara and proceeded to Havana, Fidel directed him to exclude from his column the Directorio guerrillas who had formed a front in the Escambray.

———

The controversy surrounding the role of the llano and the role of the sierra in the 26th of July Movement came to a head after April 1958 in the immediate aftermath of the long-anticipated and disastrous April 9th general strike.

In the plans of the 26th of July Movement, as they had been laid out by Frank País and Fidel Castro in 1957, and up until the poststrike meeting in May 1958 in the sierra at Altos de Mompié, the strike, which was to take place in every city and town on the island, was understood as the event that would be the coup de grâce for the Batista regime and mark the triumph of the revolution. But the strike did not mean a workers' walkout alone. The object was to bring the cities openly into the war to topple the Batista regime. As Sweig observes, the insurgents defined "huelga" much like certain underground groups among Cuban revolutionaries in the 1930s described urban insurrection, and they began to speak of it as "total war," an all-out extended effort in which the 26th of July Movement would come to power throughout the country.[48] In Havana these actions were to involve seizing armories stocked with weapons; blowing up the central street power outlet as well as sabotaging selected targets, particularly transportation terminals; burning gas stations and vehicles; interrupting all transit into and out of the city; and spreading a massive propaganda campaign that would blanket the city. Workers would leave their workplaces and then disperse or join the battle. In expectation of a significant number of wounded, emergency medical centers were to be set up in cooperating churches.[49] The 26th of July Movement, writes Sweig, "would orchestrate a crescendo of walkouts, industrial and agricultural sabotage, violence, selective assassinations of government figures, attacks on symbols of the regime and generalized mayhem to destabilize the Batista regime and expose its inability to maintain public and economic order."[50]

The April 9th strike in the narrative of the making of the revolution is always portrayed in the literature as a failure—indeed, as a disastrous failure.[51] The controversy around it focused and continues to focus almost entirely on the issue of who was to blame. And almost unanimously, the guilty were deemed to be the leaders of the 26th of July Movement underground, particularly in Havana. Raúl Castro expressed this succinctly: The llano leadership were a bunch of amateurs. As he said, "Let's talk for once with revolutionary sincerity!!! Much blood has been spilled, much will continue to be spilled and more than what has already been spilled for us to still not have sufficient merit to solve our amateur problems!"[52] Thus, one of the strike's results and perhaps the most important one was the transfer of authority: the restructuring of the 26th of

July Movement in May 1958, which formally situated Fidel as the unitary leader of the movement, and the sierra as the primary arena of battle.

The llano was now reduced to a secondary role, subordinated entirely to the sierra and to a strategy centering decisively on the sierra. Given the overwhelming number of clandestinas fighting in the llano, the import if not the actual fact of what they would engage in was equivalently diminished. In effect, for these clandestinas it was a double demotion. It therefore seems appropriate to attempt to understand what precisely was happening on the streets during the strike, particularly because every clandestina in Havana was involved in some way in preparations for the strike and in the strike itself.

There is little question that the strike was poorly organized. First, the national leadership decided to postpone the date on which it was to begin from March 30th to April and finally to April 9th, and many insurgents in the llano had no notice of when it was to begin until the preceding day, if then. This postponement must clearly have played a role in the disorganization. It was made even worse by the inexplicable decision to announce the call to strike on radio at 11 a.m. that day when, among others, people at work would not be listening. The level of disorganization was such that key figures in Action and Sabotage did not know that the strike had started. Pilar Sa remembers: "I was already working with Morúa [in Action and Sabotage] by the time of the April strike. Morúa did not know on April 9th that it had begun in spite of being one of the 'big shots.' That day he sent me to a cafeteria that sometimes gave us free food and that was where I found out what was going on."[53]

Juan Valdés Paz gives this picture of the day:

My brother called and warned me to be ready, because the strike was about to be declared. I went to my workplace and then he told me not to go home, so I went to a friend's house and there I waited for his call. He phoned me again and told me to go to his office, a photo shop, because it was a concentration point where weapons would be distributed to those who were joining the uprising. There, I met a group of people I did not know; no one knew each other; there was no leader nor authority. There we were, eleven compañeros ready to join the uprising and no weapons, only a revolver.[54]

Clandestinas were excluded from the 26th of July Movement's militia groups who were to carry out armed actions: These were once again exclusively male terrain. But probably the most organized insurgents were the groups almost entirely made up of women who had for months prepared to give medical assistance to wounded insurgents. Pastorita Núñez was given charge of the Comando Femenino, which was to make Molotov cocktails, transport arms and men, and organize and operate emergency hospitals in churches. These medical stations, set up by Pastorita with her usual efficiency, received no customers, however. Sonnia Moro, a young militant in the 26th of July Movement's youth brigades (the Frente Estudiantil Nacional, FEN), trained over several months on how to treat wounds by a doctor in the Calixto García Hospital sympathetic to the insurgents. She organized her group in a church in Old Havana and waited for word of what was happening. In the end, the day's most challenging job was getting the assembled medical supplies out of the church and to safety, so that they could be later used elsewhere.[55]

There were almost no wounds to cure: Virtually nothing was happening on the streets of Havana. Promised weapons had not arrived from Mexico or had not made it to Havana; the distribution of what there was of weapons was haphazard and last minute at best, particularly given the confusion about when the strike was to be staged.

Thelma Bornot, a clandestina quemada in Guantánamo and Santiago, had been sent to Havana just before April 9th. She gives a sense both of the disorganization on that day and its terrible consequences, telling the story of the assassination of Marcelo Salado, the head of Action and Sabotage in El Vedado:

When I arrived [in Havana] we stayed in an apartment where several compañeros lived. They were planning the actions for the next few days [during the strike]. We all thought the strike would take place on April 1st, but it actually happened on the 9th. We spent the days organizing all the weapons, preparing the 26th of July armbands for the compañeros who would be going to pick up the weapons with which to take the armory. I remember Marcelo Salado exiting the building in G Street once the strike had begun because not much was going on and he wanted to stir things up. Two compañeras, Esperanza Sanjurjo and Ramona, told me, "Listen, you stay here because you are not from Havana." Marcelo went out and this was fatal: He ran into a patrol car whose occupants recognized him and killed him. He was with Ramona; she was saved by someone working on the construction of a garage on the corner who managed to hide her in the garage.[56]

But if there was confusion about the date or the call to strike, the strike itself was widely anticipated. And not just by those who were to be its participants. In the two preceding months, the Batista regime brought to Havana as its police chief one of his most efficient torturers, Pilar García, and his son, Irenaldo. García's instruction upon assuming his post was "I want neither wounded nor prisoners."[57]

The shift in power to the sierra at the meeting at Altos de Mompié was further compounded by the impact of the strike on the llano. As the guerrillas in the sierra successfully beat off Batista's offensive and began to take their struggle out of the mountains, life for the insurgents in the llano became ever more tenuous. The April 9th strike and its aftermath spelled the end of what Sweig calls the "golden age" of the llano: February through March 1958.[58] In Havana, in the wake of the strike Batista's esbirros carried out a wave of assassinations of rebels whose tortured bodies were sometimes purposefully put on public display. The resultant disarticulation of the clandestinidad and the transfer of all authority and decision-making power to the sierra and particularly to Fidel meant that the rebels in Havana never again had anything close to the means or the capacity to plan and execute major actions. Police cars, their sirens blasting, patrolled Havana's streets randomly at all hours of the day and night, instilling such fear that some of those who experienced it say they still jump at the sound of sirens. Clandestinos in those very few safe houses still open to them were virtually in forced confinement, given the terror in the streets; this served to make attempts to reestablish communications even more difficult. In her book *Rogito*, Dolores Nieves wistfully recalls sensing that Rogelio Perea Suárez (Rogito), who would be killed in Havana in November 1958 at the age of twenty-one, was plagued by the feeling that he was doing nothing. One day she found him alone and he told her he was determined to assassinate a judge on the electoral tribunal in the weeks before the elections scheduled by Batista to be held in early November:

> He told me that he was in Old Havana and that he had been checking the movements [of the judge] for several days. He was sitting near the El Cristo church on a doorstep. When I asked him why he had chosen to kill that poor old man instead of a police officer or a soldier, he replied angrily that they were all guilty. Everyone supporting the regime was as guilty as those who carry guns. That man who offered his services to provide a legal facade to the regime was as guilty as the rest of them and even more than most.[59]

Rogito never carried out the execution, but the sense of despair and isolation of those in the llano in the wake of the failure of the April strike is almost tangible in Nieves's description. Her account evidences individual rebels' impulses to attempt on their own initiative almost suicidal actions in the strike's aftermath and the seeming absence of collective options.

The unleashed, sadistic rampage of torture and murder in Havana—from April to December, Batista's men killed 143 insurgents—added to the widespread despair and desperation among remaining clandestinos in the city.[60] Carmen Castro describes what it was like on the island during these months: "Myriads of assassins from the repressive bodies, the army and the police raided cities everywhere throughout the country, perpetrating the most horrendous crimes. Young men, ages 18 to 25, appeared dead each day, after being brutally tortured, beaten to death or hung. Some of them were murdered with their arms and legs tied, hundreds were riddled with bullets. The barbaric repression expanded even to minors under 15 years of age."[61] In Havana, Sonnia Moro remembers painfully, "everything was completely disrupted because it was butchery, plain and simple. It was a huge holocaust, a very hard blow."[62]

The leadership, particularly those in Action and Sabotage, had to continually be replaced, given these assassinations. In Havana it became virtually impossible to find houses that might provide even temporary refuge to insurgents, given the terror felt by people who once would have or indeed had opened their doors. This was as true for clandestinas as it was for their male counterparts. Mariíta Trasancos had been sent to Santa Clara after her second arrest since it was clear that she would not have survived a third one. When she returned to Havana in November 1958 on a mission for the 26th of July Movement, the Martiana lawyer Margot Aniceto had found her a house in which she could stay, but its owners asked her to leave after Directorio insurgents, including Natalia Bolívar, attacked the nearby Seventeenth Police Station.[63] On December 31, the night Batista would flee the island, Trasancos wandered the streets of the city without any place she might be able to find refuge. Clandestinas/os, increasingly desperate, having nowhere to go, spent nights in funeral parlors where they got temporary shelter. Funeral parlors were open all night and their occupants were by tradition given a cup of chocolate, more than likely these clandestinos' only food for the day.

In contrast to the bonding in battle in the sierra during this time period, in the llano and particularly in Havana, there was disarticulation, a shattering of whatever bonds had existed. As Julio César Rosabal García concludes, "The human cost of the strike in the llano was insuperable."[64]

The story of the llano as central in the insurrection now fades from history, and with it, inevitably, the story of urban female insurrectionaries. The revolution becomes for Cubans and for the world outside Cuba exclusively the tale of the bearded young men in the mountains.

The official narrative of the revolution solidified in the first year following the taking of power. This is another story, but suffice it to say here that the multiple conflicts and potential or actual differing visions of the insurrection presented a fundamental challenge to any projection of unity, both among the leadership and in the Cuban population in the aftermath of the triumph. Unity, in Fidel's reading of Cuban history and particularly of Martí, was central and critical to the success of the revolution. And unity, he determined, had been forged only in the bonding of the (male) guerrillas in the sierra. As he had done in the sierra, after January 1, 1959, Fidel positioned himself and was positioned as the embodiment of unity. And he surrounded himself with those whom he embraced and with those who had embraced him in the sierra. Unity in this construction then required the solidification of a specific homosocial framing of the tale of the making of the revolution.

Lest anyone think that a more complex, more truthful version of the making of the revolution might now, with the passage of more than fifty years, be possible to write on the island, one has only to read *Historia de una gesta libertadora, 1952–1959*, a book about the insurrection in the llano. Its author, Georgina Leyva Pagan, once more puts forward the historically inaccurate idea that the primary task of the llano in the making of the revolution was to supply the sierra with arms. But the book's prologue, written by Fidel Castro in 2013 two years before his death, is particularly revealing. In his discussion of the landing of the *Granma*, he reflects on Faustino Pérez, who came with him on the *Granma* and was then sent by Fidel to be head of the llano in Havana. Fidel remembers his great disappointment with Pérez's attitude in the days immediately following the landing, writing that he realized, in the midst of the attack by Batista's air force, that Pérez, finding Fidel and one other survivor, had not only lost his gun but insisted that the three shield themselves from the bombings by seeking refuge in a cane field rather than searching for other survivors with whom they could continue the battle:

> In that instant, I felt so deeply outraged that I could barely utter a word. . . . I perceived almost instinctively, the enormous strength of the "petit-bourgeois spirit," allergic to Marxism to Leninism and socialism. Even if they did not show it openly, their previous and subsequent actions proved it. They were in line with that mentality that the Yankees had spread throughout the world since the October Revolution came to power in Russia. This, of course, did not prevent the "petit bourgeoisie" from opposing the brutal coup d'état which had been repudiated by the people. How much I learned, and how much I had to swallow about this reality![65]

These words, along with a qualifying remark, "I regret to say this because Faustino was a brave man who was happy fighting in the clandestinidad," must be read not simply as an attack on Pérez but on the "petit bourgeois" attitude of the llano as a whole, where, as Fidel concludes, Faustino, as a petit bourgeois, was happiest.

This scorn some fifty-four years after the fact and surely among Fidel Castro's final published words serves yet again to distinguish those who fought in the sierra from those who fought in the llano. The "purity" of the sierra required that Pérez be excluded definitively from the realm of the close-knit male construction of the revolution, despite the fact that his insurrectionary activity preceded Fidel's; that he was one of the eighty-two men aboard the *Granma*; or that he was recalled to the sierra following the April 9th strike. The essential, individualistic nature of Pérez must therefore already be evident, even in the landing of the *Granma*, even before his time in Havana. It is fixed and unalterable. The fact that he finds his place, that he is "happy," among those in the llano defines all those in the llano along with him. So, in the myth of the making of the Cuban revolution, the llano is once again doomed to erasure and with it, in equal measure and with few exceptions, the stories of the women who fought there.

If the official tale of the sierra versus the llano provides the foundations for silence around the roles played by women, it does not by any means entirely account for it. The stories told about the llano itself, in positioning women combatants on the sidelines of the insurrection as aides to the men who were the indispensable insurgents, add yet another layer to this silence. The llano narratives play their part in reconstituting the historical positioning of women as in the battles for Cuban independence. In the chapters that follow, I seek to use the accounts told to me by women who fought in the underground movement in Havana to challenge and to redefine their positioning. In this telling, women emerge as equal protagonists in the insurrection and, as such, transgressors upon the male homosocial (re)construction of the nation.

THE CLANDESTINAS
WHY THEY WERE, WHO THEY WERE, HOW THEY WERE

The following chapters draw principally on my interviews with thirty-one clandestinas who, during the insurrection, were ages thirteen to twenty-five. The ages provided in the following list are the ages the clandestinas were when they first joined the insurgency:

María (Mariíta) Trasancos (26th of July Movement and Frente Cívico de Mujeres Martianas [FCMM]), fifteen

Sonnia Moro (26th of July Movement and Frente Estudiantil Nacional), seventeen

Pilar Sa (26th of July Movement and FCMM), eighteen

Hidelisa Esperón (26th of July Movement and FCMM), sixteen

Nilda Ravelo (26th of July Movement), seventeen

Nélida Álvarez (26th of July Movement), twenty-two

Xiomara Blanco (26th of July Movement), sixteen

Natalia Bolívar (Directorio Revolucionario [DR] and Mujeres Oposicionistas Unidas [MOU]), nineteen

Thelma Bornot (26th of July Movement), twenty-four

Marta Jiménez (DR), eighteen

Mirta Rodríguez Calderón (26th of July Movement, Civic Resistance Movement, and FCMM), seventeen

Elvira Díaz Vallina (Federación de Estudiantes Universitarios [FEU], 26th of July Movement, and Civic Resistance Movement), twenty

Digna Abreu (26th of July Movement), nineteen

Graciela Aguiar (she had been a militant with Frank País's Acción Revolucionaria Oriental [ARO] until it merged with the 26th of July Movement), sixteen when she joined the 26th of July Movement

Esperanza Sanjurjo (26th of July Movement), seventeen

Blanca Mercedes Mesa (26th of July Movement), twenty-four

Consuelo Elba (Partido Socialista Popular [PSP] Juventud and 26th of July Movement), thirteen

Carmen Berro (DR), seventeen

Verena Pino (26th of July Movement), twenty-two

Niurka Lipiz (26th of July Movement), sixteen

Yolanda Alfonso (DR), nineteen

Rosa Mier (26th of July Movement and FCMM), twenty-three

Selma Díaz (PSP Juventud), seventeen

Magaly Olivera (26th of July Movement), twenty

Magaly Martínez (DR, 26th of July Movement, and FCMM), nineteen

Josefina (Fifi) Rodríguez (26th of July Movement and FCMM), seventeen

Aimée de los Angeles Afón (26th of July Movement), seventeen

Zobeida (Mimi) Rodríguez (26th of July Movement), twenty

Limbania Jiménez (PSP), eighteen

Ercilia Gutiérrez (DR), early twenties

Zoila Lapique (DR and MOU), twenty-six[1]

Why did these women, mostly girls, some still in their teens and almost all still in secondary schools, risk their young lives to bring down the Batista regime, transgressing in so doing the norms of the society into which most were born? How was it that in the course of the insurrection and following it in the narratives about it there is an abiding silence about their very presence? Michelle Chase reports that some three thousand women were involved in the clandestine movement.[2] And with almost no exceptions they are always positioned as those who facilitated in some manner the men, portrayed explicitly or implicitly in the narratives of the revolution as those who do the real work to overthrow the regime. That is, women and what they engaged in are understood as secondary, as those who enabled the insurrection. Like their nineteenth-century forebears, although in a vastly different context and on a vastly different terrain, their role is to facilitate. The women in the 1950s insurrection carried the mantle of these forebears. And like them their marginality served to further legitimate the unchallenged and unchallengeable right of male combatants to define and determine the reconstruction of the nation.

My objective in this and the following chapters is to understand the manner in which the 1950s revolution (specifically in this study, its urban underground) reprised the male homosocial construct that framed the nineteenth-century wars. And to do this by redefining the content and concept of women as "enabling" and in examining what women actually did in the Clandestine movement.

In the context of this re-reading, I reexamine two of the operations that, in the narratives of the urban insurrection in Havana, are cited as its greatest successes. Both of these—the Night of One Hundred Bombs and the kidnapping of the Argentine race-car driver Juan Manuel Fangio—are invariably described in terms of their male protagonists. In these re-readings I use the experiences of the women with whom I spoke to paint a picture of them that disrupts a construction that underscores the right of men to be the sole arbiters of the nation reborn.

SITES OF INVOLVEMENT

For all but three of the women with whom I spoke, secondary schools and pre-universities provided the terrain on which they became involved in the insurgency. For men by contrast the terrain was significantly broader and unbounded. It included the schools they attended but also the streets of the barrios in which they lived and the freedom to cross into other areas of the city. This unrestricted movement meant that they could come into contact with diverse groups of young men in different barrios who shared like-minded views about the regime and equally like-minded ideas about what to do about it. But girls did not have this same freedom to roam the streets: The streets were not available in the same way.

The women I interviewed, with five exceptions, described their families as lower middle class. During the insurrection they were in their formative years intellectually, emotionally, and sexually. Until they entered secondary school at least, their lives were largely bounded by their barrios and their friends were almost always other girls. At least for some, the degree of their freedom of movement was monitored by their mothers. Where mothers did not work or worked in the home, there were greater restrictions and even at times informal chaperoning. The elementary schools that the young girls attended in their barrios were segregated by sex through third grade. But beyond this, schooling for women as it developed and expanded in the course of the twentieth century had opened up greater freedom of movement. Entering secondary school and more so a pre-university or in some cases the workforce radically altered the geography of their lives.[3] It put them into close contact with girls from other environments, experiences, family lives, and to some degree socioeconomic class. They interacted on a daily basis with male schoolmates. In entering into the insurgency they took advantage of this altered geography and pushed its frontiers unimaginably out.

This new freedom and the schools they attended allowed them as well the space and the context within which to develop relationships with classmates at different levels of political awareness. These relationships surely were important vehicles for leading them into oppositional actions. Mirta Rodríguez Calderón, a student at the Escuela Normal de Maestros (a teacher training school) recalls that her girlfriend Niurka Lipiz helped her understand why she had to join the fight against Batista.[4] In turn, Sonnia Moro, a student at Pittman, a private secondary school, writes that, when she met Mirta Rodríguez Calderón through a mutual girlfriend, "I was desperate to do something and Mirta helped me join the Movement of Civic Resistance. To test whether or not I was ready to carry out activities outside the law, the first assignment she gave me was to paint with black crayons the number 26 on city walls. Actually, in those days you could see the number 26 written all over Havana. Small tasks, but they made me feel I was part of a wider group."[5]

Girls' first steps into insurrectionary action usually involved visits to male prisoners in El Príncipe. Such visits were at the outset more or less personal. Girls went to visit friends or "novios" who were interred.

But rapidly these visits became synchronized and organized into student brigades. It was in the Escuela Profesional de Comercio de La Habana, one of the hotbeds of anti-Batista organizing, that the first of the student brigades was formed by ten students, including three women in this study: Pilar Sa, Nilda Ravelo, and Mariíta Trasancos. All three, while still in school, would join the underground insurgency.

WHY THEY WERE

If the channels through which girls and young women became involved in the urban insurrection were more circumscribed than those of the men with whom they would fight, their motivations were generally shared. History itself served as the moral imperative for youth to fight against the Batista regime. Cubans, Louis Pérez Jr. observes, live their history: "The past," he writes, "is never fully past, literally. . . . [It] is presented as a presence . . . learned at home; taught in the classroom; eulogized in poetry and celebrated in song; dramatized in film and narrated in fiction; memorialized in the form of monuments and statuary; commemorated on national holidays and observed on patriotic anniversaries."[6] This almost organic sense of a commonly shared history and of one's responsibility to it had roots even in childhood. It was passed down in the family, in family lore, and, in some cases, family traditions of resistance. And even when parents or relatives were resigned or apathetic, what got communicated with the Batista coup was a sense of his dictatorship as yet another in the series of violations of the patria against which the legendary heroes of the nineteenth century had fought.

Almost all the women I interviewed had heard through their primary school years and afterward stories about the heroes of the nineteenth-century struggles for independence. These stories were framed by a male telling of the wars and who fought them. Chief among these was José Martí; his ideas, ideals, and vision of the Cuba that could be were central to their formation even as young children. Thus Mariíta, who was eleven at the moment of the coup:

> I studied at the Sociedad Económica Amigos del País School, which was sort of a public school with a board of trustees. I had very good teachers who taught me a lot about Cuban history, about the mambises, who for me were like gods; I simply idealized them. When I was in sixth grade we

celebrated the centennial of Martí's birth and at roll call, every day, [we said,] "present, present"; but in our [school], doing so was like saying one of Marti's phrases. At home, in a magazine that Martí wrote for children, *La edad de oro* [The golden age] we read his phrases. My father had many of Martí's books with many of his speeches. In 1952 I read a lot about Martí with the mindset of a twelve-year-old; I adored Marti.[7]

And Sonnia Moro:

For me, the presence of Martí was even a physical one, because in my parents' bedroom there was a head sculpted by Sicre that we worshiped.[8] So, immersed in legends and myths, we learned to love and to respect Martí as if he were still alive, as if he hadn't died. That feeling persists in me to the present day. But I believe it was in my teens, after Batista's coup, that I understood that his texts might very well have been written for us, so obvious was their present-day importance. Nevertheless, above all, [I valued] the anecdotes of how ethical, modest, humble, and especially how talented he was, his patriotic nature and that love for Cuba that we shared.[9]

There are many Martís: Martí the poet, Martí the prose writer, Martí the political organizer, Martí the social justice warrior, Martí the nationalist, Martí the anti-imperialist, Martí the redeemer of the nation. Mariíta's and Sonnia's childhood memories evidence the manner in which Martí impacted their young lives. The very fact that they were immersed in Martí, that Martí's *Edad de oro* was regular reading for children meant that he was embedded in their consciousness even before they contemplated the world around them. In Nicaragua and El Salvador, the major Latin American revolutionary movements of the 1970s and 1980s took the names of their countries' iconic historical revolutionary heroes. The Frente Sandinista in Nicaragua named itself for Augusto César Sandino who famously took on the United States in the 1920s. And the Farabundo Martí National Liberation Front in El Salvador named itself after Farabundo Martí, who led the resistance to the Martínez dictatorship in the 1930s. But neither figure drew close in meaning to what Martí meant to Cubans. And neither left an enormous body of writing from which young revolutionaries could seemingly infinitely draw on to confirm the justice and the rightness of their actions. The thread that wove together the opposition to Batista among these girls was Martí, and in the insurrection, above all, Martí the radical nationalist and his project of social justice and national dignity. His was the voice that was, as it had been for earlier generations, so powerful a force in women's and men's entry into the clandestinidad. Claiming Martí and denying the dictatorship's claim to him at every turn was critical for the insurrectionaries. Not for nothing did the FCMM name itself after Martí.

Living history served to reinforce the legendary tales of the wars of independence. Everyone, directly in the case of the older generation or indirectly in the case of their children, knew someone who had been involved in the nineteenth-century anticolonial wars or the 1930s anti-Machado uprising. These networks of historical and contemporary resistance were ubiquitous. Batista's 1952 coup followed the 1930 revolution in which he himself had been a principal actor by fewer than twenty years. And it followed the end of the final war of independence by only fifty-four years. The physical presence of surviving old mambises from the 1895–98 war in everyday life nourished this sense of historical continuity. Sonnia Moro relates: "For my generation, during our childhood we were able to meet veterans of the independence wars, old men who always wore a medal on their chests and told us things about the wars."[10]

Traditions of resistance and the reasons for which one's antecedents fought in short had a very real, tangible currency. For some young clandestinas this history had flesh-and-blood roots. Grandparents and for some even parents who were in the mambí army in the 1895–98 war of independence were remembered with great pride in family lore. The children in these families, both male and female, were immersed in and understood themselves as the inheritors of its traditions of resistance and as responsible to honor them. Magaly Martínez's father, an older man, fought with Maceo in Pinar del Río.[11] As had Carmen Berro's father: She relates that the stories he told her of the war infused her childhood and impelled her to join the clandestine movement. In the aftermath of the final independence war, her father was a founder of the Association of Veterans of the War. He took her along with him to whatever patriotic ceremonies she was allowed to attend. In her first year of medical school at the University of Havana she joined a cell of the Directorio.[12] When Mirta Rodríguez Calderón's parents, fearing for her safety, tried to keep her from going to a clandestine meeting, she replied that they had told her about Maceo and Céspedes and Martí and various other heroes of the nineteenth century: How could they now tell her not to act against the Batista dictatorship?[13]

At the university, for both women and men who joined the clandestine movements, the tradition of university student leadership in protest against dictatorial rule and political corruption and for radical change weighed heavily. Students at the University of Havana had been in the forefront of the 1930 revolution; assuming this role again was experienced by many of them as both a badge of honor and an obligation. It was hardly a coincidence that the University of Havana was the site of the first gathering in reaction to the coup on the night of March 10, 1952. Even those who were not university students or students at any level looked to the university in immediate response to it. As their involvement in anti-Batista protest deepened, many students came to believe it required of them any sacrifice. A considerable proportion of those at the University of Havana who would become leaders in the Directorio and the 26th of July Movement were students in the schools of architecture, medicine, and education, where women were most numerous. But the leadership ranks of these schools with the exception of the school of education were male.[14]

University autonomy, achieved in 1934, meant that, at least in the days and weeks directly following the coup, police forces could not enter campuses to quell protests and terminate meetings. But this did not hold true for manifestations that went from the university into the streets around it. The Batista regime's violent response to these early demonstrations led by the Federation of University students swelled the number of demonstrators and consolidated groups that had already begun to form clandestinely to plan or to take far more militant actions.

By taking on the mantle of resistance, individual student leaders were viewed as inheritors of the legendary figures of earlier resistances and as such drew other students into active opposition to the dictatorship. José Antonio Echeverría, the charismatic young man who became president of the FEU in 1954 and head of the Directorio in 1956, played a major role in giving form and definition to this university opposition. Héctor Terry, a Directorio militant, recounts: "When I enrolled in the University I felt a deep respect for José Antonio, for Fructuoso [Rodríguez], for Carbó [Serviá]. I saw them as tireless; they were always on the front line despite the beatings they endured. They formed in us that quality of giving ourselves fully to the struggle no matter what."[15]

But the impact Echeverría had went beyond male university students. It was felt by secondary school students like Sonnia Moro, who remembers the effect Echeverría's assassination and funeral had on her as a sixteen-year-old: "I think that the one death that really had a deep impact on me was José Antonio Echeverría's. I did not see his body. It was [wrapped] in a banner. His death had to be put to use."[16]

The figure of Eduardo Chibás loomed over virtually all the students at the university who would form and join the Directorio and the 26th of July Movement. Nearly all the women with whom I spoke recalled that their parents, along with a vast swathe of the Cuban population, had been ardent supporters of Chibás, the charismatic founder and leader of the Ortodoxo Party. His weekly radio addresses condemning political and economic corruption and his promise to cleanse Cuba of it tied him to the persistent but always frustrated promise of the unrealized Cuban nation. The symbol of the party was a broom that would sweep out corruption; its motto was "Vergüenza contra dinero" (Dignity against corruption). Nilda Ravelo's entire extended family, the Villafrancas, were fervent Chibasistas. They saw in him the man who would guide Cuba's future. Nilda and her family lived on a finca on the outskirts of Havana that had no electricity. Every Sunday the entire family walked part of the way and hitched the rest of it to the Reparto Baluarte where they could listen to Chibás's radio program. For Nilda and her family as well as many others, the coup, by strangling any hope that decades of corruption would be ended, left only a single option: armed struggle to bring down the Batista regime.[17] The profound impact Chibás had on those who would later join the insurgency remained evident sixty-five years later. Melba Hernández had been one of the two women who were part of the 1953 attack led by Fidel Castro on the Moncada fortress. At her wake in 2015 Melba Hernández's coffin with ashes was covered with two banners: one flag of the 26th of July Movement and the other banner reading "Vergüenza contra dinero."

At the moment of Batista's coup Fidel Castro was a young lawyer involved in Ortodoxo Party politics in Havana. Outside of these circles in the city, he was largely unknown. The attack on the Moncada and its immediate aftermath made him into a national figure and converted what had been the "movement," a small group of men and women around him, into the 26th of July Movement, setting it on its path to become the dominant insurrectionary force intent on overthrowing the dictatorship. At his trial following the attack, Fidel transformed his defense into a systematic denunciation of the dictatorship: detailing conditions on the island, the brutality of the regime, and therefore the necessity and right to overthrow it. While imprisoned, Fidel, well known for his prodigious memory, committed this defense to paper in what came to be known as "History Will Absolve Me." And he directed that it be distributed through whatever movement channels were possible.

Years later Vilma Espín, in one of her last interviews, celebrated "History Will Absolve Me" as "the clarion call which awakened the nation." With it, she declared, "Fidel was presenting something entirely new . . . a program around which we could all come together and fight." It was "a new language being spoken."[18] Vilma's characterization of the document as a "clarion call," as a key if not the key motivating force for those opposed to Batista to rise up against him, is problematic. No matter what its importance as what Louis Pérez Jr. understands as the "foundational text of the 26th of July Movement" and its enshrinement after 1959,[19] it is doubtful that the majority of urban militants had actually seen it either before or during the insurrectionary years. Not one of the women in this study read it until after January 1959. Copies of the unbound work or even just single pages containing parts of it circulated secretly in an uneven and disparate fashion.

Perhaps the informal, interconnected, and interwoven nature of Cuban social structure and daily life was key to the growing numbers of young women joining the insurgency. Before they began to involve themselves in clandestine activities, every woman I interviewed had some connection to the insurrection against Batista: a neighbor or a neighbor of a neighbor, or the son of a friend, or an aunt or cousin, or godparents whose son had been arrested, tortured, and even murdered. Or a classmate or friend or neighbor who already was in the clandestinidad with whom they began to actively participate. Nélida Álvarez relates:

> At the time of Batista's coup my grandmother's house became a hotbed of action because Oscar Alcalde, one of the Moncada attackers and a very close friend of our family, had his laboratory next door to us. And although he did not tell us he was going to attack the Moncada there were constant talks at home about Batista and there was plotting against Batista and I grew up in that environment. . . . From the Moncada onwards my home turned into a hotbed because every individual coming from Manzanillo or from Niquero or from Media Luna to Havana came by my grandmother's house bringing news about what had happened in Santiago.[20]

In one of those distinctly Cuban coincidences, Nélida's family were neighbors of Chibás in the last years of his life and Chibás often played with her and her sister when they were children. And yet another coincidence: After he was released from prison Fidel moved into the building in which the family then resided. Nélida reports that Fidel came to their apartment every afternoon for coffee and recited almost word for word "History Will Absolve Me."[21]

This network of ties and familiarity served to greatly magnify and personalize the impact of the Batista regime's escalating employment of terror, particularly in the days following the Directorio's attack on the Presidential Palace and the months before and after the 26th of July Movement's April 9, 1958, strike when its public expression became most gruesomely displayed in the appearance of mutilated bodies of young men on the streets.

WHO THEY WERE

Mariíta Trasancos was one of the young girls for whom contact with the Martianas was fundamental to her entry into the Clandestinad. She was born into a family of Spanish immigrants. Her mother was only partially literate and her father worked as a stevedore in one of Julio Lobo's warehouses.[22] When Lobo closed the warehouse in which he was working, her father lost this job and remained mostly unemployed. The family lived in an impoverished barrio in Old Havana. As a child, Mariíta's father talked to her a great deal about the blatant corruption and greed of successive Cuban governments and above all fumed about their continuous violations of the 1940 Cuban constitution. As a ten-year-old she listened with her parents every Sunday evening to Chibás's radio broadcasts. She began to be politically involved after entering the Escuela de Comercio: "When I first began to work in the insurgency what I thought about was that Batista had staged a coup, abolished the 1940 constitution, and implanted a regime of force. I did not know the larger implications of this and joined [the cause] to fight a man who had abolished every law."[23] Conversations about the country's political and economic situation with a girlfriend who had been her classmate in primary and secondary schools deepened her grasp of the situation. With other students in the school she began by identifying profesores de dedo, arbitrarily designated professors who had gotten their jobs through political connections and were completely unqualified to teach: "We channeled our political struggle around demands concerning these professors and we staged protest rallies and small demonstrations in and around the school."[24]

With the members of her school's student brigade, which she had been instrumental in forming, Mariíta joined in regularly planned visits to prisoners in El Príncipe. Prison visits were almost always undertaken by girls and women because men were likely to be looked upon with suspicion by prison guards. Young women visited different prisoners usually under the guise of being girlfriends or family members. These visits provided the critical link between the men in El Príncipe and the outside insurgency and for the girls involved: major points of contact with male insurgents engaged in Action and Sabotage cells and therefore the route by which the girls entered into this front.

Of the women I interviewed, only five had entered into the underground insurgency through routes involving not simply the schools they attended but their workplaces or the barrios in which they lived. Nélida Álvarez was working in a beauty parlor and formed a 26th of July Movement grouping with clients. Another was the rebellious Mariíta Trasancos. Mariíta entered into the insurgency through her secondary school, through the FCMM, and also through her barrio. Neighborhood formations of insurgents almost always involved men exclusively. As I have written, the streets were the domain of males; they had freedom of movement on these streets and between barrios where they could form wide-ranging friendships. Young girls did not have the same possibilities. But in her barrio Mariíta became very close to one of the 26th of July Movement heads of an Action and Sabotage cell, Fernando Alfonso Torices, or, as he was known in the underground, Morúa, who with Aida Pelayo had been a member of the Acción Revolucionaria Guiteras during the 1940s. With Morúa, Mariíta began to frequent Industria #260, Aida's apartment. Discussions in these spaces with Aida, Carmen, and other FCMM members were the turning point for Mariíta in her decision to take more dangerous action against the regime. "That is when I began to see that the revolution was much more than overthrowing Batista, that it also meant ending inequalities and all the corruption.[25] . . . I officially joined the FCMM. I had seen her [Aida] in action at the Castillo de El Príncipe prison. I also visited Carmen Castro's apartment many times."[26] Her interactions with the FCMM convinced her that as Aida had once said, "Batista would not be overthrown by writing on small bits of paper. He had to be unseated in some other way and I learned about other activities which were no longer just simple street rallies but other forms of struggle. This led me to Action and Sabotage."[27] The women of FCMM, as we shall see, would continue to play a key role in her life.

By the age of fifteen then, Mariíta was involved simultaneously with the FCMM, with the student brigade at the Escuela de Comercio, with a clandestine group headed by Morúa in her barrio, and through these in short order, with 26th of July Movement insurgents involved in Action and Sabotage. Mariíta's story makes it clear that the routes through which young women joined the clandestine movement were not necessarily separate but interwoven, linked by personal, social, and political relationships.

Mariíta had been working in a cell of Action and Sabotage headed by Morúa. After her first arrest (he was at that moment a prisoner in El Príncipe), it was no longer safe for them to work together closely. Pilar Sa, who had been involved with forming that first student brigade in the Escuela de Comercio with Mariíta, substituted for her. Morúa was black; accompanied by Pilar because she was a mulata, they would attract far less attention on the street. Pilar had been introduced to him while on a visit to El Príncipe and after he was released, she began to accompany him, to become, as she says, his shadow. "From the moment he got out of prison, I was permanently at his side."[28]

Pilar was born into a family, as she says, "of many colors." Her mother was black and her father white, and his family had rejected the marriage. The family lived through periods in which her mother's work as a seamstress was what they subsisted on. Inequities conditioned Pilar's daily life as she was growing up. Her mother was stricken with polio, and the combination of poverty, her mother's infirmity, and her ideas about what was proper for young girls limited Pilar's contact with the world outside her family. "I wanted to go out," she recalls, but her mother did not let her: "Men's honor," her mother asserted, "is located at the worst smelling spot of women."[29]

Pilar began her studies at the Instituto de Comercio de La Habana when she was thirteen and several years later while finishing her second bachelor's degree at the Instituto de La Habana she entered into Action and Sabotage. She was eighteen when she began to work in the insurgency, but she says that eighteen does not fully describe just how young she was. "At eighteen I had the mindset of a ten-year-old, because I was a virgin in every sense of the word. Due to my mother's disability she could not take us to the beach, to the movies or anywhere else; those spots were unknown to me. I only became familiar with all that after I turned twenty."[30]

While still in school Pilar got a job as a secretary in Anuncios Cubatráfico, a US-owned company that produced advertisements for bus stops. Pilar was already working with the 26th of July Movement, and the telephone in her office became a point of communication and coordination for the insurgents.[31] By the time Pilar was fired for using the telephone for personal reasons her involvement had deepened. She began working with Morúa. When her father learned through a friend, a mechanic who worked on Pilar García's car, that the police were looking for her, she left her parents' home and moved into a safe house with Morúa.[32]

Teresa Abreu and her sister Digna worked with Morúa as well. The sisters were born and raised in Santa Clara; their name, Abreu, indicates their slave ancestry.[33] The two were inseparable. After finishing secondary school, they moved to Havana in search of work. Teresa found a job in a shoe factory and Digna worked as a clerk in a shop selling buttons, lace, and other items for sewing. Their aunt, María Abreu, had preceded them to Havana where her son, Julio, a 26th of July Movement militant, was in jail. María herself had joined the Martianas. Julio, released from jail, found himself without any contacts who could arrange somewhere for him to sleep. He called Digna and Teresa and went to their apartment for the night. The night stretched out to weeks; the apartment became a site for clandestine meetings and finally a "cuartel" for weapons. Teresa and Digna were now fully integrated into the 26th of July Movement. Although Julio was the channel through which the sisters joined in the clandestinidad, Teresa was the motivating force. Digna remembers: "Anything, that we were fighting for, a just cause and just causes had to be fought for, no matter who did the fighting, no matter whether you were black or white. She explained things to me and I understood and learned with her and we became involved. What little I learned, I learned from her."[34] Teresa and Digna would be caught in a trap, imprisoned and tortured.

In chapter 3 I noted that it was highly unusual for a girl, or for that matter anyone, to be a member of the PSP or its youth branch and at the same time join in actions of the 26th of July Movement or the Directorio. The PSP was explicit about this and expelled anyone found to be collaborating in these groups, which it deemed terrorist. Selma Díaz, a member of the Juventud of the PSP at the university, was severely criticized simply for having a boyfriend who was a member of the Juventud but also acted at times with 26th of July Movement insurgents.[35] While informally individuals who were PSP members or members of its Juventud and insurgents in the 26th of July Movement carried out actions together, specifically perhaps in workplaces, this was certainly not true for young girls.[36] Consuelo Elba broke this rule. Consuelo was thirteen when she joined in actions against the dictatorship. The beginnings of her involvement had nothing to do with her school or her relations with young female friends. Nor was she inspired by any of Cuba's legendary heroes or by listening to Chibás's weekly radio shows. She was raised in a solar by a single mother, a black woman who was functionally illiterate and worked as a maid for a white family (Consuelo herself appears white).[37] She had no father and no other relatives and spent a good part of everyday alone and often in conversations with Ricardo, a black PSP member who worked in a tailor's shop below her solar who, she said, became like a father to her. He gave her children's books to read: *El peque*, about a child who is a revolutionary and *Simplemente amore*, about a girl who is tortured. "I believed in god, attended catechism meetings. For me communists ate children; that is what they told us. When I perceived that they [Ricardo and his friends] were communists it was shocking news." But, as she says, she drew a conclusion logical for a child: "They are practically my family; if they are communists, they cannot be bad people."[38] Consuelo joined the Juventud. Shortly thereafter, through the young people she met while working as a child model at the Cuban Institute of Radio and Television, she began to collaborate with the 26th of July Movement.[39] She was first arrested in 1956 during a demonstration in Parque Central. After her second arrest (she has told no one what was done to her during this arrest), she escaped to the sierra and joined Fidel's column.

RACE AND THE CLANDESTINAS

Devyn Spence Benson notes the widely held and broadly circulated belief during the years of the insurgency and into the present that black Cubans favored Batista because he was black (he was generally described as mulato). Searching through the ephemera of the period, she documents the fact that "some members of the anti-Batista coalition routinely portrayed Afro-Cubans as supporters of the besieged dictator and used racist epithets like 'black monkey' and 'el mulato malo' to attack Batista."[40] She reports that Batista did indeed attempt to coopt various black societies, using lottery money to do so.[41]

Of the women I interviewed, all but two were white or white in appearance with one exception, and they denied that there were racial distinctions among insurrectionaries. Elvira Díaz Vallina and colleagues put the number of black women involved in the clandestinidad in the municipality of Plaza in Havana during the period from 1952 to 1959 as 18 percent of the total. But this figure is problematic: It does not consider the racial makeup of Plaza as a whole and does not explain its criteria for determining who was white and who was black.[42] Every clandestina discussed in this work, no matter what her color was, thinks the figure of 18 percent is significantly inflated.[43] But even had the Díaz Vallina study taken account of these various qualifications, it is clear that black and mulata women were extremely underrepresented in the clandestinidad. As Digna Abreu, one of the black and mulata clandestinas I interviewed, described it, she and her sister Teresa were "black flies in a sea of milk."[44] This was probably truer of women than it was of men; in Havana, a number of insurgents in the leadership, particularly of the 26th of July Movement, were black or mulato. There are no studies of female participants that would elucidate why this was so, so we are left to hypothesize about the reasons.

The first and most obvious explanation relates to access to schooling. The beginnings of collective agitation against the Batista regime and with it the development of clandestine resistance, particularly among girls, happened, as I have written, mainly in certain secondary and pre-university schools and in the University of Havana itself. And these schools were overwhelmingly white. Given the economic circumstances of the majority of their families, young black girls were regularly forced to cut off their schooling after their primary years. Black and mulata girls and women generally found employment as servants, clerks in small shops, seamstresses working out of their homes, nannies, or sometimes perhaps nurses. When Digna, Teresa, and Pilar were captured by Batista's esbirros, a policeman at the station to which they were taken said to them, "I expected to see the daughters of Martí here, but not the daughters of Maceo."[45]

Second, we might look to the myth of a nonracial Cuba. The trope of unity at the heart of the construction of the nation, passed down from Martí, served to make publicly invisible questions related to race even among those seeking radical change. A thundering silence about race in most accounts of the struggles for change in twentieth-century Cuba settled in during the decades after the 1912 massacre of blacks.[46] And this silence occurs in accounts of the massacre in writings not just by Cuban historians but also among black Cubans themselves, given the way in which the fear it had evoked among them echoed even into the following decades.[47] And with good reason: Anecdotal evidence shows that during the 1950s insurgency, black revolutionaries received treatment far harsher than whites at the hands of their captors. Certainly Cuban history with regard to the differential treatment of blacks and whites supports this. Digna reflects that she could not tell whether the brutality of the beatings inflicted on her and her sister by their captors had to do with the fact that they were black or the fact that they were insurgents.[48] Juan Almeida, a storied black comandante in the sierra, noted that Armando Mestre, black and among those in the 1953 assault on Moncada, was the most harshly treated of those captured: "They kept on telling him 'Come over here. You are a revolutionary? Don't you know negros can't be revolutionaries? Negros are either thieves or Batista supporters, but never revolutionaries.'"[49]

This same silence concerning race shaped political opposition to and rebellion against corrupt political and economic regimes on the island in the first half of the twentieth century. White male voices and actors populate and overwhelmingly dominate the narrative of these years. Even in the Communist Party, which did speak out about the issue of race, the emphasis on workers as the primary category of analysis meant that the unique oppression of black workers was not its focal point.[50] Neither the 26th of July Movement nor the Directorio moved to correct this: Race and racial inequality were not on the agenda of either movement. The issue of race was never mentioned by Fidel Castro in his denunciation of the economic and political distortions of Cuban society in "History Will Absolve Me," and it is alluded to only slightly in the 1957 Program Manifesto of the 26th of July Movement.[51] Spence Benson concludes that "ultimately it was easier and less divisive for the predominant middle class and white leadership of the 26th of July Movement (and I might add, the Directorio) to maintain a vague Martian platform about race as they navigated the ever-changing social milieu of the anti-Batista struggle."[52] Whether for strategic reasons or ideological ones, the 26th of July Movement, in positioning itself as the inheritors of Martí and claiming continuity with the wars of independence, portrayed themselves as the champions of a Cuba in Martí's terms, in which all were citizens above all rather than racially distinct. Why then should blacks expect to see the 1952–59 insurrection as anything different? Why, as Digna pointed out, "should they sacrifice themselves yet again?"[53] As an esbirro said to Carlos Fonseca, a black clandestino arrested while transporting arms and brought to the Servicio de Intelligencia Militar, "After Maceo fought for la patria, who has seen a negro making a revolution?"[54]

FORMS OF FAMILY RESISTANCE

For the young women who became clandestinas the whole structure of their lives altered not only socially but also physically; they entered into wholly new realms of being. This was a very different life than what their parents had fully expected them to lead or indeed what they expected to lead during their adolescence. It inevitably resulted in conflicts with parents, some so severe that they caused permanent breaks.

Those clandestinas living in their parents' homes led double lives. Others lived elsewhere and without their parents' consent for the first time. Some were living in movement-rented apartments under the guise of being married to one of the male clandestinos living with them: this in a society just decades away from a time when no decent young (white) woman would be seen on the street without a chaperone, and not simply those from upper-class families. Living this life, Pilar said, was really something: "Imagine, I was a girl of eighteen who was never allowed to go out alone, never . . . given the rules of that rigid Spanish upbringing that did not allow us any freedoms. Suddenly, it was like a maelstrom for me, a grand vertigo."[55]

Four of the women with whom I spoke were involved in the insurgency along with their entire families. María de los Ángeles Afón and her sister and mother were 26th of July Movement militants. In their house, as I shall elaborate in chapter 5, the Argentine race-car driver Juan Manuel Fangio was sequestered.[56] Ercilia Gutiérrez and her family provided refuge for Guillermo Jiménez, a Directorio militant, following the failed attack on the Presidential Palace until the collapse of the Batista regime. During this entire period, her nine-year old son, Godeardo, ran interference for the Directorio in a number of ways.[57] Magaly Martínez, at the moment she was arrested, had been helping her mother by searching out places of refuge, renting apartments for Directorio insurgents, and hiding weapons.[58] And Xiomara Blanco served as a messenger for her father to leaders of both the 26th of July Movement and the Directorio.[59]

But this kind of collaborative family involvement was not the case for the other women in this study. Some who lived with their parents tried to hide what they were involved with. Others went openly against the will of their parents, not because their parents were pro-Batista; to the contrary in most cases they opposed the dictatorship. Rather, they feared what might happen to their daughters. Or they feared what might happen to family members as a result of their daughters' participation in the insurgency.

Parents reacted in various ways to restrict their daughters' activities. Niurka Lipiz's father and mother had fought on the Republican side in the Spanish civil war and had remained politically active in Cuba. But when her father became aware of his daughter's involvement in clandestine activities, he literally took away her clothes in his effort to stop her.[60] Sonnia Moro led a double life between school and her 26th of July Movement activities. Her mother knew what she was doing; her father pretended he didn't until after the triumph when he proudly claimed his own (proxy) involvement by boasting of the actions of his daughter.[61] Following the April 9, 1958, strike, her father suffered a heart attack, which she firmly believes he invented to keep her from continuing her involvement. Her mother appealed to her that it would be "disrespectful" to her father to leave her home for the ten days he was laid up in bed.[62]

Pilar Sa's parents were both in favor of the insurgency. But when she learned that the police were searching for her, Pilar left her parents' home to live in a safe house with Morúa, giving them the address of the house in which she would be living. "My father went there and made such a scandal, demanding to know why I was there that we had to leave the house. He simply could not understand. My mother did, but he did not. The next time she [my mother] saw me, I was in jail. It was the macho mentality, dictating that boys could do it, but girls could not."[63]

Mariíta Trasanco's mother begged Carmen Castro to convince her daughter "to get this thing of action groups out of her head." When Mariíta was arrested for the second time and brutally tortured, Carmen relates that her mother, "desperate, planted herself in the Ninth Police Station, headquarters of the ubiquitous torturer Esteban Ventura and asked when they would release her. Ventura went into a rage: 'If you ever come back here, I am going to kick your ass so hard that it will send you back to Spain' [where she had been born]."[64] In Mariíta's case her father's fears centered not so much around his daughter but rather what her underground actions would mean for his family, particularly his three sons. He feared that Mariíta would put her brothers in far more danger than herself. When the then head of Action and Sabotage in Havana proposed to her that the movement rent her family a house, given that as a family of eight the comings and goings of different people would not be suspicious, Mariíta's father flatly refused: "They will kill all of us," he said.[65]

Parents of those women already in the workforce reacted in similar fashion to their daughters' militancy. The family of Natalia Bolívar, a Directorio militant, belonged to the Cuban aristocracy. Her father had been involved and nearly killed in the struggle against Machado in the 1930s. In reaction to what he had lived through, any discussion of politics in their home was forbidden. Therefore, Natalia too led a double life. Her work in the Museum of Bellas Artes gave her some degree of freedom from the society to which her family belonged in which young women alone or in couples still had to be accompanied by a chaperone when they went out. And it gave her the possibility of escape from the life she had already rebelled against. Most importantly, it gave her cover for her deepening involvement with the Directorio. Her parents knew nothing of her activities until she was arrested.[66]

For one of the women I interviewed, the family rift lasted far beyond January 1, 1959. Hidelisa Esperón relates that her family had no idea about her activities until they saw her in a television report about the Martianas' demonstration on Galiano and the ensuing clash with the police. Her mother, a rabid Chibasista as Hidelisa describes her, was the most horrified by her involvement in the movement, particularly as her commitment deepened. In October 1958 Hidelisa was captured and taken to the Ninth Police Station and brutally tortured.[67] Because she was a minor she was released conditionally to her father; he was silent when she informed him she intended to continue in the clandestinidad. She went to live with the mother of the clandestino whom she had married in a hasty ceremony while he was still in jail.[68] She reconciled with her parents only years after the triumph.[69]

THE NOVIAS ARGUMENT

In much of the literature about clandestinas, there is either explicitly or implicitly yet another reason put forth about why young women joined their lives to the movements: the idea that they became involved not so much out of any conviction or commitment to an idea or ideal of a redeemed and just Cuba, but because they were simply following the lead of or were deeply influenced and convinced or even tricked by their boyfriends (who, of course, had ulterior motives in romancing them). The regime's repressive apparatus assumed this as well, and it would frame the torture they inflicted upon captured clandestinas. I discuss this in chapter 6. These boyfriends, according to this logic, were the ones who were truly committed to the revolution, whatever the cost. In situating them in this fashion, the very question of clandestinas as protagonists in the insurrection becomes moot and the centrality of men in the insurgency and the subsequent reconstruction of the nation is once more confirmed. But perhaps equally disturbing, in the aftermath of the taking of power this is what is implied in many of the portrayals of clandestinas: It virtually defines them. Any mention of their names in books, in the media, and in popular parlance is almost mechanically followed by "Oh, yes, the novia of . . ." Thereby, clandestinas' identities in the insurrection were contained entirely within and reduced to their relationships with often-martyred male insurgents. They become the twentieth-century versions of the "abnegada viudas" of the nineteenth-century wars. And, like them, they were stripped of their own identities.[70]

ABSTINENCE AND TRANSGRESSION: THE DILEMMA
OF SEXUAL RELATIONS IN THE CLANDESTINIDAD

The girls who became clandestinas grew up in the 1940s and 1950s in family homes where the subject of sexuality was taboo. As Carrie Hamilton notes, unspoken traditions of silence and prohibition surrounded the subject of sex.[71] Not one of the women with whom I spoke had had a conversation about anything related to sex or sexuality with their mothers or with older female family members. Mirta Rodríguez Calderón recalls that when she was about twelve years old she asked her mother, who was a devout Catholic, how Eve and Adam had reproduced. "For my mother this was insolence, these were things you didn't ask about, things of faith. From then on I did not ask her any more questions about it."[72]

But it was virtually inevitable that during the insurrection, given the ages of the clandestinas/os and the intensity of what they were living, romantic relationships would develop. As Mirta comments, "We were living life in the present." And Ángela Alonso: "We were young, and there was nothing to hold us back."[73] Yet interestingly the women I spoke with almost unanimously denied that there were any tensions around or even discussions about sexual relations between female and male insurgents or among female insurgents themselves. The norms and continued operation of the patriarchal order in Cuba, which for centuries had governed women's sexuality and required female virginity as key to its maintenance, were, of course, at work here. They reflect the centuries' long concerns around female virginity, which continued to prevail in the 1950s.[74]

But there was another constraint on female sexual activity: a specific response to life in the insurgency. For clandestinas sexual relations were implicitly understood as a violation of the insurrection, a betrayal of the patria. Given this formulation, the revolution itself was dangerously imperiled by the intimate male-female contacts necessitated by the insurrection. Pilar's relationship with Morúa, with whom she was living, is illustrative:

After working together for some time, a mutual attraction sparked between the two of us. We fell in love. Well, he fell in love and I did not want
to. I did not realize that he was falling for me. I thought, "How could
we fall in love when we are in the fight?" Our cause could not allow it,
but love came anyway, although I did not realize it because I was very
naïve. Once, when we were at a bar, he kissed me and I was petrified. I
was shocked and felt guilty because how could I be falling for a man if
we were fighting for our country? It was a very respectful affair, almost
platonic. In the house where we were hiding we slept on the same bed
putting a pillow between us. We were never lovers. That would have been
a betrayal of our ideals.[75]

"The betrayal" Pilar identifies here directly echoes the stories of the
abnegada wives and widows of the heroes of the nineteenth-century
wars. As with Pilar, their unbroken sexual fidelity to the patria required
and was measured and defined for women by their unbroken fidelity to
their dead husbands. The norms and unstated prohibitions concerning
female sexual activity during the 1950s insurrection, whether in fact they
were observed in private, echo this conflation of sexual purity and purity
of commitment to the insurrection to redeem the patria. Chase notes
that "the relationship between young men and women involved in the
urban underground was supposed to be 'sacred'; violating that relationship would be sacrilege."[76]

In the 1950s insurgency there must certainly have been much greater
ambiguity than in the nineteenth century about what was sexually per-
missible, both because of the passage of time and because the insurrection itself fostered the kind of intimate contact with men that few young
clandestinas had ever experienced. The place where one would think
tensions around sex would be most fraught should have been among
those young women whose positioning in the clandestine movement
required them to share the same space with their male counterparts in
Action and Sabotage, living as their "wives" in order to give cover to a
base of insurgent operations. Hidelisa Esperón's life in a safe house with
two male militants speaks to these tensions. Hidelisa's narration of her
experiences in the clandestinidad is instructive. The relationships in the
household the three shared re-created in an entirely other context the
patriarchal order that she had rebelled against in leaving her parents'
home to join the insurrection. She came into contact with Ángel Ameijeiras (Machaco) and Tony Fernández in visits to El Príncipe. Machaco

asked her to join them in the clandestinidad in Action and Sabotage when the two got out of prison. Machaco, the head of Action and Sabotage in Havana after the April 9th strike, along with Tony Fernández, his second in command, were important targets for Batista. Therefore Hidelisa, living with them, was in effect equally so. In their constructed household Machaco took on the role of her father. As Hidelisa tells it, both of her parents were horrified by the idea that she would go off to live with two men. When she insisted, ready to do this without her parents' assent, Machaco said no. He knew her father and he went to speak with him and in what amounted to a transfer of paternal authority, her father agreed to the arrangement. In the story that the three told, they formalized this in a sense in the barrio into which they moved. Hidelisa was presented as Machaco's wife, taken without permission from her parents' house and wed (he was thirty-three; she was sixteen but looked even younger). Tony was presented as Machaco's cousin and a university student. Hidelisa's life changed dramatically: "I really experienced hardships. I had to sleep on the floor. We had no money to buy food, whereas I had never gone hungry before. I had not truly faced pressing needs. We slept there, spreading newspapers on the floor, something I had never done before."[77] In this apartment they re-created a traditional household. Hidelisa learned to cook; she did the shopping, flirting with the grocer in order to get desperately needed supplies. Hidelisa was most effective with the tactical use of flirting: She employed it with guards at El Príncipe in order to get around waiting in lines and to extend the length of her visits to prisoners. When her friendship with him grew to be something else, Tony asked Machaco's permission to be her novio, and Machaco presided over a ceremony formalizing this, acting once more as her father. And as she tells it, his paternal monitoring of her "purity" continued: He strictly forbade them even to kiss.[78]

Machaco himself was not restrained by these prohibitions against sexual relations in the insurrection. Chase remarked that "male insurrectionaries were not bound by the restraints of parents in engaging in sexual relations and engaged in relations with women who were not in the insurrection."[79] But at least one of Machaco's sexual relationships was with a clandestina: Norma Porras.

The case of Norma Porras is instructive. Like every other young girl who joined the insurgency, she had transgressed against the norms of the society in which she had been brought up and in so doing rejected the life she had been supposed to live. Her second transgression involved her sexual relationship with Machaco. This relationship is memorialized in Fernando Pérez's film *Clandestinos* with the romance at its very heart. As I have noted, for women in the insurgency, such relationships violated the very cause for which they had committed their lives. As Pilar declared, the goal of overthrowing the dictatorship required abstinence from a relationship, which would inevitably result in a deviation from this goal and a betrayal of the insurgency. But more: According to women who had lived in close quarters with her, Porras was guilty of a third transgression—she engaged in more than one sexual relationship in the underground. In the late 1980s when Fernando Pérez was in the process of making *Clandestinos* he mentioned to his much-respected professor Dolores Nieves, herself a clandestina, that the film would center around a fictionalized version of Porras and Machaco's relationship, Nieves dismissed Porras, declaring her "a prostitute."[80] Others labeled her as "a girl looking for a boyfriend."[81] Still others remembered that Porras would have been excluded from the movement, given these activities, but had not been because she had a cousin who was an important figure in Batista's police. Despite the many years that had passed since the insurgency, these comments were made almost spontaneously by women. But given that Porras was in fact an active participant in the underground, and given the passage of time and changes in social mores, clandestinas now dismiss epithets as something of the distant past and irrelevant.[82] Nonetheless, situating Porras's story in the context of life in the underground reflects the manner in which the bodies of young women were positioned in the urban insurrection.

CLANDESTINAS IN HAVANA
WHAT THEY DID

In May 2014 the Club Martiano de Herencia Rebelde held one in its series of meetings on the clandestinidad in Havana. As I noted in the introduction, the club's main objective was to revive the memory of the insurrection in Havana. Discussion in this meeting centered on the attacks carried out by Action and Sabotage cells during the period from November 30, 1956, to January 1, 1959. The recitation of these actions evidenced the scope of the struggle undertaken by clandestinas/os in Havana. It was in a sense a record made for a history that has minimized both the extent and the import of what occurred in the city during these years.

But at the same time, by focusing solely on armed actions, it reinscribed in this history a narrative that recognizes only the story of these actions and their results, rather than the story of all that was necessary to produce them. Because armed actions were usually carried out by male clandestinos, what emerges in this recitation is a hero-ology: a history in which men (clandestinos) in battle with other men (Batista's battery of repressors) become the protagonists of the tale. The male homosocial construct that frames the narrative of the revolution as a whole is replicated in the story of the llano.

What is missing here is the dailiness of living and fighting in the insurgent movement. This dailiness, as Chantal Mouffe so perceptively notes, is at the (missing) heart of history.[1] Without a comprehension of this, and even in the case of those women involved in Action and Sabotage, clandestinas are inevitably reduced to supportive roles within the bounds of what was appropriate for women (albeit in a very inappropriate context). They enabled the men who did the actual work of overthrowing the tyranny and therefore almost by definition they were secondary in importance.

There were tactical considerations involved in some of what female insurgents did. As women they could employ themselves or be employed in certain kinds of operations more easily than men. The normative assumptions at the time about women in Cuban society allowed them to inhabit and move in certain spaces that would have been dangerous or even deadly for male insurgents. Women delivering and distributing weapons would be far less subject to any kind of search; visits to prisons other than by family members were women's work. Women made up most of the processions that followed the coffins of assassinated male insurgents, and they witnessed their burials. Michelle Chase notes the manner in which these processions were converted into "performances . . . of protest."[2] Women's clothes or even their bodies could be employed to transport both messages and weapons. Police searches of a young woman would in most circumstances be off limits. Women for instance were not searched when they visited male insurgents jailed in El Príncipe. Touching in any way the bodies of women who were supposedly pregnant would be yet more inconceivable. But a more complete and complex reading of what are generally understood as acts of assistance is revealing. For instance, women accompanying men to plant explosives were in reality equally involved (and equally endangered) in these acts of sabotage.

My intention is not to challenge the range of the actions undertaken by women. Rather, it is to resignify them and, in so doing, to surface the transgressive nature of what women did in the clandestine movement. My intention is to erase the idea that actions involving some form of direct engagement between the (male) enemy and the (male) insurgents define the degree of one's centrality in the project of national reconstruction or redemption.

In what follows in this chapter, I seek to do this, first, by reconsidering the actions seen generally as "women's work" in the insurrection, using the testimonies of the clandestinas who undertook these actions. Second, by reconsidering the gendered roles in the portrayal of two of the major offensives undertaken by Action and Sabotage groups in Havana: the Night of One Hundred Bombs in November 1957 and the kidnapping of the internationally famous Argentine race-car driver Juan Manuel Fangio in February 1958. Each action was planned and carried out by the 26th of July Movement. And each is understood as a high point in the narrative of the urban insurrection in Havana.

WOMEN'S WORK RECONSIDERED 1: THE CONTEXT

The subordinate nature of clandestinas' involvement was formally shaped by the structure (or lack thereof) of the insurgent movements, which in theory determined who would dictate what actions were to be undertaken by whom. On paper in each city, for example, the 26th of July Movement was organized in "cells" that replicated the movement's structure at the provincial and national levels. These cells, again theoretically, were tied to and under the direction of the leadership of the various fronts: Propaganda, Finance, Action and Sabotage, and so on, as well as the National Workers Front and the National Students Front. Underground cells also functioned as part of the Movement of Civic Resistance (MRC), whose public face was purportedly to bring together people (professionals, etc.) who opposed the Batista regime but were not involved actively in the insurgency.

Elvira Díaz Vallina, the head of a cell in the MRC in Havana, describes this structure of the underground movement:

> The structure was radial. There was a leader and nine subordinates and each one of these subordinates had in turn nine other people under them and those nine had another nine and this is how the structure expanded. By doing this, Frank [País] aimed at protecting the maximum leaders of the organization. If a person who belonged to the third or fourth level was arrested, he would not know the rest of the structure. That is to say, that person only knew the one person with whom he was in direct contact but did not know who the main leader of the whole structure was.[3]

At the upper levels and in Action and Sabotage, this description has resonance. Its leadership for the city as a whole was always men and was selected by the head of the 26th of July Movement in the city.

But in practice ground operations rarely corresponded, or better said, did not obey the orderly structure Vallina describes. Pilar Sa, as noted in chapter 4, who lived in a safe house with Morúa, one of the heads of Action and Sabotage in Havana until his assassination and her arrest in October 1958, flatly dismisses the notion that at the street level any sort of cell structure regularly determined and controlled insurgents' actions or even existed:

> These people who tell you that there was a group, an organization: They are lying! It is all a fabrication because it was not like that at all. There was no such a thing as an organization. In fact, there was nothing. It was all very spontaneous, very loose, from the heart. And when I hear people say those things I do not argue with them. What for? It is not worth it. It is what it is. All those people who speak about an organization, that he was the leader, that he had a cell: Forget it! The one who had a gun was the leader because he was the one who could make the decisions. Those who did not have a gun followed the one with the gun.[4]

The idea that the insurgents operated within a carefully laid out structure as described by Elvira, Pilar insists, is something dreamed up in the wake of January 1, 1959. Actual daily realities of the struggle had little to do with organized cell structures.[5]

The truth probably lies somewhere between these two assertions. At its upper levels the underground movement in Havana modeled itself on a classic insurrectionary structure. Faustino Pérez was designated by the 26th of July Movement leadership to be in charge of the insurrection in Havana as a whole. He was removed from this position in the aftermath of the April 9, 1958, strike and replaced by Delio Gómez Ochoa, who up to that point had been with the guerrilla forces in the sierra. Sergio González (El Curita) headed Action and Sabotage cells in Havana until his assassination in March 1958. In May 1958 Ángel Ameijeiras (Machaco) took over the role that had been El Curita's until he was killed in November of that year.[6] But if this begins to sound like the cell structure true of other insurgencies, in practice it was far more flexible. This would seem to be particularly true for women. Pilar Sa, speaking from her own experiences in Action and Sabotage, seemingly adheres to a universal rule of all underground cell insurgencies. For Pilar, working with Morúa and accompanying him everywhere he went meant asking no questions. Among other things the danger involved in knowing the specifics of what he was doing was too great should she be caught, as she eventually was. Nor did different Action and Sabotage groups living in safe houses, which were in some cases sites for arms storage, necessarily know where others were located for the same reason.[7]

Hidelisa Esperón's entry into the underground movement appears by contrast extremely informal and subject to no rules at all. Hidelisa had no prior experience in the underground movement and was presumably an unknown entity when she was recruited directly during a prison visit to live in a safe house as Machaco's fictive wife.

But Pilar certainly voices what other clandestinas/os in virtually every account of the insurrection attested to: The on-the-ground structure was submerged by events and actions. The heads of Action and Sabotage cells in different municipalities in Havana, or the organizers of different actions, would most often draw together small assemblages of clandestinas/os for each action they intended to carry out. At this level then, "cells" might better be described as groups or groupings. They were extremely fluid. Indeed, in some instances groups of insurgents formed themselves, sometimes in the context of prison visits, sometimes in neighborhoods, sometimes in workplaces, and then claimed allegiance to the movement to bring down the dictatorship, carrying out actions of sabotage. Nélida Álvarez, who worked in the Lancaster Institute of Beauty, relates that after they knew of the landing of the *Granma* she, two other employees, a client, and the client's husband formed a "cell" of the 26th of July Movement, which undertook various tasks in the insurgency including sabotage. There was no "head" appointed from above who initially directed what this group did.[8] As Juan Valdés Paz asserts, "The fact that the main group of Action and Sabotage, with a central leadership assigned by the movement, was more or less organized had nothing to do with the large number of sympathizers, supporters, and activists who on their own and on behalf of the 26th of July Movement carried out actions against Batista. That is to say, for each one of those organized groups there were hundreds of people who, if you asked them, would tell you that they belonged to the 26th of July Movement but actually they were not a part of any organized structure."[9]

Valdés Paz remembers how he and his brother got together with a group of their friends in the barrio in which they lived: "A compañero in our neighborhood asked my brother, who he knew was an anti-Batista radical, to carry out actions with him against the regime. And my brother invited his little brother, who was me, to join him in these actions. It did not matter who I was, what mattered was that I was against Batista. He proposed what to do and I, who was anxious to do anything against Batista, joined in; in fact, anybody could."[10]

Among students in the secondary schools and pre-universities where the 26th of July Movement clandestine groups were active, Sonnia Moro points out that it would have been extremely difficult to establish "walls of secrecy," given that "conspiracy language" was always in operation: "Everyone knew each other's position." That is, whether or not they were already involved or might be involved in the future there was no secret about where individuals stood vis-à-vis the dictatorship or the struggle against it.[11] Sonnia and other female insurgents in this study relate that they undertook daily not one but a range of different actions: selling bonos, accompanying male clandestinos in the street, distributing propaganda, carrying messages to and from prisoners. If we employed Elvira Diaz Vallina's organizational chart, this range of actions would be carried out by different "cells." But Sonnia recalls that every night, despite the fact that she was no longer going to classes, she would put on her uniform to keep what she was doing hidden from her family and go the Instituto de la Víbora where she would meet her compañeros to learn what was happening and decide what they should do next.[12]

WOMEN'S WORK RECONSIDERED 2: RE-READING WOMEN'S ROLES AS MESSENGERS

Young clandestinas transgressively used the expanded geography in which they now moved in multiple ways to directly service the insurrection. These lines of communication between individuals and groups of clandestinas/os were indispensable. Keeping these lines open was almost exclusively dependent on women: messages from the urban underground to the sierra and back; messages from prisoners in both El Príncipe and Mantilla to other prisoners and to those outside the prisons; the identification of informants among the prison populations; messengers between disparate groups of insurgents; messengers to warn about impending police raids; messengers to gather, carry, and distribute weapons. Yet the image of "messenger" conjures up someone who is simply the intermediary for the principals (almost always male), sending and receiving material of various sorts. We know about the authors of these messages and about their recipients but virtually nothing about the messengers themselves. Yet these women who were actually in the greatest peril are nameless and thereby assigned to oblivion.[13]

Visits to prisoners were perhaps the most critical of these lines of communication, organized and systematically carried out almost exclusively by women. These visits were generally channeled through the student brigades and the Martianas. What was delivered in these visits was not simply food and so on, as it is often indicated in the literature, but messages and occasionally even weapons. Sonnia relates how these visits proceeded:

> In El Príncipe, visitors, mostly women, stood in a long line. At the time there was no identity card; they searched your purse, but not meticulously, and asked for your full name and address. The first time I went, right after the April 9 strike, I gave a false address and name for obvious reasons. The first one that crossed my mind was "Zoila Lara." And even though it made me giggle later because it sounded silly, I had to continue to use it. The room where all visits took place was big and not private. There was a counter between us but we were allowed to touch each other and even to kiss. We took this opportunity to pass on messages. Prisoners came in when the guards called their names. I never gave the name of the person I was actually visiting. Rather, I asked for someone we suspected was a snitch or an infiltrator. This was the agreed-upon signal for a specific man in my group to come meet me, thereby avoiding being associated with each other. Perhaps this sounds naïve but it worked for us. I was once given for safeguarding the verbatim of a trial the clandestinos had conducted in the prison against someone who had given information during an interrogation because he could not stand the torture or was too afraid.[14]

Sonnia relates a time when she was asked to carry parts of a weapon in need of repair out of El Príncipe. The means of doing this was more or less to duplicate the manner in which messages were transferred. Sonnia would lean over the counter separating a prisoner from his visitor, and in a semi-embrace, the gun part would be transferred: "I was going to be given a gun, part of which needed to be recalibrated. They intended to slip it into my bosom while they gave me a goodbye hug but they changed their minds when I pointed out that I was so skinny it might slip through my clothes to the floor."[15]

While male insurgents confiscated in almost all cases the actual use of weapons, their distribution was women's work. Given the dire scarcity of weapons in the cities, the result of frustrated and unfulfilled promises of arms from abroad and the constant demand for arms by the sierra leadership, locating and transporting available weapons was critical. The literature on the clandestinidad points in particular to the advantages that styles of skirts in 1950s Cuba had for carrying various forms of arms. Multilayered crinolines, which were supposed to underpin bouffant skirts, left a good deal of space with which to work. Hidelisa Esperon describes the skirts she and other clandestinas fabricated to transport weapons and explosives of various kinds: "They were wide, rigid underskirts, which had deep pockets on the front side. We could not sit and we made these long and thin explosive materials to fit into the pockets. We carried about four dynamite cartridges. Later on we put a fuse on them and they were ready to be thrown. But it was a heavy load for a bus ride."[16]

Women accompanying men with large shipments of arms from abroad destined for the sierra provided a cover for such shipments. Magaly Olivero and her fiancé were assigned to travel to Miami to bring the money to pay for two carloads of arms arranged by Haydée Santamaría. As a cover, they married and went on their honeymoon to Miami. Magaly returned from Miami with a message from Haydée to Fidel, which she carried in her vagina. And then two weeks later when the cars in which the arms were hidden arrived by ferry in Havana, she and her now-husband continued, as it were, their honeymoon, traveling in one of these cars supposedly to Varadero. She went dressed as a tourist, wearing high heels, which proved a hazard when, after driving as far as they could into a cane field, they had then to carry the arms the remainder of the way to the appointed meeting place.[17]

Implicit in these actions undertaken by women is the assumption that using women's bodies or the clothes and accessories associated with these bodies as vehicles for the transport of messages from one place to another and for the transport of weapons was safe or rather safer. This was partly true. But this assumption requires reconsideration. Hidelisa relates what it was like carrying sticks of dynamite under her skirt on perennially crowded Cuban buses (which with walking or some combination of the two was the means by which women transported both propaganda and arms) and the danger inherent even in brushing up against other passengers:

I had to catch a bus in Párraga to go to Vedado where Ramón Perdomo was waiting for the ten petardos [bombs] that I was carrying.[18] I put them in my underskirt and tightened my skirt with a belt so that they wouldn't fall out, but buses had narrow aisles and they were packed with passengers. I had to reach the back or stay close to the door and men kept offering me their seats: "Come, señorita, take my seat." I was embarrassed, but one of them insisted, "Come." It was in the back, in a row of five, very narrow seats. I tried to slip past a boy who was sitting in the row but I hit him with my load and he exclaimed, "Your thighs are too hard, what are you carrying there, cast iron?" And I retorted, "You insolent, you were surely trying to touch me." It was a lie, of course; the truth was that I had hit him hard. Then he began saying, "No, no, señorita, you are carrying cast iron for sure!" I had to get off at the next stop to avoid attracting attention.[19]

One time Hidelisa had a straw bag containing dynamite on a bus:

I was carrying a bag full of dynamite for the boys that I had collected with Angelita [González] and Nilda [Ravelo]. The bag was especially made for that purpose by Angelita. I bought watercress and put it on top of a newspaper to make it look like a grocery bag. Then, a policeman who was sitting said to me, "Señorita, let me take that bag for you!" I told him, "Thank you, sir, but if you were really a gentleman you would offer me your seat." Then he stood up and gave me his seat and I put the bag on my lap and he kept staring at me, smoking, and I was saying to myself, "Oh, mother of God, what if all of it explodes!"[20]

These accounts begin to reveal a truth that was buried in the narrative of the urban insurrection. The insurrection on the ground and in practice can be far better understood and reconfigured as composed of collective groupings of male and female insurgents who shared in actions understood not in terms of their end results but as all that went into producing them. In this vein Linda Klouzal, in her study of the city movements, understands the urban insurgency as composed of "communities" of those fighting to bring down the Batista regime.[21]

A brief account of Nilda Ravelo's actions in the insurgency underscores this idea of understanding male and female insurgents as collective protagonists in the struggle. By September 1955 Nilda, a student at the Escuela Profesional de Comercio de La Habana, was already deeply involved in armed actions. Her first involvement came when she attended a commemoration on September 4 of Batista's first coup d'état in 1933.[22] While pretending to enjoy the party like any other Batistiano, she searched out where arms and materials were kept because the movement had plans to attack the cuartel.

In February 1957, there was another such encounter. Nilda's mother, Fela, had a small cafeteria near the Havana airport in Rancho Boyeros where agents of the Naval Intelligence Service stationed at the airport often ate lunch. Nilda overheard a conversation among them in which they mentioned that Batista was going to attend that year's cattle fair and she immediately thought about an attempt on his life. She went to an apartment in Vedado that was serving as a weapons storage, meeting place, and refuge for various clandestinos. She informed Pedro Palmero and Federico Bel Lloch of her idea and was told they had to consult the movement leaders in the area where the fair was to be held. The next day she learned that the plan would be carried out by a revolutionary cell in Boyeros. She returned to Boyeros by bus, carrying three guns in her purse. The following day, going back to the apartment in Vedado, she was caught in a police trap. Her cousin Orieta Cordeiro tells the tale:

> [Nilda] went up to the apartment, knocked on the door, and an esbirro with a gun in hand opened it. She realized that the apartment has been taken by the police and that they were waiting for people to arrive. She serenely protested that she was there to see a seamstress and had obviously knocked on the wrong door. She never altered her story, sat calmly in the apartment reading a magazine. Her presence made it impossible for the police to carry out orders to assassinate the eight men in the apartment. Taken to SIM [Servicio de Intelligencia Militar (Military Intelligence Service)], she calmly repeated her story over and over again while listening to the sounds of the men being tortured next to the room in which she was being held. But after several days her identity was discovered, turned in by the taxicab driver who had taken her to the apartment. Members of her family were arrested with her, and she was eventually sent to Mantilla. She was the first 26th of July clandestina in Mantilla.[23]

Nilda's second arrest came the night she took Delio Gómez Ochoa, who took charge of the 26th of July Movement in Havana in May 1958, to meet with Machaco Ameijeiras, then the head of Action and Sabotage in the city. Nilda served as the contact between the leadership of the movement in Havana and those in charge of Action and Sabotage. She then returned to a safe house, but esbirros raided the house and two former 26th of July Movement members who had turned on the movement identified her. She had flushed materials down the toilet and shoved bullets that would not flush into the bathtub drain and then tried to escape across the roof but they were waiting for her there: "Nilda, where are you going?" Arrested, she was taken to the Ninth Police Station, the domain of Esteban Ventura, the most infamously brutal of Batista's esbirros.[24] He appeared and greeted her attired in beige silk pajamas and said, "So here we have the bomb thrower of Rancho Boyeros." She was then transported to Mantilla where she remained until the morning after Batista fled Cuba.[25] Nilda's two arrests earned her sixteen months in Mantilla.

Various clandestinas with whom I spoke were regularly involved in making, distributing, and planting explosives. In acts of sabotage involving explosives, young female insurgents frequently targeted the major streets in the commercial center of the city, such as Galiano, which, as noted in chapter 1, offered goods for female consumption. And the insurgency understood middle-class, white women to be those most implicated in this consumption.

From the early years of the dictatorship, Galiano had regularly been a site for women's demonstrations and protests aimed at reaching both female shoppers and female sales clerks. In later years, it would also be the target for acts of sabotage. Female insurgents, because they could easily blend into the women shopping on streets such as Galiano, carried out these actions. Aida Pelayo and Olga Román, as well as younger clandestinas, were involved in acts of sabotage in shops along Galiano. In November 1957, in a plan to disrupt and thereby make a statement about the extravagant Christmas shopping going on at the same time as the insurgency, nineteen-year-old Mirta Rodríguez Calderón was given the task of organizing a group of eight women to set off fósforo vivo in El Encanto, the exclusive department store on Galiano.[26] The group, pretending to be shopping, first cased the store looking for and deciding on the most appropriate spots to set them off. Mirta herself chose fine furs, an ostentatiously class-associated item, given Havana's climate. It didn't work out well: Her group got lost and did not arrive at the scheduled spot at the scheduled time:

> I knew that we only had twenty minutes before the fósforo vivo would explode and when I realized there were only five minutes to go and that we had to act immediately, I decided to act alone. But when I went to

enter El Encanto the capsules began to react and the explosions began to set fire to my clothes, burned my thumb and destroyed my thumbnail, and burned a hole in my stomach. I couldn't make a run for it because I was so hurt. A group of chivatos surrounded me and I was taken to the Third Police Station. And in the police station they put my package, not knowing that it contained the remaining fósforo vivo, next to the gun rack where they began exploding.[27]

This was Mirta's second arrest.

In August 1958 Digna Abreu, in her night-school class in typing, heard from a friend about a job possibility in the home of one of the owners of the hardware store Feíto y Cabezón in Central Havana. The friend told her that the store owner was a lover of guns and armaments and kept a significant number of them in a locked room in his house. Digna formulated a plan, took it to Machaco, and applied and got the job cleaning in the family home. She worked for two months, carefully keeping a record of the comings and goings of the inhabitants of the house, and created a floor plan indicating the location in which the arms were kept. One night when no one was home except for an aged and sick aunt, Digna, telling the aunt that she was going to get medicine for her, left the house, leaving the door unlocked. Insurgents then entered the house, took the key from where she had indicated it would be, and made off with the stash of arms, mostly guns. No one suspected that Digna had anything to do with this until a month later when she was caught in a trap in an entirely different circumstance and arrested. This was when the owner of the house, recognizing her, realized that Digna had been the linchpin of the robbery.[28]

WOMEN'S WORK RECONSIDERED 4: COLLABORATORS

Collaborators, as they were labeled, were almost always women and usually mothers, who opened their homes to give insurgents refuge and to provide meeting places. As Dolores Nieves, a young clandestina, averred, "For the rebels our houses were vital. Their freedom of action depended on it."[29] These spaces allowed the dispersed rebels to come together in small numbers to plan and coordinate what they intended to do. In some instances the houses were sites where various forms of weapons could be stored or assembled. And most frequently they were places that provided refuge for clandestinos who were quemada, known and being hunted by Batista's forces. The women who lived in these homes often had sons or daughters who were in the clandestinidad. But often they did not.

The term *collaborator*, as it is used in the literature about the insurrection, is both unfortunate and misleading. The word carries an obvious diminution, a clear implication of lesser and only occasional importance and involvement in the anti-Batista struggle. But the distinction needs to be interrogated, because once again it is women whose roles are being envisioned as lesser.

Ercilia Gutiérrez came from Camagüey to Havana in 1956 with her husband and her young son, Godeardo. In Havana she became involved with the Directorio Revolucionario. Until January 1959 she and her family moved constantly from house to house in service to the insurgents. In the first of these houses were stored many of the weapons to be used in the March 13, 1957, attack on the Presidential Palace. After the failure of the attack, her family provided safe houses for Directorio insurgents who escaped the attack. Ercilia relates the reason why they left their first house two days after the March 13 attack:

> A policeman came to the house and he wanted me to show him the garage. I told him, "Look here, sir, I don't have the key." I told him that the owner of the house had the key because he had to throw away some rubbish that was inside. Then he told me to open the door of the apartment below us. I told him, "Look, I can't open the door to the apartment down there because it belongs to my in-laws, and I do not get along with them; I have to send them a message to bring the key here to give it to you." Then very quickly I hung a towel on the line on the porch, so that they [the insurgents] would know not to come up. By chance, Enrique Rodríguez Loeches drove by, and when he saw the towel he drove on.[30] The policeman had gone upstairs and talked with Nene [my husband] and me on the porch. But when Enrique saw the policeman standing there, he vanished into thin air and he went to warn the others.[31]

In the wake of the failed attack, the family moved once more, a security measure they took before a given house could become known to the police. In each house under a different name they set up what appeared to neighbors a normal household: husband, wife, and child. As

Guillermo Jiménez, a Directorio militant who in the wake of March 13 and the terrible retribution taken by Batista's forces, found refuge with them, relates: "That was the perfect facade because it was not something that had to be invented. They were a real married couple with a child with normal habits. This was different from renting an apartment which might be used often, thereby attracting attention. From this perspective, theirs was the best possible situation."[32]

Given this facade, Jiménez could be more easily introduced to neighbors as a relative or a friend who had just arrived from Camagüey. Ercilia and her husband carefully examined each new apartment before they rented it; each had to have, among other things, two doors in order to facilitate escape should that prove necessary. The existence of a safe house was known only to a few: meetings of Directorio clandestinos who had remained in Havana were never held there. Messages from and to Jiménez, who was now a member of the national directorate, were frequently carried by Godeardo who, because he was a child, was the perfect messenger.[33]

The frequent moves to other apartments and with that the continual upending of their household meant that their son had in effect to become a clandestino. He was instructed by his mother never to bring home friends to play. And more: As Ercilia remembers:

> Godeardo almost continually had to take on a new identity because every time we moved he went to a different school. He would change his name without anyone having to tell him to do so. He was the ideal clandestino; he never failed to observe the elementary security rules. When he went to a new school I would (re)name him, for instance, Héctor Rodríguez and when they said at roll call "Héctor Rodríguez," he said, "Present." The last house we lived in was in the Almendares neighborhood. He always had a little bit of money in his pocket so I told him, "Look, Godeardo, if you see a policeman roaming about, get into a taxi and go to El Cotorro, where my aunt lives, and later on I'll meet you there." The idea was for him not to come here.[34]

Godeardo was twelve when the revolution took power. We will return to his story in chapter 7.

WOMEN'S WORK RECONSIDERED 5: THE NIGHT OF ONE HUNDRED BOMBS

As the insurrection in Havana began to heat up, disrupting or rather intervening upon daily life in the city was central to the actions undertaken by clandestinos. In the context of a vastly unequal struggle between at best poorly armed revolutionaries and the multiple forces intent on destroying them, it was essential that the underground movement elaborate and execute plans to impress on the general population its presence and to create an imaginary of its strength and growing numbers in order to undermine whenever possible Batista's efforts to assure both Cubans on the island and its neighbor to the north that peace and stability reigned in the country. This was particularly problematic in Havana, given the city's physical layout and the size of its population. Actions were inevitably geographically contained and could not therefore serve to effectively impact or make itself known in the entire city. Even bombs set off at specific targets could not do this.

Batista's imposition of press censorship further complicated the question of how to impact the entire city in a situation in which the employment of media, at least until February 1958 when Radio Rebelde was set up in the sierra, was not an option. This required ingenuity, very dangerous undertakings, and the efforts of both clandestinas and clandestinos.

The first and among the most successful of these actions was the Night of One Hundred Bombs. On the evening of November 8, 1957, in every municipality of the city, 26th of July Movement insurgents set off bombs or something that sounded like bombs at exactly 9 p.m., timed to coincide with the cañonazo.[35] These simultaneous explosions were intended to give the city's residents, Batista's forces, and tourists the impression that the insurrectionaries were not simply present in the city but everywhere. They were most effective in this. The filmmaker Fernando Pérez was twelve years old and out walking with his father in the municipality of Guanabacoa where his family lived. The sounds of the explosions marked the moment when he first became aware that something was afoot. Those sounds and that night opened the path to *Clandestinos*, the film he would make later in his life.[36]

The city was electrified; the military, thinking the city was being bombed, was in complete disarray. Police cars circulated wildly throughout the city, sirens blasting, not knowing where exactly to go next. People flooded the local radio stations with calls, believing the city was being bombed; streetlights in which explosives of some sort had been placed went out, darkening some areas of the city. Reporters in the streets from various points in the capital called into their station Radio Reloj, the popular and seemingly innocuous station that ticked off every second, to report that "two petardos went off on the corner in such and such barrio; one bomb blew out the window store in the Calzada of Diez de Octubre." The pile-up of these reports led to a brief suspension of broadcasts on Radio Reloj. No one was captured, killed, or injured.[37]

The Night of One Hundred Bombs was the idea of Sergio González, or El Curita as he was known in the insurgency. González, whom I mentioned earlier, was then the head of Action and Sabotage in Havana. Lillian Guerra rightly notes that González was certainly among the most original and creative of the underground insurgents.[38] But if the Night of One Hundred Bombs was his idea, it was in every aspect of its preparation and execution the work of two people: El Curita and Mariíta Trasancos, who at the age of fifteen was already involved in Action and Sabotage. Mariíta had met El Curita during one of her visits to El Príncipe, arranged through the Frente Cívico de Mujeres Martianas and had helped him escape the prison. As I described it earlier in this chapter, there was nothing but a counter separating prisoners from their visitors and Mariíta was, as she says, very small. "When Sergio escaped from prison he said to me, 'Don't move.' And he jumped over the counter and disappeared, camouflaged among the visitors."[39]

El Curita escaped two weeks before the Night of One Hundred Bombs and during those two weeks he planned and organized the entire action. To carry it off, enough explosives needed to be collected from various locales throughout Havana. El Curita gave the task of gathering much of this material to Mariíta. He instructed her: "Well, Mariíta do this. We are going to get dynamite in Guanabacoa." With a male insurgent she went off in the middle of the night by bus with only the vaguest notion of how to find "El Guajiro de Minas," the man who had the ingredients for the explosives: "As it happened, we were in luck because the first person we spoke with turned out to be our man." Actually, he was a young boy. When she told him "casually as always" what she was there for, he took one look at this small, slight girl and asked: "Are you crazy? Do you know what you are talking about?"[40]

Mariíta then set to work on assembling the explosive materials. In this she was joined by four other young women: Norma Porras, who with Mariíta was a member of the FCMM; Digna Abreu; Teresa Abreu; and Pilar Sa. Once they were assembled, out of the cache of explosives Mariíta grabbed 25 petardos to distribute to insurgents in municipalities around the city. But shortly before the action, "El Curita asked me to whom I had given the bombs. I named the person and he said: 'You better make sure that these bombs explode.' He had strict criteria for who should have each bomb and I went running to take back some of the petardos that I had given to certain people and redistribute them to others."[41] The bombs were exploded mainly by youths in student brigades supervised by Gerardo Abreu Fontán and clandestinos in the ranks of the MRC and insurgents in barrio groups of Action and Sabotage.

On January 6, 1958, Mariíta was taken prisoner for the second time in an apartment that El Curita had rented where she and a male combatant were preparing petardos. The apartment had been staked out; just before the police entered it, one of the explosives misfired, burning her face and neck. In this state Mariíta was brought to the Ninth Police Station.[42]

El Curita was killed on March 18, 1958, after an intense manhunt that followed the execution of the head of the chivatos in the Second Police Station. His corpse, along with those of two other clandestinos, was found on a street in Alta Habana the following day.[43] Mariíta would be snatched off the streets a third time in the month before the end of the dictatorship.

THE GOLDEN AGE OF THE LLANO

The brief periods during which Batista lifted censorship opened a different range of possibilities, which the revolutionaries in the llano could mine, and they were both daring and creative in doing this. Thus, the events of what Julia Sweig labels "the golden age of the llano," from February through March 1958.[44] Batista had lifted press censorship in February in an effort to create among Cubans and in the world at large the imaginary of an island at peace under his leadership. He was determined to move the presidential election up from November to June as part of this effort.[45]

But once more his plans came back to bite him. These months were punctuated by a series of actions against the dictatorship undertaken in almost staccato fashion. The insurgents used press freedom to make known this sequence of actions, intent on impressing upon the public the extent of the insurgency in Havana.

In the month before he lifted censorship, things in Havana heated up. In January insurgents in the city set fire to 400,000 gallons of jet fuel in an oil refinery owned by Esso Standard. Dense smoke was visible over the city for three days.[46] In February, insurgents in both El Príncipe and Mantilla went on a ten-day hunger strike to protest the re-arrest of nineteen rebels at the doors of El Príncipe as they were being released, and the strikers succeeded in getting habeas corpus rights reinstated. The February hunger strike worked to publicize nationally the regime's violation of constitutional rights, despite its (brief) restoration of the Constitution. Later in February a clandestina who was an employee at the Cámara de Compensaciones del Banco Nacional worked out a plan by which insurgents got into the bank and set fire to checks and bank drafts that were being cleared. Their aim, as one of the participants relates, was "to create instability among the rich who should feel that in Cuba there were no guarantees for growing capital or business." In the following week, the popular weekly *Bohemia* printed a full account of the raid written by one of its participants.[47] In March, the Student Revolutionary Directorate and the 26th of July Movement organized a nationwide student strike, which closed down both public and private secondary schools in protest of the murder of two seventh-grade students in Santiago.[48]

United States embassy officials reported back to the State Department that "rebels and terrorists continued to harass the [Batista] Government from one end of the island to the other" in incidents that were "too many to attempt to catalogue."[49]

WOMEN'S WORK RECONSIDERED 6: OPERATION FANGIO

The February 23, 1958, kidnapping of Juan Manuel Fangio, the internationally renowned Argentine race-car champion, represented the crowning jewel in the story of the Havana insurgency. As part of his effort to paint Cuba on the world stage as a peaceful country thriving under his rule, Batista decided to reprise the Gran Premio de Cuba, the automobile race that had been held in Havana the previous year. The star of the show was to be Juan Manuel Fangio, five times the world auto-racing champion and winner of the prior Gran Premio race. Batista's intention was to make the race as big a spectacle as he could. Publicity about the event was aimed at drawing the widest audience of international press and tourists.

As it turned out, this was not a great idea. Spectacle it indeed proved to be, but hardly the kind the dictator had hoped for. The 26th of July Movement insurgents hatched a plan to kidnap the race-car driver in order to undermine Batista's celebration and to demonstrate their strength. They intended to use the kidnapping to maximize their message about what they were fighting against and fighting for. Marcelo Salado, the head of Action and Sabotage in the neighborhood of El Vedado, had the idea of carrying out the kidnapping a year earlier in the context of the 1957 race but although this is not the manner in which it is generally explained, there clearly was no way at that point that such an action could be pulled off. Nor was success in any way sure in 1958: Accounts of it by participants make it clear that they themselves were shocked by its success.

The first task was the actual kidnapping itself. Insurgents cased the places on Fangio's schedule and chose the Lincoln Hotel, in which Fangio was to have dinner the night before the race. Manuel Uziel and Oscar Lucero managed to enter the lobby of the hotel and mill around in it during the predinner reception. Before anyone, including his bodyguard, knew what was happening, Lucero escorted Fangio out of the lobby at gunpoint, finally landing at a safe house in the Havana suburb of Nuevo Vedado. The house belonged to the "norteñas" Silvina Morán and her two daughters, Agnes (seventeen) and Aimée (twenty-one).[50] It had been used on occasion by the leaders of the movement in Havana for meetings. All three women were members of the 26th of July Movement. Silvina was reluctant at first because she thought the kidnapping had to do with collecting ransom, which she did not favor. It did not. And because she knew the extreme danger into which Fangio's presence would put her family. In the end Agnes and her sister convinced their mother. Fangio remained remarkably calm as he was driven to the norteñas' home (indeed, far calmer than those in the car with him). Ángel Fernández Vila ("Horacio" in the insurgency), who was driving the car in which Fangio was transported, gives this now humorous account: "Fangio was seated in the rear of the car, between two insurgents armed with guns. The young Cubans were very nervous, not the least of them himself, who was almost hurtling through the streets. At which point Fangio leaned forward, tapped him on the shoulder and suggested that he 'slow down.'"[51]

Fangio maintained that calm for virtually the entire twenty-six hours of his sequester. At the first house to which he was taken (where it was decided it was not safe), he took out a pack of Chesterfield cigarettes and offered them around. When he reached the house of the norteñas, dinner was waiting for him (because, as the rebels realized, he had been kidnapped before he had a chance to eat). He then refused to go immediately to the room in which he was to sleep. As he said, "It's not healthy to go to bed on a full stomach." Rather, he chose to remain awake in conversation until 1 a.m. The 26th of July Movement insurgents informed the Argentine embassy, and through them Fangio's family were notified that he was in no danger. With Agnes and Silvina and a small contingent of the men involved in the kidnapping, Fangio spent the evening and the next day—the day of the race—sequestered in the house in Nuevo Vedado.

The press and radio stations were given immediate and dramatic notice. Radio Rebelde, which had just begun to broadcast from the Sierra Maestra, announced, "This is the 26th of July. Fangio is in our custody and he won't be competing tomorrow." To Batista's further embarrassment, the kidnapping was reported publicly before he himself knew about it. And worse still for Batista, after he was released the day after the race to diplomats from the Argentine embassy, Fangio, smiling, referred to his former captors as "my friends, the kidnappers."[52] The kidnappers then apologized to Fangio's family and to the Argentine nation for "the hours of anguish" they had caused them.[53] Nor did the kidnapping disappear quickly from the pages of the international press. In his first post-kidnapping interview with a Mexican journalist, Fangio lamented the fact that he had missed the race but went on to declare that, otherwise, he had been taken care of magnificently: "If my kidnapping can serve a good purpose as an Argentinian, I support them."[54] Or as he later commented, "My kidnappers treated me as family."[55]

The insurgents had achieved their goal. They had in a most dramatic manner disrupted Batista's "show"; they gave an impression of the insurgency's capacities and in doing so had pulled off what was to that point perhaps the most widespread diffusion internationally of awareness of the anti-Batista insurrection on the island; and they had created a vivid picture of the movement's presence in the llano, particularly in Havana, for national as well as international audiences. As Arnol Rodríguez, an advertising agent and member of the 26th of July Movement, reported, "For several days national and international press agencies kept the names of Fangio and Cuba on their headlines. Never before had the names of Fidel and Havana been broadcast in so many different parts of the world. References to this action in the news lingered on much longer in magazines." The US Embassy, affirming the 26th of July

Movement's media victory, reflected that "widespread publicity (in the United States, Europe and Latin America) will probably cast the (Cuban) government in a bad light as incapable of maintaining order in its own house." And the Embassy was right. Articles about the kidnapping appeared in newspapers worldwide, such as the *New York Times*, *Excelsior* (in Mexico), *O'Globo* (in Brazil), *Paris Match* and *Le Monde* (in France), the *Daily Mail* (in England), as well as papers in the USSR and Japan. The widely read British journal the *Economist* reported: "Not frequently new political techniques get invented. But Cuban rebels have invented a new one with the kidnapping of the champion race car driver Fangio. The kidnapping of the famous athlete is something different. International press articles highlighted the huge amount of money that Batista squandered in the high-speed circuit while people went hungry. Had they kidnapped the President, they wouldn't have been as effective in the international political arena which is highly saturated by publicity."[56]

In accounts and testimonies about it, Operation Fangio is always a male affair: Lucero took Fangio at gunpoint from the Lincoln Hotel lobby; clandestinos drove him to two different houses; clandestinos spent the night talking with him about their determination to rid the island of a brutal dictatorship and convincing him of the rightness of their actions, including his own kidnapping. Clandestinos in short, had the idea for, planned, and carried out the kidnapping, and they converted Fangio into a supporter of the insurgency. Despite the fact that Fangio spent the night of his kidnapping and the next day in the house of three women, there is a strange familiarity in the descriptions of that first evening. Silvina prepared dinner for the men who sat around the table talking. After dinner the men continued their conversation. Fangio again pulled out his pack of Chesterfields and offered them around.[57] In short, the actors in the drama were at the table and were all male; the women were the support staff, providing the usual womanly things of room and board.

However, a reexamination of the sequences of the kidnapping reveals clearly that women were indispensable to the action. Ramona Balber was one of the two insurgents who in the days prior to the kidnapping was assigned to check out all the possible sites where the action could be carried out.[58] Ramona entered the Lincoln Hotel alone to observe Fangio's movements. That provided the groundwork for the kidnapping of Fangio from the hotel lobby. What is almost never mentioned in accounts of the kidnapping itself is that Oscar Lucero was able to move unnoticed around the lobby of the Lincoln Hotel without arousing suspicion because he was accompanied by his pregnant wife, Blanca Niubo. Blanca thus put herself in the same situation of supreme danger as the male insurgents who carried the guns. Then, for more than twenty-six hours, dozens upon dozens of patrol cars circulated throughout the city while the kidnappers and kidnapped were holed up in the house of three women.[59] Every person in that house, male and female, was well aware that if they were discovered, they would all be killed, including Fangio, and his murder would have been attributed to the 26th of July Movement. Seventeen-year-old Agnes de los Angeles spent hours with Fangio, talking to him about the situation on the island, about Fidel, and even showing him the Herbert Mathews 1957 *New York Times* interview with Fidel, which she had preserved from an old issue of *Bohemia*. One can but imagine what the effect of this conversation with a very young yet very determined girl had on the race-car driver. In the story of Operation Fangio, we are told that the journalist Carlos Lechuga arranged Fangio's release and that Arnol Rodríguez was in charge of taking him to the functionaries of the Argentine embassy. What is not related in this story is that Dr. Ada Curí was equally involved in coordinating Fangio's release and that two women accompanied Fangio to meet the Argentine functionaries.[60]

But the film *Operation Fangio*, a Spanish-Argentinian coproduction that appeared in Cuban movie theaters in 1987, put a whole new spin on the kidnapping. The film might have served to resurface awareness, three decades later, of a climactic event in the insurgency among an older population that might have forgotten it and a younger population who were not yet born when it took place. Despite its obvious dramatic potential, it was a box office flop. But its depiction of the kidnapping is worth commenting on. In it, one woman plays a critical if not the critical role, but it is as the object of sexual desire for Fangio. Pilar, apparently standing in for all the women involved in the kidnapping wrapped into one, is portrayed as central to it. She is the first to attempt to lure Fangio out of the hotel from which he would be taken by the kidnappers and the last to say farewell to him at the press conference at the Argentine embassy after his release. And she accomplishes this all through prolonged eye contact with him. Every time they look at each other, their eyes emanate an unrequited and unrequitable love, or, better said, an unrealized and unrealizable sexual intimacy. She explains nothing to him about the reasons for the kidnapping; apparently this is not her role. Nor is it necessary: Fangio's geniality about being kidnapped has nothing to do with the revolution in the film; rather, it has to do almost entirely with

Fangio's attraction to Pilar. So obvious is this shared visual intimacy that, at one point, when one of the chief males involved in the kidnapping and apparently her boyfriend sees it, he grabs her and proposes marriage. It is she who convinces her mother, the only other woman portrayed in the film, to allow the kidnappers to sequester Fangio in her house despite her mother's fears. But this is only after Pilar's mother tries to convince Pilar to grow out of the phase her mother appears to think she is in, to dress more appropriately, and to stop all her involvement with anti-Batista groups. Upon Fangio's arrival at her house, the mother transforms into the perfect middle-class hostess, welcoming him with motherly care, fussing over whether he is eating enough. As he leaves to be taken to the Argentine embassy, she assures him with a hug that "mi casa es tu casa." This film represents the worst of portrayals of women in revolutionary movements. Their role in these portrayals is presented entirely in terms of their sexuality. The contrast between the mother and daughter in the film and the actual mother and daughters who were central to the kidnapping of Fangio, all three militants in the 26th of July Movement, could not have been greater. At the film's conclusion, some of those involved in the actual kidnapping appear to talk briefly about the kidnapping but do not comment on the film itself. Among those speaking the only woman is Silvana, the mother, and then only briefly.

Oscar Lucero was captured in April 1958 and was subsequently disappeared. His body was never found. Sometime after the revolution took power, Agnes de los Ángeles Afón, working at the Institute for Friendship with the Peoples, would be purposefully denounced and discharged from her job, as part of her preparation to infiltrate a group suspected of counterrevolutionary activities, which she did.

But the golden age of the llano came to an end in the wake of the April 9, 1958, strike. All authority rested in the hands of Fidel both in the sierra and the llano. While actions continued in Havana, the insurgency's presence was marked by the almost weekly appearance of the bodies of clandestinos, tortured and displayed in public spaces. The llano would never recover.

THE USES OF TORTURE

Batista's dictatorship has been referred to by one scholar writing about it as a "dictablanda," particularly in comparison to the vicious dictatorships that in the decades following the Cuban revolution took power in the southern cone of South America.[1] In fact, however, from 1957 through 1958 Cuba was a sort of experimental laboratory in terms of both do's and don'ts for a good deal of what would follow in Latin America in the 1970s and 1980s. In the llano, state violence, if somewhat sporadic during the years up to 1957, would dramatically intensify in the aftermath of the Directorio's attack on the Presidential Palace in March 1957 and in the months after the April 9, 1958, strike. Insurrectionaries experienced these months as a virtual war of terror.

In the wake of the strike, as noted in chapter 3, Batista's forces launched an offensive not simply against the guerrillas in the Sierra Maestra mountains, but against the clandestine movement throughout the country. Life for insurgents in the urban underground became ever more precarious. In the sierra, the guerrillas who successfully fought off the massive army that Batista sent in June 1958 to finish them off were organized into different fronts, concentrated in given areas and, relative to the llano, armed. In the llano, none of this was so.

Given that those in charge in the llano were always male insurgents, it was they who were specifically targeted by the regime around these key moments during the final years of the insurrection. Male bodies, often horribly tortured, would appear almost weekly on city streets.[2] These unbearable displays were aimed in large part to terrify and subdue the general population. Others were simply disappeared, a technique widely employed in later years by Latin American dictatorships. Torture and assassinations became increasingly random in the weeks leading up to Batista's exit, when it was becoming ever clearer that the end of the regime was near.

As I noted in my introduction, death, and even suicide, in the service of the nation has always occupied center stage in the narrative of Cuban history.[3] Not by chance is the word *die* embedded in the national anthem, written in 1869 at the very moment of the first war of independence: "To die for the nation is to live." In Havana five women were murdered by the regime. As martyrs, the stories of four of these women become incorporated into the official accounts of the revolution. But the indispensable *Semillas de fuego*, a compilation of testimonies about the urban insurrection published in Cuban newspapers and in the weekly *Bohemia* magazine in the 1980s, reads like a male martyrology. In it the people whose stories are told by those who knew and fought with them are stories of the heroes killed by Batista's various agencies of repression; that is, with a very few exceptions, men. Hero and martyr become synonymous and interchangeable. These stories of men become the narratives of the insurrection.[4] Women's voices enter mainly in their telling and as such are in effect complicit in validating their own invisibilization. In this manner the clandestinas and other insurgent women are situated and situate themselves on the periphery in the narrative. As did their nineteenth-century forebears, they tell the stories of the heroes/martyrs and, in so doing, center them in the narrative of the insurrection. Given the melding of martyr and hero in this narrative and the fact that men, as its protagonists, were those most likely to suffer death, the extent and discussion of the regime's use of torture on captured clandestinas receives almost no attention. The violence wreaked by the regime on the bodies of captured female insurgents disappears from public discourse.

One general explanation given for the scarcity of accounts about regime violence against women—that there were fewer clandestinas, and therefore presumably fewer female targets—seems too facile and reductionist.[5] Michelle Chase draws on the work of Begoña Aretxaga on Northern Ireland to surface a more resonant, if generalized, interpretation of the disparities in violence imposed on the bodies of male and female insurgents. Aretxaga writes: "Men encounter suffering in the violent death generated by an unjust social order. . . . [M]en's suffering is inscribed in their own bodies through their fighting; women's [suffering] is inscribed in the bodies of others; fathers, sons, brothers, husbands or friends."[6] In what follows, I seek to explore the uses made by the regime in its torture of the women, drawn from the experiences of the clandestinas with whom I spoke, almost all of whom had been imprisoned, in most cases more than once. I begin by laying out the parameters of what I will argue in this chapter: that is, the balance between the random infliction of pain on the bodies of women and the logic informing these acts. I then lay out the context: the sites of torture, their purveyors, and the common vocabulary in the methods these purveyors employed in torturing captive clandestinas. Third, by examining in detail individual experiences, I attempt to flesh out in greater depth what I note as the logic underpinning the differential application of torture upon women. Employing a brief comparative framework, I discuss the limitations the regime faced in inflicting violence on women's bodies. I end this chapter with a discussion of clandestinas' lives in the women's holding prison, Mantilla.

THE MELDING OF RANDOMNESS AND LOGIC

An examination of the nature of the violence wreaked upon any individual woman makes it clear that it would be a mistake to underrate the factor of randomness. One has only to survey the major torturers and sites of torture in Havana to grasp this randomness, which was in itself a terrible form of torture. But it would equally be a mistake to fail to note a certain logic enmeshed in the application of torture. The logic is perhaps most easily identified in the targeting of four of the women who were murdered by the regime's agents in Havana. But in fact it can be understood as having had wider implications, deeply rooted in the particularities of the patriarchal order, intrinsically of a piece with the male homosocial construction of the nation, which framed the 1950s insurgency as it had the nineteenth-century wars of independence.

For the regime and its agents, the girls and women who were active participants in the urban insurrection had removed themselves from this patriarchal order; worse still, they had consciously and openly violated it. They were therefore disposable: no longer women in the manner in which they were defined within the Cuban social structure: mothers, daughters, wives, or sisters. Therefore they were legitimate, indeed necessary, targets for torture. If the order was to be restored, they had to be denied their "rightful" place in it and, even if they were forced back into it in some form, shamed forever by their violation. Captured clandestinas with a few notable exceptions had to be understood by their torturers as peripheral. Their most obvious use when captured was to provide information in the form of names and locales of those whom the regime saw as the real actors in the insurrection: men. Clandestinas, or, as esbirros unfailingly referred to them, putas (whores), had entered into the insurrection purely to service in multiple ways these real actors.

If we look beyond the obvious, using Gayle Rubin's classical formulation in "The Traffic in Women," these women were exchangeable, tradeable between men: the male insurrectionaries and the male regime with its various arms, both contesting for control of the nation. The esbirros' degradation and torture therefore served a dual purpose: It physically marked the bodies of deviant women and at the same time functioned to emasculate male insurgents. Demasculinization, then, involved not simply the brutalization of male prisoners. It involved torture inflicted on the bodies of women whom those prisoners were unable to protect.

THE SITES OF TORTURE, THE PURVEYORS, AND THEIR VOCABULARY

In Havana the torture of captured insurgents was enabled by the concentration in the city of the multiple arms of state violence, secret, civil, and military: the police in nineteen police stations; the Buro para Represion de las Actividades Coimunistas (BRAC; Bureau for the Repression of Communist Activities); the Servicio de Intelligencia Militar (SIM; Military Intelligence Service), or, as its esbirros called it, the "University of Life"; and the Servicio de Intelligencia Naval (SIN; Naval Intelligence Service).[7] Further, Havana was home to the General Staff of the War Marine; La Cabaña Fortress Artillery Regiment; the Campo Columbia barracks with the general staff of the army; the Fifth Regiment of the rural guards; the central division of the National Police; and the Managua Military Academy. These were supplemented by paramilitary groups, including the Tigres de Masferrer, as well as union members charged with informing on workers to Military High Command.[8]

Torture was supervised and carried out by a bevy of sadists to whom Batista had given free rein. Pilar García, among the most celebrated torturers on the island, was brought by Batista to Havana on the eve of the expected April 1958 strike to head the National Police. It was said he had the name of a woman and the heart of an assassin. He brought with him to Havana his son, Irenaldo García, whom he had trained well. Irenaldo was put in charge of SIM.

Esteban Ventura, who by 1958 had made his way up the military ranks to Inspecting Commander and Head of District, was Havana's most ubiquitous torturer and Cuba's archetypal assassin.[9] His jurisdiction was formally two police stations in Havana and in Havana Campo, but in practice he was free to go wherever he chose. He was infamous for liking to watch:

> Very rarely did he stain his clothes or hands with the blood of his detainees. He watched his subordinates do the work. He had true specialists in beatings, in pulling out nails, and other horrendous methods of torture. He only intervened to psychologically soften up the tortured or try to get them to talk. Those who were close to him or knew him slightly describe him as tall and slim, not bad looking, always elegantly dressed, wearing a tailor-made white linen suit or his impeccable blue police uniform. One might think that with the care he put into his personal appearance he would never have wanted to touch other people or be brushed by them. And it is said that although he was present during the torture sessions, he did not take part in them to avoid hurting himself and dirtying his clothes. He could give orders to force someone to talk or kill them with a mere sign or word, or ask his close friend, Dr. Pedro García Mellado, to come and judge how presentable his prisoners were before showing them in public. "This one will die. This one will only go blind. This one is okay, only a few punches." Those were Mellado's diagnoses.[10]

These men and the various intelligence services and paramilitary forces used informers—chivatos, or 33.33s—who were drawn from the unemployed and were ubiquitous.[11] And they were mobile; they could move their fruit or vegetable carts from place to place in different areas of the city to observe and report on movements of suspected insurgents, could be on street corners selling lottery tickets, could hang out in shops and cafés near suspected houses, or could be used even as the regime's informants in prison. Some were ex-insurgents whom the police, usually through torture and/or fear of torture, had themselves or through family members managed to turn.

Those women seized were first taken to one of the nineteen police stations in Havana and then in some cases to the BRAC or SIM or SIN. In the police stations they were in purgatory, essentially disappeared. Entirely vulnerable and unprotected by any legal mechanism, they were without defenses against the whims, inclinations, and brutality of the men who held them. As long as no one knew where they were, there were no limits to what could be done to them. And no limits on what they could imagine might be done to them. Limits came into play only when it became publicly known in some manner that they had been arrested, or until they had been formally booked and taken to the women's holding prison in Mantilla.

The men who supervised or did the torturing employed a toolbox commonly used by torturers everywhere. Variations in the choice of methods appeared to be seemingly random, each one aimed at extracting the names and locales of male insurgents. Virtually all those brought into police stations were subjected to multiple beatings to various degrees of severity, depending on who was doing the beating. In some cases women were taken from their cells in the middle of the night and told that they were about to be shot. Women were regularly threatened with rape or, as their captors called it, "echar un palo."[12] Arrested clandestinas were initially held in rooms in police stations where they could hear the agonizing tortures of male clandestinos: Their torturers called this "listening to opera."[13]

Pilar Sa was seized on orders of Ventura by a bevy of his esbirros, and spent October 2 to November 6, 1958, in one of these purgatories. She had been caught in a trap set by an informer in the ranks of the 26th of July Movement. Pilar was delivering the gun of Morúa, with whom she had lived as his fictive wife, to Machaco Ameijeiras, then the head of Action and Sabotage in Havana. Morúa had been murdered nine days before. Some fifty-five years later, returning to the house in which she had been captured, Pilar forced herself to remember:

It was a beautiful October night. There was a full moon, shining high like a big round cheese. I was walking down the street and I sensed danger, at about half a block from here. I stopped. I crouched down and looked behind me, thinking the police were following me, but everything seemed normal. So I got to the door [of the apartment], and the police were expecting me. They said: "Shoot the next one [who came to the door] down." And the next one was Ángel Rosell, who was instantly riddled with bullets. He fell right there. When they took us out, I walked past him and touched his body with my foot. I could still feel his death throes—that very peculiar sound that human beings make when they are dying.[14]

From that night of the full moon, she says, "I began to lose awareness of myself, until November 6 [the day when she was transferred to Mantilla], in dark dungeons filled with screams, beatings, terror and impotence":

When Ventura was beating us he kept on saying: "Cry, cry!" But I did not cry. Then he said, "These black maids, instead of supporting Batista who's also black!" So I told him: "I am not a maid; I am a high school graduate!" "You can't be a high school graduate," he responded. [So I said,] "My high school graduate ring was taken away from me by one of your men." He didn't hit me any more after I said that. And then he stood up towering over me, at the doorstep, and "boom!" [One of Ventura's men] threw me the ring. He had been ordered to give me back the ring. I have honestly erased all those memories from my hard drive, so to speak. I threw all that information out because those are deep wounds. Even now, when I talk about this, I feel sick.[15]

Race clearly entered into the freedom exercised by those doing the battering. While the evidence of her educational achievement (Pilar had two bachelor's degrees) seemed to have saved Pilar, a mulata, from further physical beatings despite her color, it was not so for Digna Abreu and her sister, Teresa, both black women, who were in the same apartment and arrested with Pilar. They were taken first to the Ninth Police Station, then to the Fifth Police Station, and then to BRAC, before being booked and sent to Mantilla. It was a journey through hell for them. In the Ninth Police Station, they were put in a small room where they were beaten in turn by fourteen esbirros. Digna asserts that these beatings were worse than any men could have received, given the number of esbirros involved. Their blackness clearly framed the severity of what they were subjected to. Their torture was punctuated by a constant stream of epithets: "Black communists, black this, black that." They were beaten with fists, feet, and elbows. Finally, Ventura arrived and asked them, "How is it possible that little black maids like you are fighting against Batista, who is black as well?" And then, unusual for Ventura, he himself took a turn. Digna says, "He stuck his fingers in my nose making the blood run like rivers all over my dress; our clothes were in tatters and stained with blood."[16]

In the Fifth Police Station, Digna says, she "passed the most bitter moments of my life." Their mother, who came to Havana immediately upon hearing via Margot Aniceto that Digna and Teresa had been arrested, was never allowed to see them and was permitted to send them some food only once during the last days they spent in the Fifth Police Station.[17] This meant that the threat of further torture or even murder hung over them for the entire time they were in the station.

And another standard practice in the vocabulary of torture was the terror of anticipating interrogations and beatings carried out at random during the night. Nélida Álvarez was dragged from her basement cell in the Ninth Police Station on five consecutive nights after she was arrested and before she was taken to Mantilla:

> Perhaps I shouldn't talk about the tortures they inflicted on me. Beside the beatings, [Ventura] constantly threatened me that he was going to kill me, that he was going to do to me what he had done to Abreu Fontán, that he was going to put a bullet in my head and throw me in the Plaza Cívica [now Revolution Square]. Once they took me out during the night, but what I am proud of is the fact that I was only twenty-two and weighed ninety pounds, and I never revealed even my own name, because I did not want to. I told myself, I'm going to die here, but with dignity. And that will be the end of it.[18]

Conditions in these police stations magnified the treatment of those held in them. Carmen Castro, Aida Pelayo and two other Martianas in the first of their many arrests during the insurrection, were taken to the Fifth Police Station. Ventura had been informed by a chivata of the location of the safe house in which they were living. They were put in what Carmen described as "a filthy room whose walls were spattered with blood." Aida was separated from the other three, repeatedly brought up from the basement in which she was being held and questioned about the terrorist activities of the Frente Civico de Martianas. Carmen describes the "infernal" conditions in the Fifth Police Station during the one and a half months they were incarcerated: "When we arrived at the holding prison they confined all four of us in a small dark cell that lacked ventilation. The stench of a toilet, close to our heads, made us nauseous. There were legions of mosquitoes swarming over the rickety old beds. The food was inedible, the water undrinkable."[19] Aida was held for another three months. When released, her health was seriously shattered; she had lost thirty pounds.

The use of family members to extract information, another general practice of torturers everywhere, was employed in a variety of contexts. Xiomara Blanco's family was prominent in Bauta, a small town close to Havana. Her father had been in opposition groups virtually from the moment of the coup, first with the Movimiento Nacional Revolucionario and then the 26th of July Movement. When he was arrested and taken to the Second Police Station, his family members—Xiomara, then fourteen years old; her brother, twelve; and her mother—were brought to the station, put in separate rooms, and questioned without a break from dawn until 2 a.m. the following morning. Their interrogators demanded that they reveal the names of the insurgents who frequented their home, and they were told they would be killed if they did not talk. At some point in the night they were put in a covered van loaded with picks, shovels, and other farm instruments and sacks full of earth. Seeing this, Xiomara told herself, "This is to bury us." They were driven around in circles for three hours, losing all sense of where they were. Finally, they were delivered to the police station in Bauta and then forbidden to leave their house. For the following weeks, every night, a policeman wearing boots with metal toes (which he used, he said, in order not to have to dirty his hands when he was killing someone) walked back and forth on the roof of the house to terrorize the family.[20]

When Mirta Rodríguez Calderón, then nineteen, was captured setting off fósforo vivo at El Encanto and taken to the Third Police Station, its chief, Zamora, asked her who her boyfriend was, as he must have planned the action. "They told me that this man was leading me astray because they wouldn't believe that women could make their own choices. There always had to be a man behind it. They told me I was a hyena. I only knew a hyena was a ferocious animal but that's it. They demanded that I tell them who my boyfriend was, the one who had gotten me into this mess."[21]

The punishment inflicted on Mirta went further than beatings. Her violation of the norms governing a daughter's place in the family meant not simply that she was guilty and therefore disposable; her family and particularly her father were as well. Her father was in this scenario a weakling. Because fathers were supposedly the guardians of their daughters' conduct, Mirta's involvement in the insurrection was evidence that her father had failed to exercise his paternal duties. He was therefore a legitimate target. Mirta was given the choice of betraying her "boyfriend"—that is, giving names of male insurrectionaries—or seeing her actions result directly in the destruction of the family she had betrayed through these actions. Her father was brought in and she was forced to hear him supposedly being tortured. She was then told that because she had refused to cooperate they were going to kill him: "They took my father away and pretended to kill him. I heard the cocking of guns, followed by shots and the simulation of the sound of a body falling to the floor." She knew she could not live with this and made the decision to kill herself. It was only two days later, after she arrived at Mantilla, she received word from Pastorita Núñez that her father had in fact not been murdered.[22] In this same vein, when Hidelisa Esperón was released from the Ninth Police Station, Ventura cupped his hands in front of her and told her that the next time she saw him her father's heart would be in his hands.[23]

DEVIANT WOMEN AND THE LOGIC OF TORTURE

Rape and gang rape were the most severe punishments short of murder that could be wreaked upon women. First, it marked them indelibly and permanently as outcasts from a society in which female virginity was required. In 1950s Cuban society, rape under any circumstances was a thing of shame for girls and women. It would make them outcasts even from their own families. And who in the family would determine this expulsion? As Mirta Rodriguez Calderon explains, "How could a young girl tell her parents, but especially her father, that she had been raped? How could she expect that any man would want to marry her?"[24] Rape was not to be admitted to or talked about publicly or openly. Lorraine Bayard de Volo underscores the holding power of this "internalized shame." She cites a never-realized plan by a group of women being held in the Fifth Police Station to produce a signed document detailing "how women were defamed and abused when they fell into Ventura's claws." They intended "to keep the document secret until the dictatorship falls because otherwise they would be shamed, and to deliver the document to the Tribunal which is going to judge that monster called Ventura after Batista is overthrown." Unfortunately they decided against it because "the things to be told are such that they cannot be told."[25]

This may in part explain why there are only a few documented personal accounts of rape by clandestinas. In later decades, following the collapse of the brutal dictatorial regimes in Chile, Argentina, Uruguay, and Brazil, women's testimonies of their rape would be central to public condemnation of the regimes in these countries and in the world as a whole.

Second, the rape of female insurgents was understood by their rapists as a profound form of physical revenge against male insurgents. Given that those directing and carrying out the torture of women took it for granted that female insurgents who had entered into the movement were these men's property, the violation, the physical possession of female insurgents' bodies profoundly undermined male insurgents' very manhood, as perhaps nothing else could. Thus brutalization and rape of three women, each of whom had been involved in Action and Sabotage. The three were entrapped in an apartment in Vedado in October 1958. Two of these women, Angela González and Mercedes Nibot, were in their thirties; the third woman, Hidelisa Esperón, was seventeen. A roster of esbirros led by Ramón Calviño filled the apartment.[26] They stripped and savagely beat the women. Angela, the oldest of the three, gives this account of what was done to her: "Calviño recognized (me) and he went insane. . . . [A]fter he stripped me I was handed off (to the other officers) so they could rape and humiliate me."[27] Hidelisa relates, "I tell you, they did to us what was later done to the Iraqis in Abu Ghraib."[28]

Hidelisa, as I wrote in chapter 4, had been living in a safe house with the then head of Action and Sabotage in the city. Her captors dragged her naked and by her hair up the long flight of stairs into the Ninth Police Station to Ventura's office. Seeing his gun left on his desk, she picked it up, thinking to shoot him, but was subdued. (The gun was empty: This was apparently among the little games Ventura enjoyed playing.) Ventura turned to two of the esbirros who had brought her to the station and told them, "Do what you want to with her, but don't kill her."[29] Hidelisa was instead taken to a small windowless room and raped by members of Ventura's entourage. As she was being raped, Ventura laughed: "Look at this little beauty, so pretty, but she's going to leave here looking very different."[30] Hidelisa, crying fifty-seven years later as she relived what happened to her in the police station, remembers its brutality: "I left the room with my thighs and legs bathed in blood." She was then taken, still naked, to a cell in which thirty-two male insurgents were being held. These men "closed their eyes and I tried to cover myself with my long hair." Michelle Chase, in writing about Hidelisa, suggests that this treatment was intended to extend yet further the trauma of her sexual humiliation, as surely it did. She surmises that her torturers' intent was to force Hidelisa "to imagine being gang raped by her own compañeros."[31] But Ventura certainly had a second objective in humiliating her in this manner: the further demasculinization of the thirty-two men who inhabited the cell. On top of falling into the hands of Batista's agents they were now yet further emasculated: The presence of Hidelisa's violated, naked body was intended to bring home to them their inability and helplessness to live up to their responsibility as men to protect and save her.

From the filthy basement cell to which she was then taken, Hidelisa could see a small window and remembers thinking longingly that from the window, she could see houses on Zapata Street: "I thought, 'If only someone could see me from a balcony, maybe someone hanging their laundry. Oh, if they only glanced down and saw me. Oh, if I could only scream.'"[32] Then, still naked, she was taken before dawn (Hidelisa says that "when they took us out it was never during the day") to the Colon cemetery and told to give names and locations. When she refused, she was ordered to run: "Run, whore, run." She assumed she would be shot in the back. She was far too physically broken and too afraid to run anywhere. But she was not shot; rather, she was shoved again into the car and onto the floor, all the while being hit with the butt of a machine gun. "I thought I was dead. And when I realized I was still living, I had a strange sensation of happiness." She was then taken back to the police station. Hidelisa was subjected to this terror two times. The third time she was driven once again through Colon and taken to the BRAC.

In 1958, during the two-month period in which Batista had lifted censorship, a first-person account of Esterlina Milanés's rape and severe brutalization, accompanied by the report of the doctor who treated her, scandalized the general population. Milanés, a forty-year-old Catholic schoolteacher, had worked with both the Directorio and the 26th of July Movement as a driver, and she occasionally delivered weapons. Unlike Hidelisa, she was not in direct daily contact with a hunted clandestine leader. What she was forced to undergo therefore had little to do with her positioning in the clandestinidad. Like others, she was subject to the will and desires of the particular men who had her in their power. But there is perhaps a further explanation for the degree and the severity of what they inflicted on her. Esterlina was arrested and beaten brutally in the car taking her to the Twelfth Police Station: "They dragged me (into the police station) holding me by my armpits, pulling me." There, in the course of subsequent beatings, her mandible was broken and her teeth, with the exception of three upper molars, were knocked out of her mouth. She passed out; men in hoods injected her to bring her back to consciousness and the beating began again.

The "vieja cochina" (dirty old pig), as they called her, had violated two critical norms. First, she had degraded her place as a middle-aged woman in Cuban society to "seduce" multiple young men: She was, as her torturers declared, "the old woman who has so many young lovers." By extension then, she had corrupted—ruined—these young men and was responsible for what was to be done to them. Other clandestinas, when captured, were usually made to listen to the screams of male insurgents in adjoining rooms as electric shocks were applied to their genitals. In Esterlina's case this was not enough: She was forced to watch one of her "young lovers"—the insurgent with whom she was arrested— undergo this torture.

Second, and perhaps even more threatening to those in charge of her torture, Esterlina had broken the most sacred rule of the patriarchal order: She had abandoned her role as mother in favor of her "young lovers." This, for her torturers, was unforgivable; she was beyond the pale in their eyes. She no longer had claim to be a mother. The degree and the nature of the violence inflicted upon her surely had a great deal to do with this. She was told that if she did not talk, that is, give up her "young lovers," her three children would be taken from her and killed. The manner in which she was raped was just punishment for her violation: The source of her motherhood, her uterus, had to be destroyed. Ventura appeared at the police station to supervise: "They held me by my arms and legs and pulled my underpants down—they had already removed my clothes. I cannot explain it clearly, I felt such excruciating pain that I thought I was dying. They stuck the plastic end of an umbrella inside me and tore my uterus. They ripped up all my insides including my large intestine."

When she was returned to her cell, she asked for water and was brought urine to drink, which was then thrown in her face when she refused it. The Colombian ambassador who had come to the prison in search of his nephew got her out of the station and to a hospital. After emergency treatment, dressed in nun's clothes, she was taken to the Ecuadorian embassy.[33]

There was as well logic for the murder of the women that the regime specifically targeted for assassination. Each had put themselves beyond the pale by committing specific acts in the service of the most important of the male leadership.

Clodomira Acosta and Lidia Doce, forty-one and twenty-two years old respectively, were messengers from the comandancia in the sierra to the comandancia in the llano. They arrived in Havana with a note from Che Guevara concerning two officers in Batista's army who were deserting to the 26th of July Movement. Various women with whom I spoke explained their capture: Given their lives in the sierra, they were not accustomed to the constant precautions that for clandestinos in the llano were virtually instinctive. They were arrested and went through the purgatory of torture in Ventura's Fifth and Ninth Police Stations and then taken to the SIM where its chief, Julio Laurent, continued their torture, finally disappearing them in the sea. Their bodies were never recovered.[34]

Lourdes and Cristina Giralt, eighteen and twenty-two years old, respectively, were taken upon their return to their apartment. The apartment was as well a storehouse for weapons, and was at the moment of their return being ransacked by the police. Bayard de Volo documents their murder and the body of evidence that they had been brutally raped before being killed.[35]

There was a fifth woman murdered by the regime's agents. Aleida Fernández Chardiet, who spoke fluent English, got a job as an operator in the Compañía Telefónica Internacional. Telephone operators in Havana were mainly women, among them clandestinas whose jobs as operators served as vital links of communication. Aleida taped a conversation between a high-ranking functionary in Batista's regime and Earl Smith, the US ambassador to Cuba, who was then in Washington. In the phone call Smith was asked to intercede with the US government to increase military aid to the regime to try to stop the advance of the revolutionary army in the mountains of eastern Cuba. Aleida gave this tape to the 26th of July Movement, which made it public. A police investigation determined that she had been the direct intermediary, but because she came from a prominent family it was decided to make her murder look like a random automobile accident. She was killed by the police, who stopped her car as she was driving to her parents' home in Güines.[36]

━━━━━

Other clandestinas were specifically hunted and almost certainly targeted for death. All were women who, in the eyes of the esbirros, had operated on what was understood to be male terrain. Essentially, they fell out of the boundaries of the "traffic in women" and thereby directly challenged the male construction of the conflict. Each played central roles in planning and carrying out acts of sabotage, and they had earned a reputation among the esbirros in their own right. Nilda Ravelo worked directly with Faustino Pérez and then with Delio Gómez Ochoa, Pérez's replacement as head of the movement in Havana following the May 1958 meeting in Altos de Mompié. Mariíta Trasancos was, as I described in chapter 5, El Curita's "right-hand woman" in realizing the Night of One Hundred Bombs, among other actions. Ángela Alonso shared informally the direction of Action and Sabotage with Orlando Nodarse, the head of these operations in Pinar del Río. Verena Pino was a major figure in a prominent rebel family in the Santa Clara clandestinidad. Natalia Bolívar took on a yet more prominent role in the Directorio after its failed attack on the Presidential Palace and the exit of its surviving leadership—all male—from the island.

Given the extent of their violation, even of the norms of the insurgents themselves, these women, according to their own testimonies or the testimonies of those who knew them well in the insurgency, most probably would have been assassinated or disappeared had fate in different forms not intervened.[37]

The brutality to which each of them was subjected when captured reflected at least in part the extent to which they were deemed to have transgressed. Mariíta Trasancos, only sixteen years old, was caught for the first time in January 1958 in an apartment, in which as I write in chapter 4, she was in the middle of fabricating explosives. She was taken to Ventura's office in the Ninth Police Station. The police radioed ahead that the "package" was on its way: They clearly knew exactly who she was. Jean Franco notes the regular use of that term "paquete" (package) for those captured during the Pinochet dictatorship as the beginning of the process of dehumanization by which those who torture are released from any compulsion to moderate their brutality.[38]

Ventura looked at this small childlike girl whose eyebrows and lashes were burnt off shortly before her arrest in the course of (mis)preparing the explosives, and given that she was already legendary among the esbirros, exclaimed, "And this little shit is Mariíta?" In an unusual move, since I noted earlier he himself only occasionally did the physical work of torturing prisoners, Ventura grabbed Mariíta's hair and "twisted my neck as if I were a chicken." She was then beaten viciously. She fully expected to be killed. At which point Margot Aniceto, having gotten word of where Mariíta was being held through one of her various informal legal networks, intervened. The Martianas, as noted in chapter 2, made a habit of using every connection they had to save imprisoned and tortured insurrectionaries, and in doing this Aniceto was no slouch. She contacted Julio Laurent, the head of the SIN, who during the 1930s had been a student in the movement to bring down the Machado dictatorship. During that time, Laurent had been her sister's boyfriend but now he was among the most celebrated of Batista's contingent of torturers and murderers. Margot asked him to intervene with Ventura. Said Margot, "She is just a young girl who has nothing to do with all this." What follows is Mariíta's account of what happened next:

> [Laurent] showed up at Ventura's office and Ventura asked me: "Do you know who this is?" And I had said: "No." I honestly did not know him, all dressed in white and red as he was. But suddenly, something came spontaneously out of my mouth: "This guy is Lieutenant Laurent, the assassin of Jorge Agostini." [Laurent] had a reddish complexion, but he turned pale white. After a while I no longer cared about what they did to me, because [I thought] they were going to kill me right here, I never thought they would let me go.

Mariita assumed that Laurent had been called in to kill her. But in the end she was not killed; rather, horribly beaten, she was transferred to the police hospital and to relative safety. And then to the women's prison at Mantilla. Because Mariíta was a minor, Aniceto got her released on conditional liberty to the custody of her parents. "I understood after, when I was in Mantilla, what had happened when Margot asked me what I had said to Laurent. What did I say? That he was Agostini's assassin. Said Margot, 'No wonder he told me "She is no poor little girl: She's an hija de puta."'"[39]

After her release, given that her parents' house was continually raided by the police who had ransacked it, taking even her clothes, Mariíta could no longer live there and, as she remembers, she lived wherever she could, usually in places found for her by the FCMM. On August 1, 1958, she was again captured, literally taken off the street and to Ventura's office in the Ninth Police Station where an assorted group of his most infamous torturers was gathered. Ventura asked her, "Do you know where we are coming from?" She replied, "If you don't tell me I don't know." He said, "From killing your husbands in prison."[40] She noted, "They were celebrating, drinking alcohol, and so he did not beat me."[41]

By chance, someone had seen her being loaded into an unmarked car and called her mother, who immediately called Aida. Like Aniceto, Aida had no scruples at all in employing whatever contacts she had made over the years. She called an Auténtico Party politician she knew from her days as a member of that party in the 1930s, who intended to run for office in the November 1958 elections scheduled by Batista. This politician appeared at the station and Mariíta was released to him after some days. As she was being released Ventura warned, "Be careful, because there won't be a third time. You won't even make it here a third time."[42]

Natalia Bolivar was caught in a trap going to a meeting between insurgents of the 26th of July Movement and the Directorio. The building in which the meeting was to take place as well as the blocks around it had been staked out by police. In the subsequent search of her parents' house and unknown to her parents, the police found hidden weapons of clandestinos who had been killed, uniforms and handcuffs, issues of the Partido Socialista Popular's *Carta Semanal*, and bonos of the Directorio and the 26th of July Movement.

> First they took me to El Laguito in a caravan of cars to beat me.[43] They fractured my ribs. Then, immediately after that, they brought me to BRAC, where they interrogated me. They called me "the witch" and began beating me again and poking inside my ears with a sharp wire and punching my ribs, which were already broken. They took me to a jetty and told me that they were going to put cement shoes on me and throw me into Havana's harbor, which really scared me because I had been a champion swimmer and I knew what death by drowning felt like, and then they decided to call Laurent, the head of SIN.[44]

What saved her, Natalia asserts, was her "collar religioso," given to her by one of the most famous babalawos in Matanzas a week earlier, who had told her, "Death is following you." He made her a necklace of Ogun and instructed her: "Girl, you will be taken prisoner and taken to a man who might either kill you or let you go, but if he sees this necklace he will ask you what Santería house you come from and you will tell him this and that. Then he will be forced to grant you one wish, only one, so girl, use that wish because your life depends on it." And so she did. Taken to Laurent and bleeding profusely, in her struggle to free herself from the grasp of the two esbirros holding her by her arms, her blouse opened slightly. Laurent, it turned out, was himself a believer. He saw her necklace and asked her what Santería house she was from. Natalia recited what the babalawo had instructed her to recite, and Laurent then commanded the esbirros holding her to leave and asked her what she wanted. She answered that she wanted her mother and "a chocolate suero—because it was my passion." She could not drink the suero because her mouth had been ripped. "Being with my mother made me feel peaceful. I knew nothing was going to happen to me. I clung onto her for dear life." Laurent called Ventura and told him: "We have to let her go. We have to let her go."[45]

This and her family's very influential connections got her refuge in the Brazilian embassy, which Ventura then circled continuously in his car, hoping to catch her out. After fifteen days, her wounds cared for, instead of going into exile as her mother had arranged with the Brazilian ambassador, she cut her hair, left the embassy, and joined her compañeros in the clandestinidad.[46]

Verena Pino and her entire family—her mother, Margot; her two brothers, Quintín and Julio; and her sister, Bertica—were combatants. Julio, while a medical student at the University of Havana, had joined the Directorio, and when he returned home to Santa Clara after the university closed in November 1956 he joined the 26th of July Movement. He died in a bomb explosion. Verena, quemada in Santa Clara, went to Havana and then to Matanzas. She was caught on December 23, 1958, by police in Matanzas and taken to the BRAC where she was tortured so brutally that she attempted to cut her wrists with a plastic ornamental comb. They sewed up her wrists and continued her torture. They kept her alive because Rolando Masferrer was looking for her: "He didn't want someone else to kill me. He wanted to personally torture me." She survived only because the Batista regime collapsed a week after her detention.[47]

There were limitations the regime faced in the torture of women that did not apply to male clandestinos. These limitations were rooted in two intertwined realities faced by the regime, having to do with what I discussed in chapter 1: the nature of Cuban civil society and the issue of the legitimacy of the regime. Why was it, for instance, that the Batista regime did not simply use the tactics of murder and disappearing employed by later dictatorships in Chile or Argentina to eliminate both male and female opposition or potential opposition? In these countries the word "disappear" became a verb. After all, Chile and Argentina, much like Cuba, were characterized by substantial civil societies. Indeed, in the case of Chile the 1973 military coup had been preceded by nearly half a century of electoral rule. Yet in both countries this seemed not an impediment to the systematic use of rape, assassination, and disappearance, even of very young women.

Multiple external and internal factors need to be taken into account here. First, the coups in Chile and Argentina occurred in a much different world and at a much different time than did Batista's takeover in Cuba. Lessons had been learned; methods were more sophisticated; support from outside, and in the case of Chile particularly from the United States, was far more calibrated, inclusive, and subtle.

But we can identify something perhaps far more critical. In contrast to Cuba, in both Argentina and Chile civil society was torn against itself. In both countries, significant and powerful sectors actively supported the military takeovers and viewed the elimination of the opposition by whatever means as necessary and even justified.

These dictatorships seem to have taken some lessons from Batista's debacle; among these were that the public display of tortured bodies was counterproductive. The escalating appearance of the brutally marked bodies served to create terror on the one hand and horror and disgust on the other. One can only imagine the reaction had young female bodies been similarly posed. The publication alone of pictures or even written reports about battered young women proved scandalous for Batista and were received by Cuban civil society as yet a further humiliation, another act by the dictatorship that violated Cubans' sense of themselves, their history, and that was seen as demeaning their country in the outside world. The first such photograph, the beaten face of Enélida González, a student in the Faculty of Social Sciences and Public Law at the University of Havana, appeared on the front page of the daily newspaper *La Prensa Libre* on February 9, 1956, and it resulted in a public uproar. The Federación de Estudiantes Universitarios called a twenty-four-hour universitywide strike. The FCMM wrote that the attack was part of a wave of violence and pandemonium that damaged the prestige of Cuban society and had no place in a civilized, generous, and noble country that for America and the world, was the homeland of José Martí, a champion of human rights.

In a public denunciation of Enélida's kidnapping and beating, the much-respected dean of the Faculty of Social Sciences, Raúl Roa, described to the Cuban public what had happened to her: "Arbitrarily arrested near her home, Señorita González was taken blindfolded to a distant place where she was disrobed, brutally beaten; her eyebrows shaved and then she was forced to drink castor oil, finally be abandoned in the vicinity of El Rincón half-naked and without money. . . . This event, exceedingly critical in itself, is even more demeaning because it involved a woman."[48] And when in February 1958 about one hundred men in El Príncipe staged their second hunger strike, publicity about the strike was filtered through stories of the women in Mantilla who staged a parallel strike. Photographs of these women, taken to hospitals in deteriorating condition, were, above anything else, the public face of the strikes.[49]

Even worse were the published and subsequently widely reprinted and circulated newspaper and televised accounts about Esterlina Milanés and the doctors who treated her. Her story shocked the sensibilities of those Cubans who wanted to continue thinking of their country, despite the dictatorship, as a civilized place where such things could not occur.[50] The story of her rape and torture was broadcast not simply in Cuba but in the international press as well. *Bohemia* entitled its account as the "History of Horrors." *El Mundo*, one of Cuba's leading dailies, published a commentary by Carlos Lechuga, a member of the Movimiento de Resistencia Civil (MRC): "It is difficult to believe that we have fallen so low, that there are Cubans so devoid of human feelings and so immoral. It is shameful that in our country the deeds that Sra. Milanés, a forty-year old Catholic school teacher who accuses Captain Sosa, the chief of the Twelfth Police Station and various of his subordinates of raping and torturing her for three days until the Ambassador of Colombia saved her from this hell."[51]

Esterlina's transgression against her condition of motherhood was thus reversed: Her torturers were now the transgressors. In violating her, they and not Esterlina had violated the inviolable: motherhood. And the violation was yet more profound. In torturing her sexually, they had gone beyond all bounds. As in multiple other societies in Cuba historically and into the 1950s motherhood and sex had no place in the same sentence. Batista quickly reimposed censorship.

FEMALE BONDING: MANTILLA

After they were formally charged with a crime, girls and women who had been arrested and held in purgatory in a police station or in the BRAC or SIM or SIN were taken to the women's holding prison, Mantilla. Somewhat ironically, given that it was a prison, Mantilla was in effect the most important site in which female insurgents could come together in a community of women. In the early years of resistance to the regime, public demonstrations by women allowed for such spaces, but only during the time of the demonstrations themselves. Mantilla, on the other hand, provided the time and space for a far more extended development of a community.

The severe trauma experienced by many of those who arrived finally in Mantilla did not easily heal. Ángela Alonso, twenty-seven, captured with her fiancé, Orlando Nodarse, was accused of illegal possession of explosives, weapons, and propaganda, and assisting in the suicide (of Nodarse). Ángela lived with the guilt that she had murdered her novio. Nodarse had been so severely tortured during his previous arrests that he had brain damage, which among other things made him subject to periods of unconsciousness. Sure that he would not survive another arrest, another round of torture, and probable assassination, he and Angela had made a suicide pact. They hid one of the extremely toxic pills they used to kill pigs while sabotaging nativity celebrations on fincas owned by Batista supporters in Pinar del Rio. Should the police once more come, they planned to split the pill. And the police did indeed come again. Angela retrieved the pill and gave it first to Nodarse, but he swallowed it whole. She found out only after the triumph that he had not died from the pill; rather, his stomach had been pumped so that he could be subjected again to torture. When Nodarse's body was exhumed they found bullets among his remains. Arrested and in Mantilla, Ángela was ridden by guilt that haunted her nightly. Mirta Rodriguez Calderon, who was imprisoned with her, recalls that Ángela arrived in Mantilla "destroyed both inside and out": "She saw Nodarse in her dreams and spoke to him and asked him, 'When are you coming for me, my darling? Are you coming to get me? Why don't you look so tall? Why don't you have feet? I can't see your feet.'"[52]

After her release from Mantilla, quemada, Ángela was sent by the leadership in Havana to the sierra, where she worked with Faustino Pérez in the Asociaciones Campesinas de Territorio Libre, an experiment that sought to involve the peasantry in civil government. Her story was made into the opera *La hija de Cuba*, or *Lila* (her name in the clandestinidad), by a Russian composer.[53]

Nonetheless, Mantilla guaranteed real and effective safety to those who entered into what was, in effect, a nascent female-only bounded space. Concretely, arrival at Mantilla meant that it was now publicly known that one had been arrested. For those who had endured extended confinement in the cellars of police stations, never knowing what they might be subjected to, being taken to Mantilla ended the horrible uncertainty about one's fate. Now, as Pilar Sa says, "At least you could not be disappeared, you have survived, you are finally safe. You are in paradise."[54]

This sense of safety was perhaps most tangible for those who arrived at Mantilla severely tortured. Nélida Alvarez was twenty-two when she was arrested after a long search by Ventura's esbirros. She had been subjected to days and nights of endless interrogation sessions in the Fifth Police Station and then in SIM, accused of plotting to furnish provisions to the 26th of July Movement guerrilla front forming in the mountains of Pinar del Río. Says Nélida, "When I arrived [in Mantilla], it seemed to me that I had arrived at a palace. It felt to me like a haven of peace."[55]

Pilar describes Nélida's appearance when she arrived in Mantilla: "No one recognized her. They thought she was a común [a regular prisoner], because she was in such bad shape, so filthy, so destroyed, in pieces."[56] Nélida speaks of Mantilla and what followed: "When I saw two or three familiar faces I felt a great sense of relief. I was terrified after being subjected at the police station to all kinds of torture, both physical and psychological, for five straight days, and with that animal Ventura and his esbirros. My nerves were very bad and I could barely get up or walk."[57]

What Pilar recalls as "the overwhelming sense of calm and purity" that has stayed with her to this day came in part from the unspoken physical and emotional support that those who arrived in the prison received from the women and girls there. Again, Nélida:

> When I saw the faces of Pilar [Sa] and Nilda [Ravelo] I breathed again, because I had thought they were going to kill me [in the police station]. Seeing them again renewed my strength. Pilar was in the upper bunk and offered it to me, but I could not climb up, because I was in such bad shape. Those other prisoners cooked for me, because I was so weak. When it was my turn to cook, once a week, they cooked for me. They gave me shots; they fed me and bathed me. The first time they had to bathe me because I had been beaten so badly that I could not raise my arms to wash my hair and I remember that a very old woman who had lost her twenty-two-year-old son in Santiago took me in as if I were her daughter.[58]

The physical layout of Mantilla and the isolation of the political prisoners from the comunes, perhaps intended to keep the comunes from being "infected," actually served to further this sense of community. Presos comunes and political prisoners were confined in separate blocks on two separate floors in the prison. Comunes were mostly transient, that is, in Mantilla for a day or days. The political prisoners lived together in close quarters. They were not confined to separate cells but rather shared a large room with cots. Except for brief periods when they were allowed walks in the central patio downstairs, they had almost no contact with the presos comunes. They were therefore literally together all the time. They cooked, shared packages as well as information brought by their families and other visitors, and listened to a small radio, which Pilar's family had snuck in, to learn what was going on in the outside world. Twice, in coordination with the male prisoners in El Príncipe, those women who were imprisoned organized and staged their own hunger strikes. And once, led by Nilda—who, having spent a total of a year and a half in Mantilla, would come to be called its dean—they collectively plotted and organized (although did not carry out) an escape.

With few exceptions the political prisoners were white; the comunes were generally black or mulata. But, given deep racial assumptions in Cuban society, when Pilar, a mulata, after twenty-seven days "being dragged from one jail to the other," arrived at Mantilla together with Digna and Teresa Abreu who were black, all three were first put in with the comunes. Pilar describes their arrival: "I weighed some eighty pounds. I was dirty, wearing the same clothes one whole month, and then Teresa and Digna arrived. We were two blacks and one mulata, so when the prison guards saw us they thought we are comunes. So they sent us in with the comunes. I did not know where I was. The compañeras [the political prisoners] were expecting us, because Margot [Aniceto] had told them that we were going to be arriving."[59]

Material life for the political prisoners further set them apart from the comunes. The clandestinas' emotional and physical daily needs were greatly ameliorated by regular visits by parents (almost always mothers), sisters, and the women of the FCMM. Mirta remembers that Pastorita Núñez came to the prison every week, sometimes loaded with cannelloni from Potín, a chain of posh Havana restaurants. This, she said, was the occasion for a feast among the prisoners.[60] Visitors were free to come every day to sit with their loved ones on benches. No bars separated them from one another.

These regular and frequent family visits provided affective contact and, as well, opportunities for the women in Mantilla to get and to share among themselves news of what was happening in the country and even to continue participating actively in the insurgency. They developed methods of passing information to and from the men in prison in El Príncipe and to movement insurgents in the outside world, by creating a chain, facilitated by female family members who served as intermediaries. Thus, confinement itself was employed to continue women's functions as messengers and even to bring other young women into the movement. Pilar's younger sister became a messenger between Pilar, the women in Mantilla, and the men in El Príncipe. Her sister relates that Pilar directed her to

> go see the tenientico [little lieutenant], the nickname of a combatiente in El Príncipe and give him a note. That was how I started the trafficking of messages from El Príncipe to Mantilla and from Mantilla to El Príncipe. Inmates communicated that way with each other. I was scared to death. I put all the notes in my bra. The tenientico told me to wait for his signal to hand him the notes. I arrived with my bra full of papers and left with it empty. Usually when I was leaving El Príncipe with my bra filled with correspondence, there was a policeman outside, but this time there were two, so I was very nervous. I began walking towards them, my head proudly raised and swinging my hips to make them check out my figure as all men do when a woman passes nearby. And that they did and glancing at my curves, they missed what was hidden inside. My heart was beating as fast as my hips were swaying. I went to El Príncipe in the morning and in the afternoon to Mantilla, taking messages back and forth.[61]

The twenty-two women who were in Mantilla on January 1, 1959, only knew that Batista had fled when Pilar's mother arrived at the jail to tell them and to demand their immediate release. Nilda wanted everyone to stand up and sing the national anthem. It is unlikely that this happened. People were beginning to come out on the streets, and the women in Mantilla joined them.

AFTERMATHS
FORGETTING AND REMEMBERING

Something ungraspable, something difficult to grasp, that was there during the strike and its occupation. Something is in the midst of happening, something is happening: just that, the feeling of that. . . . That something should come from the outsider, to meet you, to surprise you, to take you away, to raise you up, to undo you, it's there, it's now, we are beside it, we are with it, we feel the pressure and we create it, everything is happening, everything can happen, it's the present, and the world empties itself and fills up again and the walls pull back, they are transparent and they pull back they separate and they fade away, they leave room and it's now and now and now. . . . Love can create this feeling, or art; it is rare to feel it in society, where one is almost always confronted with a kind of obligatory inertia, where the activity one pursues, the activity that one can pursue, goes almost always hand in hand with the painful feeling of limitations. But during the strike we could touch it with our fingers, rub our hands across its back.

LESLIE KAPLAN / *DEPUIS MAINTENANT*

In her novel about a workers' strike and occupation in France during 1968, Leslie Kaplan captures what must have been the feeling of euphoria, of the impossible made possible. After January 1, 1959, as the news that Batista had fled began to spread and be believed, people poured onto the streets of Havana. By the time Fidel and the Caravan of Liberty reached the city on January 8, they were thronged: In photographs of the caravan's arrival, it seems as if the entire city was on hand to greet it ecstatically.

Batista was gone. The intensity of what female insurgents had for several years been engaged with began to give way to new, multiple realities. During the years of the insurgency women in the clandestine movement had not seriously asked themselves or even begun to come to terms with what was next in Cuba and, intimately related to this, in their own lives. Nor had they explicitly or seemingly implicitly contemplated the gender implications of what they had lived through with such intensity. Gender demands had nowhere been a part of the fabric of the insurrection. And yet, as Michelle Chase observes, "ideas about gender were central, not marginal, to revolutionary politics. . . . [I]t is impossible to fully understand the major political processes of the period—including insurrectionary alliances, political radicalization and polarization, mass emigration, and the rise of an internal opposition, without seeing how these were linked to gender relations. . . . [T]he political transformations of this period were suffused with references to masculinity, maternalism, sexuality, and the family."[1]

For most of the girls and young women who had fought against the regime in the clandestinidad, it was impossible to go back. They had lived these years of their youth as they never could have imagined they would, no matter the world or the social and economic milieu from which they had come. They had in some form definitively rebelled against the will of their families and transgressed against societal norms. In the actions they undertook as insurgents, they had exercised a degree of freedom of movement and self-determination that was hardly customary in 1950s Cuba. They had lived in close contact with their male compañeros, in some cases sharing the same spaces. They had participated in actions certainly inconceivable to them prior to their involvement in the insurgency. Many had been imprisoned even multiple times, beaten and in various other ways tortured. They had witnessed the horribly tortured bodies of intimate friends. Chase notes that in the accounts some have given of their experiences as clandestinas one can almost feel the boundaries of their social world extending.[2] They had moved far beyond the prescribed parameters of "decent" behavior. These years in the underground had transformed them as individuals. For most, this transformation inevitably led to a more critical awareness of the limitations of the society that in effect they had turned their backs on. And it was virtually impossible for them to somehow reintegrate themselves into their formerly preordained positions in household patriarchy or to return to the private sphere. Few went back to their parents' homes. For those like Mariíta Trasancos, who was only seventeen when the revolution took power, being once more under the rules and regulations of what was in her case the rigid patriarchal structure of her Spanish parents' household proved intolerable. Trasancos had gone back to the Escuela de Comercio to complete her studies and had returned to live with her parents, but found it impossible: "My mother wanted me to be home by 9 p.m., and said that I couldn't go to the movies alone, and I reminded her that I had been living on my own for two years. So, to avoid upsetting and fighting with them, I checked into a guest house very near Carmen Castro's apartment, in El Vedado who said: Come and work with me."[3]

For Mariíta and for most of the other former clandestinas, what happened next played itself out in diverse ways largely in the context of the inconceivably rapid movement of the revolution in power. Like Mariíta, many of the young clandestinas went back to the schools from which they had been expelled when they were arrested, but at the same time each engaged in multiple and diverse tasks determined largely by the moment. In the months directly following the taking of power, Mariíta and others engaged in naming and ferreting out individuals who had collaborated with the regime and for whatever reason were still in Havana. With various other former clandestinas she went first to work with Faustino Pérez in the Ministry of Recuperation of Embezzled Goods. As head of the 26th of July Movement in Havana until May 1958, Pérez had been a familiar presence for them.

Mirta Rodríguez Calderón got her degree from the Escuela Normal de Maestros and went to work with Ángela Alonso, her cellmate in Mantilla during their 1958 hunger strike, as general director of the Comedores Populares y Escolares. These dining rooms, which were actually holdovers from the years of the dictatorship, provided inexpensive food to those who needed it. At the same time Mirta was asked by Héctor Ravelo, the head of the 26th of July Movement in Havana Campo during the insurrection, to organize the short-lived Women's Section of the 26th of July Movement. The Women's Section is discussed later in this chapter. Suffice it to say here that its work centered on organizing poor women around the port area and supporting the rapidly evolving policies of the leadership in manifold ways.[4]

Almost all of these young clandestinas eventually took up more permanent careers that often had little or nothing to do with what their pre-revolutionary years in school were supposed to have prepared them for. Nilda Ravelo became a lawyer; Pilar Sa, a book editor; Digna Abreu and her sister, Teresa, first worked together in the Office of the National Police. Digna then worked in a medical laboratory, and Teresa in the offices of the National Trade Union. Mirta Rodriguez Calderon became a much-respected journalist whose articles were published mainly in *Bohemia*; Sonnia Moro, a historian; Consuelo Elba, a filmmaker; Xiomara Blanco wrote novelas for television.

Most married soon after the revolution took power, not uncommonly to the men with whom they shared their experiences in the anti-Batista movement. But these marriages frequently proved battlegrounds on which husbands and the families of the couple sought to reimpose traditional family norms. With a few exceptions, all of the women with whom I spoke with had been divorced at least once. Although the divorce rate in postrevolutionary Cuba is remarkably high, my discussions with these women indicated that clashes with mates, particularly in first marriages, were often rooted in the dramatic changes in self-conception women had experienced in their daily lives in the insurgency and the corresponding failure to accept these profound changes among the male ex-insurgents who were their husbands. Selma Díaz, for instance, continued her study of architecture at the University of Havana. She married Osmany Cienfuegos, the brother of Camilo, who had been her boyfriend prior to 1959. But she left him when it became clear that he expected her to be at home to greet him upon his return from whatever he was doing.[5] Most of the clandestinas who remained in Cuba are now retired; some have died. And virtually all in my study now live as single women, usually with one of their children: Their husbands have died, or they did not remarry after their last divorce. Almost all have at least one child living elsewhere, either in the United States or in Latin America or Europe.

If the lives of these women in every aspect, both personal and public, had taken a radical and profoundly different turn than that which seemed inevitable prior to Batista's coup, one key reality had not changed: The path the revolution would follow in the years after 1959 was not to be determined by women. As the official story of how the revolution had been made became ever more enshrined, those celebrated as its protagonists were male and most frequently those who had fought together and bonded in the sierra. In redeeming the violated nation, they had confirmed their right to determine its future: The 1960s reconstruction of the nation would be in their hands. In like fashion the roles played by women in bringing the Batista regime to its end were reconfigured. The out-front militancy of the Martianas became the story of a group of older women, assumed to be mothers, whose engagement in the revolution rotated around a kind of charity work (for instance, caring for the families of martyred male clandestinos). The young clandestinas in the same story become those who in a variety of ways provided assistance in keeping with traditional female positioning vis-à-vis the real fighters. This configuration re-created in essence the structure of relations of power between men and women that was reconfirmed in the wake of the nineteenth-century wars.

This exclusion of women from the most critical realms of power and decision-making was evident even in the subsequent careers of the four women whose names are engraved in the official story of the taking of power. Vilma Espín, who studied electrical engineering at MIT in the early 1950s, a time when surely she was one of the few female students at the Institute, got to use little of this education. Rather she was appointed head of the new Women's Federation by Fidel, apparently simply because she was a woman. Haydée Santamaría was allotted a new literary house, Casa de las Américas, which, through her own efforts, became a major venue for Latin American artists and writers. Only Celia Sánchez for the remainder of her life was in daily contact with Fidel, serving essentially as his personal secretary and as the key channel to him for virtually anyone. But the degree and weight of her informal role have never been clear. Melba Hernández worked in foreign affairs, serving the Organization of Solidarity with the Peoples of Asia, Africa and Latin America (OSPAAL) and as ambassador to Vietnam.

FEAR, TRAUMA, AND GENDER

A month before I finished my fieldwork, I sat in on a panel discussion that was intended to deal with or rather bring to life the history of the clandestinidad in Havana. The audience consisted of young students at the Universidad de Ciencias Médicas de La Habana (School of Medicine at the University of Havana). The panel comprised five former 26th of July Movement members, all men and all white, and one former Directorio Revolucionario (DR) militant, who was male and mulatto. One panel member dominated the presentation, with occasional interjections by the others. The session was to last for two hours. What the panelists had to say consisted of lengthy accounts of the heroic actions of various insurgents. Their recitation ended at one hour and fifty-five minutes, with five minutes left for questions. The thundering silence in the audience was broken by one young student who stepped up to the microphone and asked whether any of the panelists had ever been afraid. The audience perked up. The answer was "no, because we were fighting the most vicious dictator in world history," and so forth. Thundering silence in the auditorium took hold once again.

Two related themes emerge here. First, the revolution and those who seek to speak for it have yet to find a way to bring alive the period of its triumph for people who did not live through it, to give it a human face that might have some success in engaging younger generations of Cubans. Second, the word "fear" is taboo in the lexicon of men in the revolution and in Cuban revolutionary history. It evokes the unforgivable. The story of the heroic male or the heroic male martyr leaves no space whatsoever for any expression of fear: It is a weakness that for male insurgents from the nineteenth-century wars to the 1950s revolution cannot be spoken. It would reveal a crack in the construction of the edifice that legitimates the male right to rule. It is treason. The rules would most probably have been different for female insurgents. Should she have evidenced fear in any of the contexts in which she was present, it surely would have radically diminished the trust and the regard other insurgents held for her. But more, among male insurgents it would serve as confirmation of the generally held belief concerning women's natural weaknesses and would underscore, if this needed underscoring, the roles suitable or not suitable for women in the underground movement.

In fact however, there was no reference to fear among the former clandestinas I interviewed. Rather, the abiding emotion rooted in their time in the underground movement was trauma. In my first conversation with her about her years in the clandestine movement, Pilar Sa stated firmly that she was someone who always looked toward the future; for her, the past was the past. But as we shall see, for Pilar the past was hard to escape. In 1962, with a scholarship actually awarded to her sister, she went to study electrical engineering in the Soviet Union. She married a Russian but left him to bring her two children back to Cuba when they were five and six so that they would be raised as Cubans.

But in a later interview Pilar spoke again about the past, this time revealing something more. Her language suggested that for her the past remained forbidden to rein: unbearable and mined with wounds that would not heal. We went together back to the safe house in which she had been trapped by a squad of esbirros, where she witnessed one of them shoot and murder a young man who came to the door after her. At the gate to the house she hesitated and asked for a couple of minutes by herself. A half hour later she came back not speaking.

Almost all of the former clandestinas with whom I spoke experienced trauma in different forms. None escaped or could escape the effects of what they had lived through and what they had witnessed during their years in the clandestinidad. The past did not nor could it rest easy for any of these women. The solidifying narrative of the heroic male struggle allowed room for the public expression of this trauma during the trials of those who had tortured or been responsible for torturing and murdering insurgents. But there was little space other than the trials for dealing with trauma at an ongoing and shared level. Individual or collective trauma, much like admissions of fear, had no place in the story of the heroic male revolution. Like fear, trauma could not be spoken of. Ironically, this silence among women served to further enable a narrative of the underground movement that centered almost entirely on men as its protagonists. That is, clandestinas themselves contributed to their relative absence in the tales of the underground movement.

The absence of some sort of common space that might have allowed a degree of shared healing was joined with the absence of any awareness of the need for it. Instead, the collective bonding that women experienced in Mantilla dissipated over the course of the chaotic first years after 1959. Some former clandestinas like Digna Abreu speak of their families and particularly their mothers as providing private sources of comfort. But overwhelmingly, the women with whom I spoke absorbed in some form the trauma into themselves, unspoken and unspeakable. And in their lives following the insurrection this trauma found different forms of expression. Mirta Rodríguez Calderón relived for years the haunting sounds the esbirros employed to convince her that they had killed her father: a sack pounding to the floor, the gunshot.[6] Hidelisa Esperón married one of the men with whom she lived in a safe house in the clandestinidad only to see him die in an automobile accident the year after the revolution took power. She lives directly above the apartment from which, in 1958, she was dragged and taken to the Ninth Police Station to be tortured. Her present is infused with the past. She says that she has never had a peaceful night's sleep in her apartment: If she hears a noise she wakes up in a fright. With her second husband she visits every week the graves of the two men she lived with during the insurrection, Machaco Ameijeiras and Tony Fernández. They remain always in her present: Drawings of the two hang on her living-room wall.[7]

Nilda Ravelo lives to a great degree as if she were still in the clandestinidad. After the triumph she focused her attention on identifying those who had managed to disguise their role in the Batista regime. She then worked in the Ministry of Justice. But her life fundamentally continues to be shaped by her years in the clandestinidad. She has an encyclopedic knowledge of every detail of the insurrection in Havana, and she navigates the city with this map in her mind. She holds her memories tight; she cannot seem or want to let them recede, and her face lights up when she is in the company of the dwindling circle of people who fought with her. She remains faithful, as she says, to those who lived and those who did not: "My commitment," she states, "is to the dead."[8]

Nor did the fierce trauma produced by the years of the insurrection affect only the women who had been directly involved in underground actions. Trauma reverberated almost inevitably into the families of the "collaborators," those women who took in and gave refuge and cover to hunted insurrectionaries. Ercilia Gutiérrez and her family, as I described in chapter 5, had given cover to Guillermo Jiménez, Directorio insurgent. Following January 1, 1959, Ercilia returned to her former job. But for her son, Godeardo, who had been from the age of nine effectively a DR clandestino, and not by his own choice, life as he grew up became increasingly difficult. Guillermo had developed the greatest affection for the boy. He relates:

> Godeardo was a victim of the whole process. He remained totally traumatized. He did not have a normal life, a normal childhood [with] the normal things which children play with, a happy life. We actually created for him a situation of terrible sacrifice. I always had a bit of a guilt complex; he always had a very close attachment, a very affectionate link with me, and as far as the circumstances allowed, we always kept in contact. Godeardo always had many problems at his workplaces, because he was very rigid and wanted things to be done perfectly, something impossible. And then, he would not understand, because he had a strong personality, and he went to see me to find out if I could get him a job. But I was in a difficult situation at the time. I was [working] in a factory, and I got him a job there because it was the only thing that I could do for him. So,

I said, "I have no other way of helping you." He went to work with me for several years.[9]

Godeardo left Cuba and now lives in Tampa. He is in regular contact with his family.

And then there were the women who committed themselves and were to an extent consumed by the search for justice left unresolved by the revolution's triumph. Marta Jiménez was eight months pregnant when her husband, Fructoso Rodríguez, along with three other youths who had taken part in the March 13, 1957 Directorio attack on the Presidential Palace, was assassinated at Humboldt 7 (7 Humboldt Street) thirty-eight days later. Guillermo recalls it painfully: "The funeral of Fructoso and the three other compañeros killed at Humboldt 7 turned into the last battle of the four great horsemen and it was all Marta Jiménez's doing. Marta led the funeral procession, which was surrounded on all sides by policemen, and putting herself in front of the casket she managed to break the police siege. They didn't dare, they didn't have the courage to intervene. That image has remained indelibly etched forever in our minds."[10]

Marta continued as an insurgent in the Directorio but began immediately to gather evidence against Marcos Rodríguez (Marquitos) who she and the remaining Directorio leadership knew had led Ventura to the apartment in which the four were hiding. After January 1, 1959, with Guillermo, she continued with dogged determination to document the persons responsible for the murders at Humboldt 7. Following the triumph of the revolution, Joaquín Ordoqui, the Partido Socialista Popular (PSP) leader who with his wife, Edith García Buchaca, had been Marquitos's de facto protectors when he arrived in exile in Mexico, arranged a scholarship for Marquitos to Czechoslovakia and then a job in the Cuban embassy in Prague. Marquitos was finally brought back to Cuba on suspicion of having connections to the CIA, and in 1964 was put on trial for his role in the Humboldt 7 assassinations. He was found guilty and executed. His PSP protector, Ordoqui, was sentenced to house arrest for life, although not for his role in Humboldt 7 but for supposed collaboration with the CIA. The leadership of the old PSP never acknowledged the participation of any of its members in the murders at Humboldt 7.[11] Marquitos is now little more than a footnote in the tale of the revolution.

Marta spent most of her career working in the Ministry of Foreign Affairs and served as ambassador to Switzerland and Denmark. She lived alone and self-sufficient, she said, by her own choice. Her son—she has no other children—lives in Miami. She told me she had very little to do with him. She searched for years for the boy who, in a photograph taken directly after the assassinations, is caught looking up at the bloodstained staircase in Humboldt 7, where her husband and three others had been killed.[12] She died in March 2016, eight days short of the fifty-ninth anniversary of the attack on the Presidential Palace. Her son came from Miami for her funeral.

Xiomara Blanco got her degree in journalism and went on to work at the Instituto Cubano de Radio y Televisión (ICRT; Cuban Institute of Radio and Television) where she became popular for writing novelas. One day in 1969 a writer at ICRT came to her desk with a script and she recognized him as the esbirro who had interrogated her family and delivered them to Menocal, the notorious head of the Bauta police station. "Menocal," says Xiomara, "killed without hesitation whoever was arrested." Her father confirmed that this was the esbirro but refused to denounce him, saying that, if he did, "they are going to put him in front of the firing squad." She herself had no such qualms. When she went to court accompanied by her husband for the man's trial, his lawyer, who knew her husband, came up to him to tell him that he was in a trial where a crazy, hysterical woman had denounced his poor client. The client had been a real star as a voluntary teacher in a literacy campaign in 1961 when as a prisoner he instructed other inmates to read and write. Because of this he had been released from prison the same year. But now, said his lawyer, "this crazy woman is saying that he was an esbirro." Xiomara's husband replied, "This crazy woman happens to be my wife."[13] The man was sentenced to twenty years, but in 1984 was one of a group of prisoners released to Jesse Jackson and brought to the United States. Xiomara continues to work at ICRT.

THE AFTERMATH AND THE MARTIANAS

Among the women who had conceived and organized the Frente (the FCMM), their transition after 1959 was perhaps less dramatic than for younger clandestinas. Each had led lives that had been openly transgressive of societal norms even before the revolution took power. For Pastorita Núñez, Aida Pelayo, and Carmen Castro, the revolution was a realization of what had been for them a long history of political and personal rebellion. Following the taking of power, Pastorita worked in different contexts with the same ferocity, thoroughness, and stubborn attention to detail that had characterized her throughout her life. Her loyalty to Fidel remained unflagging until her death: She was, as her godson Pepito says, "intransigent."[14] After the triumph she was put in charge of the Instituto Nacional de Ahorro y Vivienda (INAV), where she put together teams of architects, planners, historians, construction workers, and sociologists to work on the construction of housing in Habana del Este as well as elsewhere in the city and on the island, financed not from the dwindling treasury of the revolution but from the money she raised from sales of national lottery bonds. Aida, Carmen, and Ibia Robustillo, Pastorita's partner, worked with her in INAV. In the four years of INAV's existence Pastorita supervised the construction of and assigned families to 8,533 houses.[15] The houses built under INAV's authority are popularly regarded, and not just by their residents, as the best built in the revolutionary period. Indeed, they are still referred to as "Pastorita's houses." Loren González, who grew up in the Havana municipality of Santa Fe where some of these houses were built, recalls that in Santa Fe during the first years of the revolution, Pastorita was probably more popular than Fidel.[16] Another 1,594 homes had already been assigned to families when in 1962 INAV was abruptly dissolved into the Ministry of Construction. Her project came to an end.[17]

Pastorita and Ibia then went to work in the Valle del Perú, a cattle plan in the province of Havana. When she arrived the area was a nightmarish field of marabú (sickle bush) as she described it.[18] In a short period of time under her authority, it produced more milk per annum than any cattle plan of corresponding size on the island. Following this, she returned to Havana to work on the construction of Lenin Park, and finally she worked in the Museum of Fine Arts. She went, in short, into relative obscurity. When Mirta Rodríguez Calderón, then a correspondent for *Bohemia*, wrote an article about her in 1988, Pepito remembers her reaction: "Maybe Fidel reads this magazine. You'll see, Fidel for sure will read this issue of *Bohemia*."[19]

THE FEDERATION OF CUBAN WOMEN

The Federation of Cuban Women (FMC), headed by Vilma Espín, was founded in November 1960. The 26th of July Movement, as I noted in chapter 2, was the only modern revolutionary movement that did not have a women's front. In the months directly after the taking of power, members of its leadership asked two former clandestinas to organize and head separate women's groups. Women's Section, headed by Mirta Rodriguez Calderón, was, as noted above, one of these.[20] The second was the Women's Brigades formed and headed by Gladys Marel García Pérez, who had been a 26th of July Movement clandestina in Matanzas and one of the few women in the llano in a command position in Action and Sabotage. The brigades operated in the areas surrounding the Capitol and were involved in militant actions in support of the revolution. Chase reports that the impetus to form these groups came from both the women themselves and from the male leadership in the 26th of July Movement. She writes that "the young women who led these two groups . . . identified with the radical nationalism of the insurrection and were motivated by an impassioned sense of duty toward the revolution. . . . [They] were primarily devoted to supporting new revolutionary decrees and implementing the social justice called for by Fidel Castro in the original Moncada speech."[21] When in 1961 the 26th of July Movement dissolved itself and the Organización Revolucionaria Integrada (ORI) was established (to encompass the 26th of July Movement, the DR, and the PSP), the Women's Section and the Women's Brigades, as arms of the 26th of July Movement, ceased to exist as well. Neither group had a role in organizing the FMC. Chase elaborates that, for various reasons, Vilma looked to the PSP women's front, the FDMC, to structure and staff it. This had to be particularly irksome for former 26th of July Movement and Directorio clandestinas who remembered their fraught relationship with the PSP and its youth section during the insurrection.[22] While the FMC has done important work and has expressed occasional disagreements with policies or directions taken by the state, it was and is defined by and has operated always as an arm of the male power structure. Its primary purpose, particularly during its first two decades, was to integrate women into the revolution and into agreement with the decisions determined by those in power. If the Women's Section and the Brigades had been considered in the formation and structuring of the FMC, it is tempting to imagine the difference this might have made in giving women a voice in the critical decisions made by those in power. It is equally tempting to imagine what their impact on women's positioning would have been had the Martianas not chosen to dissolve their organization a month after the revolution took power.

In 1993 two former clandestinas, Mirta Rodríguez Calderón and Xiomara Blanco, organized MAGIN, a collective of women in communications, to examine issues related to gender and sexuality and, in Joan Scott's famous words, to understand what it might mean to use gender as a tool of analysis.[23] Some of these women identified as feminists at a moment when the word "feminist" was not well looked upon among those in leadership positions, both male and female. But some did not. All were members of the FMC. Two other former clandestinas, Pilar Sa and Sonnia Moro, joined the collective in rapid order. Participation in MAGIN was completely open and communication was broadly defined: The collective came to include teachers, writers, poets, filmmakers, translators, and others from various generations and various races, steadily increasing in size during the three years of its existence. While the two women who constituted MAGIN do not connect their experiences in the urban insurgency to the formation of the collective, it is difficult to believe that it was purely coincidental. Conversations at meetings ranged widely, depending on the group's interests, from the very personal (for instance, discussions of what was and what produced female orgasms) to broader inquiries (for instance, what could be learned from women's movements elsewhere in the world and in particular in Latin America). As the poet Georgina Herrera says, "MAGIN was my university."[24] In 1996 MAGIN was deactivated (that is, told it did not have legal status) by the Communist Party's Ideological Commission on the basis that it repeated the work of the FMC and that, at a difficult moment for Cuba, MAGIN could be used as part of the enemy's efforts to seduce Cuban intellectuals.[25]

ENDINGS

Pastorita spent the last fifteen years of her life living in a small house on the grounds of the Asilo de Santovenia, a retreat maintained by nuns. At Santovenia, under a banner reading "los viejos también pueden" (old people also can), she organized the nuns and locals to plant and cultivate an organopónico, which eventually provided the food for the entire retreat and all the vegetables that Pope John Paul consumed during his 1999 visit to Cuba. She supervised the construction of a small space for contemplation on the convent grounds, built in the style of Pastorita's houses with their crenellated roofs.[26] Fidel Castro was among her friends from the old days who occasionally visited Pastorita during her years in the convent. When he dropped in, she gathered the twenty nuns living in the convent around her and talked politics. On one such visit Fidel declared that had he twenty such people around him, he could govern the country well. He did not seem to understand that they were indeed available to him. Pastorita died in 2005. Her companion, Ibia, stricken with Alzheimer's disease, died in an old age home some years later.

Carmen passed away in 1986. At her bedside when she died was her copy of Rosa Luxembourg's *Letters from Prison*, which, as I noted in chapter 2, her brother-in-law had sent to her when she was imprisoned in Isle of Pines in 1932. In the last years of her life, in failing health she moved in with Aida and Aida's son, Carlos Enrique. No plaque marks the apartment in which she lived most of her life, the site of so many personal and political discussions among young insurgents, both male and female, 26th of July Movement and Directorio, which were so critically important to the organization of the insurrection.

Every 28th of January until her death in 1998, Aida hosted a celebration of Martí's birthday, complete with what everyone who is still alive and was present reports were riotous accountings of the exploits of herself and her "accomplices" over the course of the better part of the twentieth century. They were not recorded.[27]

CHILDREN

In the years immediately following the January 1959 triumph of the revolution, there was a baby boom on the island: Many women, including those who had fought in the clandestinidad, tended to have children in fairly rapid succession. I began my discussions with the daughters and sons—eleven daughters and four sons—of some of these clandestinas not so much to illuminate their understandings of their mothers' lives in the insurrection, but rather to get at how they themselves integrated into their own lives the knowledge and experiences of their mothers. That is, I sought to get at the ways in which they incorporated or were unable to incorporate the roles their mothers played in the official narrative concerning the making of the revolution, which, along with my goddaughter, they had been taught: the story of the young bearded men who came down from the sierra. Certainly, this was the story to which they had been (over)exposed in school, through television, and in other arenas. What I discovered was not exactly what I had expected.

Of course, these children have lived in a different time, a different world, with far different personal concerns. Mariíta Trasancos has two daughters and two granddaughters, the youngest of whom is fifteen, exactly the age when Mariíta herself was first arrested. Their concerns, therefore, are inevitably very different from those that centered Mariíta's life.[1]

What was at first remarkable to me was how little most of them knew about their mothers' experiences. And they knew even less of what their grandmothers had lived through. Consuelo Elba remembers with a chuckle that once when her granddaughter answered the telephone she informed Consuelo that the Hermanos Ameijeiras hospital was calling her. It was actually Efigenio Ameijeiras, the only one of the four Ameijeiras brothers who survived the insurrection, on the phone.[2] Sonnia Moro has freely talked about her experiences in the clandestinidad in interviews, in her autobiography, and with her children.[3] And yet when her granddaughter came home from school one day and told her mother, Alina, that she had a homework assignment to interview a clandestino, she was shocked to hear that her grandmother would be a good subject.[4]

My conversations with the children of clandestinas, now themselves largely in their late forties and fifties, revealed things that were both profound and disturbing. Some of their answers to my questions echoed what my godchild had told me. In their early school years, as I mentioned earlier, they had learned the same narrative. Mariana Pita, the daughter of Mirta Rodríguez Calderón, relates her memories of this:

> As a child, you learn basically what they teach you. You question things about the world around you but you do not necessarily question the history classes received at school. On the other hand, Cuban history essentially focuses on the struggle in the mountains and spins around Fidel. Fidel's leading figure is constantly central, plus some martyrs. True, Haydée, Melba, and Celia Sánchez are present, but only a handful of women have any renown in history. Yes, I did know my mother had been in the clandestinaje. I knew that there were other women, alongside my mother, who had even tougher personal experiences but nothing. . . . If you review Cuban history textbooks you realize there is not even a slight mention; they only say in passing that the struggle in the mountains was supported by the struggle in the cities, but there are no details on that matter.[5]

Similarly, Alina González, Sonnia Moro's daughter, said, "We heard and learned references about the clandestinidad at home. Actually, if I remember, the questions in school exams revolved mostly about the heroic deeds at the sierra, the Alegría del Pío combat, the Moncada, the opening of the Second Front, the day of Che's arrival in Santa Clara, things like that.[6] The school textbooks of those days—I am a few years older now—put great emphasis on the events in the sierra, about all the battles that took place there, which were what made possible the triumph of the revolution."

For Alina, given that the school she attended in Santiago had been, before the revolution, the iconic Moncada fortress, the male martyrology particularly framed her imaginary concerning the making of the revolution:

The school was huge and each area was named after a martyr. It was as if you were seeing them because there were life-size pictures. And whenever I walked in the corridors of the school I felt overwhelmed. . . . I thought that the clandestine struggle had been important, but not as important as those men that I saw grabbing a gun and risking their lives. . . . As I got older I learned more about the clandestine struggle mainly from my mother, but this was much later. I did not learn it at school. I did not learn it through my teachers.[7]

Among the daughters with whom I spoke most had only the sketchiest knowledge of the roles their mothers played in the clandestinidad. But this was not the case for all of them. Mónica Alfonso, the daughter of Hidelisa Esperón, said that as a child she was "bathed" in the accounts her mother told her and that she herself has tried to communicate these stories to her children. Of those I interviewed, only Mónica is active in the Club Martiano de Herencia Rebelde. For Hidelisa it was critical that her daughter knew what she did and what happened to her in full detail: "If her daughter understood what it cost her to make a revolution, she would value it."[8]

Similarly, three of the sons with whom I spoke had been immersed since childhood in their families' involvement in revolutionary politics. Although these three interviews with sons of clandestinas can hardly be used to prove that mothers related something different to their sons than to their daughters, certainly their interviews do provide a contrast. Pepe Robustillo grew up as an only child in a house shared by his mother, Ibia, and his godmother, Pastorita Núñez. Following the April 9, 1958, strike, Fidel called Pastorita, by then dangerously quemada, to the sierra. Ibia, a clandestina in Santiago, led her up to Fidel's encampment and then stayed in the sierra with her. They remained together for most of the rest of their lives. Pepito relates:

My childhood was different from that of other children. When I got home, my godmother, Pastorita, was mostly responsible for my education. My mother cooked, did the laundry and other house chores. Pastorita was a woman who spent most of her life—whoever knew her can attest to this—talking about the same subject: She only talked about the revolution. The stories she told me to put me to sleep—children are usually read stories about butterflies and sheep—were about the revolution, of how they went to the sierra, of their contingents, when Fidel taught her how to shoot with a telescopic rifle [neither Pastorita nor Ibia were members of the Mariana Grajales brigade], of the air raids and bombings. . . . My godmother was a daydreamer. My mother was more realistic and avoided making references to the clandestinidad. Well, Pastorita was never mentioned at school. In my history classes they never mentioned any of that.[9]

For most of the women and daughters with whom I spoke, this openness did not hold true. Perhaps the most telling example of this involved Pilar Sa and her two daughters, Renata and Iya. Years after they had returned to Cuba from the Soviet Union, Iya, her older daughter and now an adult herself, went to see for the first time the classic 1968 Cuban film *Memorias del subdesarrollo* (Memories of underdevelopment). Its director, Tomás Gutiérrez Alea, cut into the film's narrative some documentary footage from the capture and trials of the invaders at the Bay of Pigs. In this footage, Gutiérrez Alea included a brief scene from the trial of Ramon Calviño, one of Batista's most notorious torturers, who had returned to Cuba as part of the invasion force and was taken prisoner, tried, and executed. Off camera, one hears the voice of one of his accusers, a woman who confronts him, crying, "¡Dime que no, Calviño, dime que no!" (Tell me it's not true, Calviño, tell me it's not true!). Iya, stunned, recognized her own mother's voice:

> At that time, I knew the story; that is, I knew about the trials, but listening to that voice . . . it made me shiver. My mother never talked about the past. She never said, "I did this or that. I suffered this . . ." I knew that my mother was in jail on January 1, 1959. I think it was my grandmother who told me about it, because I have no recollection of my mother telling me that story. I think it was my grandmother who told me she went to the prison to tell my mother the news about the triumph of the revolution. My mother's clandestine past was never a part of our daily lives.

In 1995, years after seeing *Memorias del subdesarrollo* (her mother has never seen the film), Iya went with Pilar to a meeting of the MAGIN collective, which Pilar had helped to form. The meeting took place on the anniversary of the invasion at the Bay of Pigs, another event, as Pilar noted in an interview with me, told only in terms of its male combatants (or, as she phrased it, another macho day). At this meeting, another colectivo member who had been in the clandestine movement insisted with Pilar that she speak of what she experienced. It was the first time she had done so. Iya describes the impact of this tale:

I was sitting next to my mother and, I don't know why, they began talking about these subjects [my mother and women in the clandestinidad]. It moved me almost to tears, I could feel a lump in my throat. Hearing about what people have lost is always a moving experience. Besides, it came as a shock to me to see my mother . . . I wasn't prepared for that . . . but it wasn't in a history class. After that conversation, instead of thinking about the revolution as a big event, I began to think about my mother . . . about what she had had to endure: That really impressed me. But it mostly made me feel extremely sad. To see that although the goal was really enormous, the struggle made sense, the idea of freedom . . . the personal suffering of others hurts me very much. However, what really pained me, instead of visualizing the big picture, was to see that my mother had suffered. . . . I was more moved by the personal suffering than by the grandiose idea, because I honestly do not see myself doing what she did. I am very far from being able to fill my mother's shoes, to be at her level.

Iya remembers the moment at the MAGIN meeting at which her mother could no longer go on telling her story: "But there came a moment when her facial expression changed as if she had reached bottom. That is, when she was asked to relive everything, even the places where everything happened, she said, 'No, no, no,' as if she were saving herself from remembering the places that could affect her."

Iya has never told her sister Renata, who lives and works in Italy, about the MAGIN meeting. And she has never talked with her in any detail about their mother's time in the clandestinidad. "I think my mother has always tried not to speak of these things and I think I have as well." She has never asked her mother questions about it: "There are things that you never talk about; I will never talk about them. My mother's most personal life, she never discussed that with us. There are things that I could have asked her but I haven't. Maybe we have found comfort in the fact that she doesn't talk about it and I never ask."[10]

Daughters all talked about their relationships with their mothers as they grew up, as all children would: Their mothers, as Iya stated, were their mothers, not the clandestinas they had been. Renata, Pilar's younger daughter, says, "I have never imagined this period of my mother's life. I think that above all, I have pictured my mother living in Russia, because those were the things closer to me, are they not? For example, my dad is not linked to that past. So there were things that I couldn't conceive. . . . I think my mother had a boyfriend who was killed in action. . . . But he was not my dad. It is a past that indirectly belongs to me, is it not?"[11]

Odalys Villafranca, Nilda Ravelo's niece, tells a story different from Iya's and Renata's but with somewhat the same outcome. What she sensed growing up, in particular from her aunt, was that there are things that still cannot be said, about both the movement in Havana and, most particularly, its relationship to the sierra. Given the age of remaining clandestinos, they may never be said. Odalys says, "I was born [in 1966] into a revolutionary family and environment. The Villafrancas in the Boyero municipality had been persecuted and hunted down."[12]

Odalys was brought up in a female-headed household by her grandmother Fela and her cousin Nilda: Given that Nilda was much older than she was, she always referred to her as her aunt. Her entire family, as I mentioned in chapter 4, had been passionate adherents of Chibás and of the Ortodoxo Party. This adherence was transferred to Fidel and to the 26th of July Movement. Some of the men who would attack the Moncada fortress practiced shooting a few kilometers from Fela's granja. When her aunt Nilda was arrested for the first time, Batista's esbirros rounded up and arrested Odalys's uncles (Nilda's brothers). Despite the fact that, as I have written, Nilda is a virtual encyclopedia concerning the insurrection in Havana, she has communicated almost nothing of her experiences in talks or in testimony, and she almost never allows herself to be interviewed.[13] It was only when Odalys asked a question that Nilda talked to her niece about the insurrection:

> [Nilda] would tell me things that were not mentioned at all in school. And when she said those things she explained, "Well, I know this because I lived through it." But in school they did not mention it either because they had no idea of it or because they did not want it to be known. Even today they are not really sure what they want to say. My daughter has a history album and since I know some stories firsthand I asked her teacher once, "How are you going to teach this part of our history to the kids? What are you going to say?" And she answered, "I am not going to tell them. It cannot be told." Did you get it? There are things that cannot be said even now, about the clandestinidad, about its interrelationship with the sierra.

Nilda's extreme reticence to talk about the clandestinidad grows directly out of the fact that her years in the insurgency frame her present life.

When Odalys had, as she put it, "some gaps that I couldn't fill, something that didn't fit into place" that didn't get filled in school, her aunt answered her questions. But no more than this. Why? Odalys concluded: "She is extremely private. She does not want to talk about what she did. She simply does not like to talk about it, does not want to. She did what she did because of her ideals. I did not ask anything because she would not answer. Nothing. . . . These are hidden stories."[14]

But there are surely other factors at play in explaining the scarcity of communication between former clandestinas and their children. One of these is certainly rooted in the drama of daily life in the tumultuous years that followed January 1959: It was a vertigo, as Pilar describes it: Former clandestinas got swept up in the whirlwind. What this meant for their daughters was the virtual absence of their mothers in their daily lives. Mónica Alfonso spoke of being dropped off at her day-care center before it was light out and being picked up by her mother only when it was dark.[15] Similarly, Sonnia Moro's daughter, Alina, recalls waiting for her mother to pick her up after school: "She was the kind of mother who was very passionate about her work and it was obvious. . . . I studied in this really, really, really huge school and sometimes she would come very late to pick me up. And people who saw me, sitting there alone in that big school, cast a pitiful glance at me. But I understood that she was teaching and I was proud that my mother was a professor at the university [of Santiago]."[16]

Sonnia, as well as other clandestinas with whom I spoke who had suspended their education in order to join the insurrection, received a scholarship to go abroad to study. Their children born elsewhere went through their early years outside of Cuba, which inevitably meant a kind of disconnect.

But in more general terms, what would it mean for a child in a schoolroom anywhere on the island to challenge the narrative of the male revolution made in the sierra? Carlos Pino is the son of Selma Díaz (Selma had been a member of the Juventud of the Partido Socialista Popular during the insurrection), and Quintín Pino's entire family had been deeply involved with the 26th of July Movement in Santa Clara. Carlos tells the story of challenging this narrative of the making of the revolution. In the tale presented in his history class, it was only in Santiago, the city always celebrated as the initiator of revolutions, that the November 30, 1956, strike, staged to coincide with the landing of *Granma*, took place:[17]

When I was in senior high school, in tenth grade, we were being taught about the uprising of November 30[, 1956], and I began to read the textbook and I said, "This is a lie. This is a lie because my father was an insurgent; he was the head of the 26th of July Movement in Santa Clara, and he organized the uprising there." You can imagine what happened, can you? A girl said, "No, how can you say that? That's a lie." And then there was this debate in the classroom . . . and then the teacher said to me, "Be quiet, be quiet, be quiet!" because some classmates were attacking me. She said, "No, no! No! He is right, the city of Santa Clara also rose up. That is the truth. I know this because I come from that city, my family is from that city. But the textbook says otherwise and what the textbook says is what I am going to teach you."[18]

Natalia Bolívar narrates a similar incident. One of her daughters, when she was eight years old, returned home from her school in tears. She had asked her teacher why they spent so little time discussing the 13th of March, the day in 1957 that the Directorio attacked the Presidential Palace. The teacher replied, "Because the Directorio betrayed the revolution." Natalia's daughter then turned on her mother, declaring that everything Natalia had told her about the Directorio was a lie. The following day, Natalia and two other compañeros who had been Directorio insurgents went to the school: "And we put up such a stink and asked that all the students meet with us to listen to what we had to say." She reflects: "That has happened constantly to me with my daughters. With my daughters and this entire problem. Because it is really shameful that they are saying those things in class, and then how can I counteract them? The fact is that there are many people who do not want to talk about it because it is still a very delicate matter."[19]

When asked why she did not similarly intervene in what her children were learning in school, Mirta Rodríguez Calderón, the author of numerous articles about the insurgency published in *Bohemia*, replied, "Do you think that I could put them into a contradiction with their situation, their reality, their school? That they go to their teacher and say: 'It was not like that, because my mother says otherwise?' . . . I could not do that."[20]

Almost all of the women I interviewed implicitly or explicitly disdained others who in any way publicized their experiences in the insurgency. It seemed to them gravely wrong to talk about what they had done. It was perceived by them as opportunistic, unprincipled, and a violation of the very reasons for which young women had joined the insurrection in the first place. It was not until decades in the armed forces, when Graciela Aguiar was promoted to be awarded a medal for her service that the people with whom she worked even knew that she had been a clandestina.

For various children of clandestinas with whom I spoke, it was not their mothers' silences that were constraining. Rather, it was the disconnect between their present and their mothers' past. And the problematic of putting together what they knew of the young woman insurrectionary with the mother with whom they grew up. For Mariana Pita Rodríguez, Mirta's daughter, the issue is not so much her mother's participation in the insurrection: She grew up, as she says, in a revolutionary household. Instead, it was the contrast that seemed to exist between the times through which her parents had lived and her own times. And perhaps more than this, how could they, the very people who risked their lives and witnessed their loved ones die to make a revolution, have done nothing to protest publicly what has happened to that revolution?

> The major issue in my life today is to analyze what happened to Cuba and to the revolution. I am proud of being a Cuban, I am proud of my roots, proud of the history of my country, proud of my commitment to my country, to my people, of putting their lives and efforts at the service of an idea or a project, and at the same time I feel sorry for my country, for my people, for what they are going through today. I grew up wondering about the grandeur of those ideals, of all that which involved so many people. And while those ideals began to cave in, to go astray, those same people did not stop to think, "What is going on here?" When I entered my teens, which is the time when you are supposed to be more aware about your looks, about being pretty, the Special Period began. At that moment, I began thinking, "If I am a good student, and if I do what I am supposed to do and my mother is a professional, what is going on here?" Because we underwent really harsh times at home, and then you grow older and start pondering about more profound things that have nothing to do with the economic crisis or lack of material things, and ask yourself more serious questions: How was it that no one realized that the revolution was taking the wrong path? How was it that my mother, who had been in prison, whom I considered to be a brilliant woman . . . how is it that none of the people [involved in the making of the revolution] did not ask themselves "something is wrong"? Or is it that they did,

and decided not to do anything about it? Or they did, but decided that the circumstances were not appropriate to say anything? And that is my big question: How was it that those clever people were not able to ask themselves what was wrong? We lived a beautiful, sublime process which did not work. For people today, that history [the era of the making of the revolution] is a mistake I think that they [the clandestinas] were lucky to have lived that process, lucky to have actively participated in the making of a project of those dimensions, which brought about important social changes, which were good for that moment, but at the same time they were very unfortunate to witness what that project turned out to be.

The 1996 deactivation of MAGIN, she says, crystallized for Mariana what the revolution had become:

MAGIN was founded when I was nineteen years old. I witnessed, with my mother, what MAGIN meant. I witnessed all their progress and also witnessed when one day they were summoned to the Council of State to be told that MAGIN could no longer be. It was at the time when I realized my mother's capacity to work, to generate projects, to generate ideas and put them into practice. I knew that they were successful and I knew they were achieving things, but they were told that they had to stop it [MAGIN]. My mother was very involved, yet she was capable of distancing herself from the problem and looking at it critically. She tried to voice her criticism, but whenever she tried to be critical, censorship mechanisms were activated to silence her and block her way to exercise her criticism constructively.[21]

For Mariana's brother, Turcio, the same questions got raised even more painfully. His mother relates:

When my children grew older, particularly the boy, he started to discover things. This is a very sad and horrible story. He began to discover that many of the things that we had taught him, that we had made him believe in, were not true. When he went to do military service, one night—I always remember that night—he came back very disappointed because they had found out that the military officer who was in charge of their unit had been stealing gas and one of the privates had been forced to do pushups until he fainted, and then they threw him a bucket of water and forced him to do some more. He was very, very depressed and I remember that he came home and sat on the floor and told me: "The revolution you taught me is not the revolution. And the reality you taught me is not the reality." That was hard. We had taught him to love what we loved. And to a certain extent, to idolize what we idolized, and to believe that things were beautiful and crystal clear, that honesty was rock solid. And suddenly they began to find out things on their own.[22]

In 2014 Pilar and her daughters, Renata and Iya, returned to the Fifth Police Station where she had been held for twenty-two days.[23] She had spent her twentieth birthday in her cell in the basement and recorded this on its walls: "Cumplí 20 años en la Quinta Estación de Policía." On the walls, as well, she recorded the passing of days, because in the station, she said, there were no days or nights. When she returned, she asked to see the cell and what she had written. But it had been turned into an apartment, and her writing—her history and a piece of the history of the clandestinidad—was gone forever, buried beneath several coats of paint.

EPILOGUE
AMÉRICA DOMITRO

Let me conclude painfully. In the course of my attempts to speak with daughters of clandestinas, I went to visit Diana-Dianita, the daughter of América Domitro. América was born in Guanabacoa into a political family who came to Cuba from Romania and Ukraine. The family migrated to Santiago, where, influenced greatly by her brother Taras, América became involved in the progressive Baptist Church and, through it, with anti-Batista activities. She met and fell in love with Frank País, also a Baptist Church member, who was at the center of actions and organizing in Santiago and the national leader of the 26th of July Movement in the llano. Frank was, at this time and by all accounts, the llano equivalent of Fidel, in terms of respect, power, and influence. On July 9, 1957, América was shopping with a friend for her wedding clothes—laughing while holding up a frivolous blue nightgown—when she heard the shots. País was assassinated on a street corner in Santiago by Batista's esbirros.[1] His wake was held at América's mother's house. And América passed into the folklore about the Cuban revolution as "the novia of Frank": This is how she is remembered in the few accounts of the revolution that mention her, by others in the clandestinidad, and when her name is brought up with those who did not know her personally. Yet this is hardly the end or indeed the beginning of her story. After Frank's murder, América, quemada in Santiago, went to Havana. She was captured, tortured, and imprisoned in Mantilla. Upon her release, she made her way back across the island and joined the Second Front in the sierra. Following the triumph of the revolution, she married an insurgent—Dianita's father—who had been put in her charge to care for when he was badly burned by the explosives he was using in a failed sabotage attempt. It was a short marriage.

Immediately as I entered her home, Dianita informed me that she did not understand why I wanted to speak with her, that she knew nothing about her mother.[2] I explained that I was there not to discuss América, but to talk about her. As we sat down I noted the bare walls of the room in which we were: There was absolutely nothing on these walls that reflected the inhabitants of the house. Dianita began again by asserting that she did not know América; her mother had died when Dianita was seven years old. Gradually, the tale emerged: After the triumph, suffering from "nerves," América spent Monday through Friday every week in a hospital, and when she returned home on the weekend, she would shut herself in her room. When Dianita was seven, América committed suicide with an overdose of pills. Some assert it was accidental; others said that she never got over Frank. Seven-year-old Dianita, indeed fifty-year-old Dianita, understood it bitterly as abandonment: Her mother did not love her enough to live for her. After her mother's death, Dianita went to live with her father. It was not a good relationship. She spent some weekends with her grandmother, América's mother. But when she asked her grandmother about América, the woman would weep.

Dianita then brought out a thick folder to show me. She had kept every article she could find that mentioned her mother, every photograph, the poems Frank had written to América. The file, for her, was her mother.

As I left she begged me to remember her, or, if I couldn't, to remember that she was Dianita, the daughter of América, who was the novia of Frank País. Two women then, given the prevailing historical narrative, stripped of their own identities.

CLANDESTINAS
A VISUAL ESSAY

From Family Collections and State Archives
Havana, Cuba, January 2023

COMPILED BY SUSAN MEISELAS

RESEARCH WITH CAROLLEE BENGELSDORF AND ROBERTO GARCÍA

PRODUCTION DESIGN BY KRISTINA SUMFLETH

THE NARRATIVE TOLD BY THESE PHOTOGRAPHS ATTEMPTS to give life to the women who populate *Clandestinas*, to situate them as protagonists in an insurrection that has been understood and related virtually exclusively in terms of its male participants. Our purpose in this photographic series is to complement the testimonies in the manuscript and reveal these young women who chose to risk their lives to defeat the dictatorship.

To do this work and create our selection, we followed four paths. We gathered personal photographs from several family collections and returned with the women to sites of memory that were the most impactful and in many senses most traumatic in their experiences as insurgents. We searched through various archives that housed material about the 1950s insurrection, most notably the Oficina de Asuntos Históricos de la Presidencia de la República de Cuba; the magazine *Bohemia*, which published before, during, and after the period of the insurrection; the archives of the Federación de Mujeres Cubanas; and the Havana archive of the Asociación Provincial de Combatientes. We simultaneously photographed publications to document our process.

In gaining access to some of these archives, we asked for and got the aid of well-placed Cubans who were key to facilitating our work. We then went back to the former clandestinas and to others we thought might assist us in identifying individuals and events pictured in the photographs to properly date them.

We have included family portraits, landscapes of memory, archival documentation of street protests, and images of women at trials and in detention cells.

THIS CHART FEATURES PICTURES OF CUBAN REVOLUTIONARIES dating from the nineteenth-century wars of independence to the 1950s insurrection. It is used by the Club Martiano de Herencia Rebelde, who are children of the 1950s insurgents, when they speak to younger generations about Havana's revolutionary history. Notably absent from the chart are any pictures of the women who participated in Cuba's centuries-long revolutionary struggles.

PATRIOTAS REPRESENTATIVOS CIUDAD DE LA HABANA

Casiguaguas	José A. Aponte y Ulabarra	Felix Varela y Morales	José de la Luz y Caballero	José M. Aguirre Valdés	Adolfo del Castillo Sánchez
Juan Bruno Zayas Alfonso	Néstor Aranguren Martínez	Juan Delgado González	Luis de Ayestarán Moliner	Manuel Sanguily Garrit	Julio A. Mella McPartland
Carlos Baliños	Alfredo López Arencibia	Rafael Trejo González	Francisco González Cueto "Paquito"	Rubén Martínez Villena	Antonio Guiteras Holmes
Aracelio Iglesias Díaz	Camilo Cienfuegos Gorriarán	Juan Manuel Márquez Rodríguez	Antonio López Fernández "Nico"	Abel Santamaría Cuadrado	Raúl Gómez García
Sergio González "El Curita" López	Gerardo Abreu "Fontán"	Juan Manuel Ameijeiras Delgado	Gustavo Ameijeiras Delgado	Angel Ameijeiras Delgado "Machaco"	Arístides Viera González "Mingolo"
José A. Echeverría Blanchi "Manzanita"	Blas Roca Calderío	Lázaro Peña González	Manuel Ascunce Domenech	Gustavo Machín Hoed Debeche	Raúl Díaz Arguelles

MIRTA RODRÍGUEZ CALDERÓN

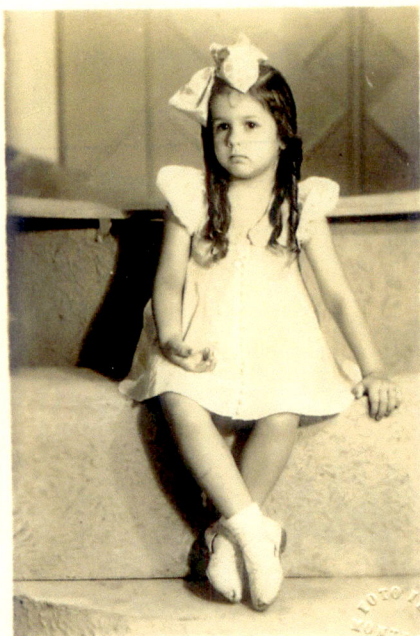

MIRTA RODRÍGUEZ CALDERÓN at ages three and six. At age seventeen, Mirta was a student in the first year at the Escuela Normal in Havana. Through her friendship with Niurka Lipiz, who was already working with the 26th of July Movement, Mirta became involved in the underground.

MIRTA RODRÍGUEZ CALDERÓN, AT NINETEEN, in Mexico in October 1958. Mirta was arrested attempting to set off fósforo vivo in the fur section of the upscale department store El Encanto. In the police station to which she was taken, she was made to hear her father being beaten and was told that he was dead. When she was released, given threats against her family, she was sent into exile in Mexico where she continued to work with 26th of July militants.

SONNIA MORO

IN THESE FAMILY PORTRAITS, Sonnia Moro is pictured at three and thirteen. As a student in Pittman, a private high school, Sonnia, through her friendship with Mirta Rodríguez Calderón, became involved in the underground. She worked with the Frente Estudiantil Nacional of the July 26th Movement, which encompassed students in secondary school.

Digna ABREU MAREGAL. "...cerca de una hora estuvieron golpeándonos con los puños". (Foto Marcelo).

Teresa ABREU MAREGAL. "...nos despertaban para describirnos torturas infames". (Foto Marcelo).

HOMBRES QUE FUERON BESTIAS

Por JESUS LOPEZ GOMEZ
Fotos de MARCELO

LA caída del batistato y la huida del tirano y su "élite" a pócó cuatro semanas, puso punto final a una horrible pesadilla de torturas y sadismos inconfesables, que difícilmente pueden encontrar paralelo en las mazmorras de la Edad Media.

Ni uno solo de los Derechos del Hombre dejó de ser hollado, ni uno solo de los refinamientos más degradantes dejó de ser utilizado, tal y como si una mentalidad nacida para el mal, hubiera estudiado minuciosamente su empleo y creado nuevos medios de suplicios.

No recuerda la historia cubana un documento más crispante y que más sobrecoja el alma que el "Presidio Político en Cuba", de nuestro José Martí; pero ahora, cuando se escriba a fondo la vesanía de los esbirros del régimen derrotado, aquellas revelaciones desgarradoras del Apóstol en sus confesiones, quedarán en un segundo término desalojadas por las más inverosímiles y bestiales realidades de nuestra época.

El mejor reportaje periodístico que pudiera darse a la publicidad nunca podrá ser escrito, al menos, tomando sus datos por relato de los que sufrieron los "arpazos de aquellos entes demoníacos, porque forman hoy día las listas de muertos o desaparecidos. Quizá alguna vez, ocultos en algún lugar ignorado aparezcan osamentas desfiguradas o quebradas con las que podrán identificarse a algunos de ellos.

Más de tres semanas han pasado y todavía continúan recibiéndose acusaciones de familiares que reclaman sus seres queridos, arrancados a viva fuerza de sus brazos para no aparecer nunca más o para ser hallados en cualquier rincón capitalino con los cuerpos balaceados y presentando signos inequívocos de perversas mutilaciones y torturas.

Muy escaso descanso han podido darse desde entonces Hirám Martínez Grave de Peralta, Ramoncito Vásquez y otros valiosos jóvenes revolucionarios a quienes se ha dado la tarea de atender cientos y cientos de casos espeluznantes muchos de los cuales, por lo atentatorio a la sensibilidad del público lector tenemos que privarnos de dar a conocer.

Teresa y Digna Abreu Maregal, fueron detenidas por agentes del chacal Ventura, tras el tiroteo de la calle Avellaneda 162, en el que fué abatido inerme, después de entregarse, José Angel Rosell, y del que lograron escapar "Machaco" Almejeira, José Antonio Fernández y Emilio Díaz Machado: el primero para caer poco después.

Las hermanas Abreu Maregal fueron conducidas a la fatídica Novena Estación. No menos de una docena de esbirros esperaban por ellas.

—Cerca de una hora estuvieron golpeándonos con los puños,

Un relato de los supervivientes de las mazmorras de Ventura, Carratalá y los grandes esbirros de la dictadura de Batista. Éstos son los testimonios de unos cuantos de los millares de víctimas de la dictadura, que ponen de manifiesto la brutalidad y criminalidad del régimen.

En el centro aparece el doctor Tomás Electo PEDROSA; a la izquierda, Ramón VÁZQUEZ, y a la derecha, el capitán Hirán MARTÍNEZ GRAVE DE PERALTA, todos ellos fueron detenidos y torturados despiadadamente. (Foto Marcelo).

54

DIGNA ABREU, NINETEEN, AND HER SISTER TERESA, TWENTY-ONE, came to Havana from their home in Santa Clara looking for work. They became involved in the 26th of July Movement through their relationship with their cousin Julio Dámaso and his mother, María Abreu. Digna proposed, planned, and executed the robbery of a house full of arms, inserting herself in the house as a cleaning woman. Teresa was among the key people carrying arms and supplies to nascent 26th of July Movement fronts in Pinar del Río. Both Digna and Teresa, along with Pilar Sa, were trapped in a house where weapons were stored and were severely tortured. Digna reflects that it was unclear whether the extreme degree to which they were beaten was in reaction to their activities in the clandestine movement or the fact that they were black. They remained imprisoned until the overthrow of the dictatorship on January 1, 1959.

NILDA RAVELO

AT AGE SEVENTEEN NILDA RAVELO began a profound involvement in the 26th of July Movement. The Escuela Provincial de Comercio de La Habana, which she attended, was one of the hotbeds of student organization in what became the youth brigades of the 26th of July Movement. Nilda, along with Pilar Sa and Mariíta Trasancos, was one of the organizers of the first student brigade. She was first arrested in a plot to assassinate Batista and was the longest-lasting prisoner in Mantilla, the women's holding prison. When told by her lawyer, Dora Rivas, that with money under the table and her agreement to go into exile in Mexico she could get out of prison, Nilda replied, "Neither in external exile [Mexico] nor in internal exile [the sierra]."

HIDELISA ESPERÓN

HIDELISA ESPERÓN, AGE SIXTEEN when she joined the underground, lived as the fictive wife of Machaco Ameijeiras, the head of Action and Sabotage in Havana from May 1958 until he was assassinated in November of that year. Hidelisa and the men with whom she lived practiced shooting in a field close to where they lived in San Miguel del Padrón. In October 1958 she was caught in a safe house with two other clandestinas who were in Action and Sabotage. Hidelisa was dragged to the notorious Ninth Police Station where under the directive of Ventura, the chief of the station, she was raped. Because she was a minor she could not be held and was released into the custody of her father.

PILAR SA

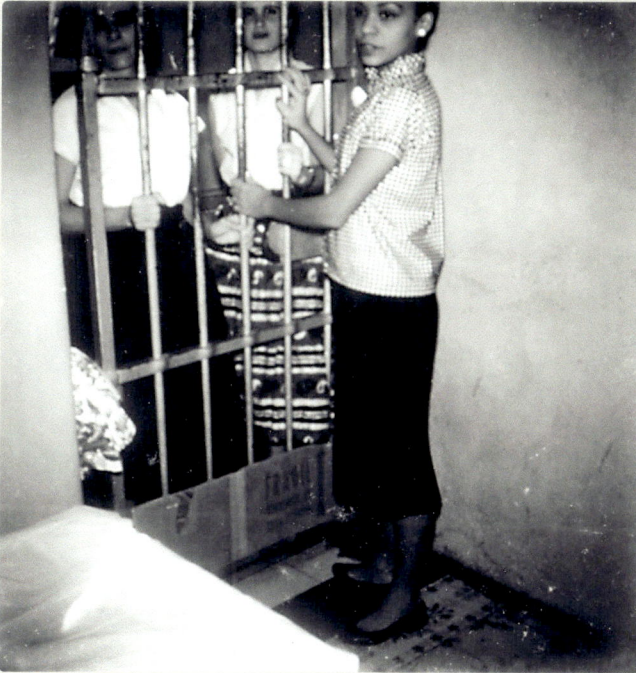

THE FIRST IMAGE IS OF PILAR SA AT AGE TWELVE at her elementary school graduation. Four years later Pilar was intensely involved in the underground movement. She lived as the fictive wife of one of its leaders. After he was assassinated, she carried his gun to a safe house where she was entrapped by Batista's esbirros. She remained in jail until the revolution took power on January 1, 1959.

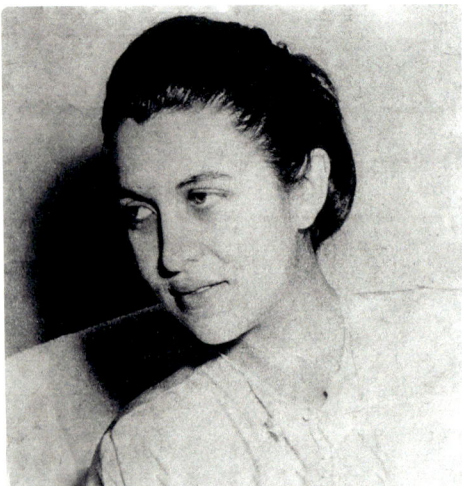

MARTA JIMÉNEZ

MARTA JIMÉNEZ, a militant in the Directorio Revolucionario, in March 1957.

MARTA WAS EIGHT MONTHS' PREGNANT when her husband, Fructuoso Rodríguez, a Directorio Revolucionario leader, was murdered with three others by Lt. Colonel Esteban Ventura's henchmen at Humbolt 7 where they were hiding after their failed attack on the Presidential Palace. Fructuoso's public funeral was the occasion for open protest against the regime. In the photograph Marta walks in front of her husband's casket, forcing her way through the line of police attempting to block the funeral procession.

A YOUNG BOY staring at a bloody staircase in the aftermath of the murders of four Directorio leaders at Humboldt 7 became a symbol of Ventura's cruelty.

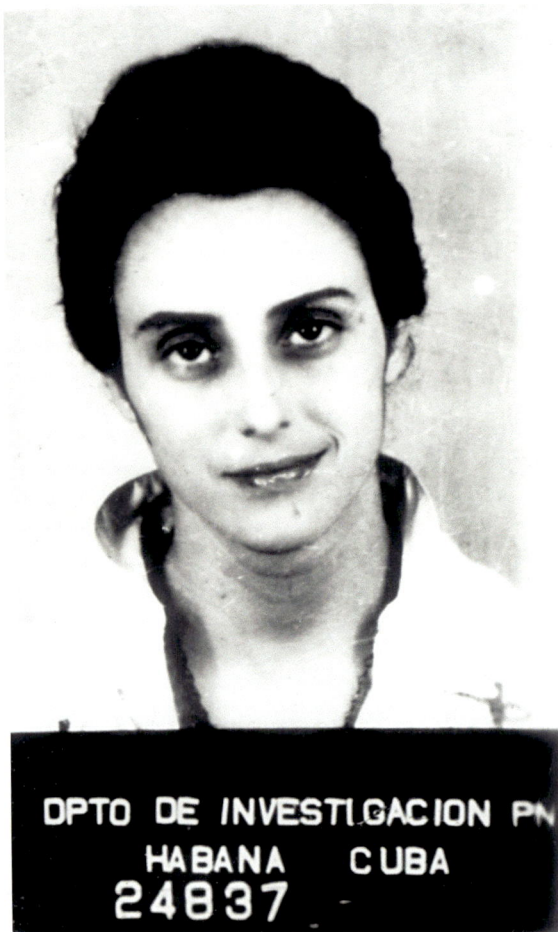

DPTO DE INVESTIGACION PN
HABANA   CUBA
24837

NATALIA BOLÍVAR ARÓSTEGUI

NATALIA BOLÍVAR ARÓSTEGUI WAS BORN into an upper-class family from which she rebelled. During the insurrection, she was a militant in the Directorio Revolucionario (DR). She was also one of the founding members of the Mujeres Oposicionistas Unidas, a woman's organization that grew out of the Frente Cívico de Mujeres Martianas. Natalia played a central role in hiding and supplying arms to the men involved in the DR's failed attack on the Presidential Palace on March 13, 1957. When Natalia was arrested in July 1958, the esbirros found incriminating papers related to her involvement with both the Directorio and the 26th of July Movement.

MARIÍTA TRASANCOS

THESE IMAGES OF MARIÍTA TRASANCOS depict her first at age six and then on her 1955 ID card for the Escuela Profesional de Comercio de La Habana. Her political activism at school began with exposing what were labeled profesores de dedo, or unqualified professors who had gotten their jobs through personal connections. With eight other students, she formed one of the first 26th of July Movement youth brigades. She was arrested twice and released only because she was a minor.

AIDA PELAYO WAS KNOWN POPULARLY AS THE "ORATOR OF THE BARRICADES." She began her revolutionary involvement in the left wing of the 1920s–1930s student insurrection. She never wavered from her course. In the months directly following the 1952 Batista coup, she and three other women formulated the idea of creating an all-women's anti-Batista organization aimed at bringing down the dictatorship. This organization was the Frente Cívico de Mujeres Martianas.

AIDA PELAYO

AIDA PELAYO, ALONG WITH MEMBERS OF THE FRENTE CÍVICO DE MUJERES MARTIANAS, played a critical role in a range of contexts in the insurrection, particularly in Havana. Aida was arrested innumerable times during the years of the dictatorship; in 1953 she was arrested for supposedly being involved in the attack on the Moncada fortress in Santiago, led by Fidel Castro. At his trial following the attack, Fidel was asked to give an account of Aida's role in the attack, and he replied, "Every time a gunshot goes off on the island, Aida is arrested."

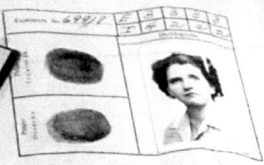

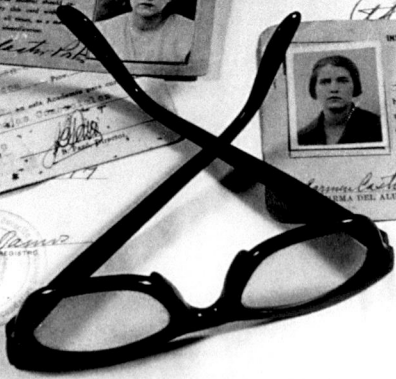

CARMEN CASTRO

CARMEN CASTRO (BACK ROW, SEVENTH FROM THE LEFT) had the distinction of being one of only thirteen women ever imprisoned in Nueva Gerona on the Isle of Pines. Later, Fidel Castro and the survivors of the 1953 attack on the Moncada fortress in Santiago would be inmates at the same jail. Carmen was in prison from 1932 to 1933, falsely accused of setting a bomb in front of a house where members of Machado's regime were meeting. Her involvement in the 1930 revolution, along with Aida Pelayo, would directly inform their idea for the 1953 organization of the Frente Cívico de Mujeres Martianas (FCMM). If Aida was the orator of the barricades, Carmen was always referred to as the brain. She organized and orchestrated marches that the FCMM led or in which they participated, and took charge of writing its public manifestos.

El encuentro con Fidel y con Celia, en la Comandancia de La Plata...

PASTORITA NÚÑEZ PARTICIPATED IN HER FIRST DEMONSTRATION against the Machado dictatorship when she was twelve. During the April 9, 1958, strike Pastorita was put in charge of the Comando Femenino, which made Molotov cocktails, transported arms and men, and organized and operated emergency medical stations. Quemada, or "burnt," that is, in too much danger to remain in Havana after the failure of the strike, she went to Fidel Castro's front in the sierra and was put in charge of collecting taxes from US businesses operating in the region. Here she is pictured in the sierra with Fidel and Celia Sanchez. In the first years after the revolution took power she organized and led the effort to rapidly build housing, including Havana del Este, which remains the finest constructed community on the island. The homes built under her authority are still recalled by their residents as "Pastorita's houses."

PASTORITA NÚÑEZ

PASTORITA NÚÑEZ SERVED ON THE NATIONAL EXECUTIVE committee of Eduardo Chibás's Ortodoxo Party, and she ardently supported him. Chibás's Sunday evening radio broadcasts denouncing corruption among government officials electrified the country. In 1951, during one of these broadcasts Chibás committed suicide. This photo shows Pastorita marching along with a contingent of male Party members to Chibás's funeral in Colon cemetery. She was one of the four women, along with Aida Pelayo, Carmen Castro, and Marta Frayde, who formulated the idea for the Frente Cívico de Mujeres Martianas.

SEARCHING THROUGH the archive of Casa de los Combatientes in Havana.

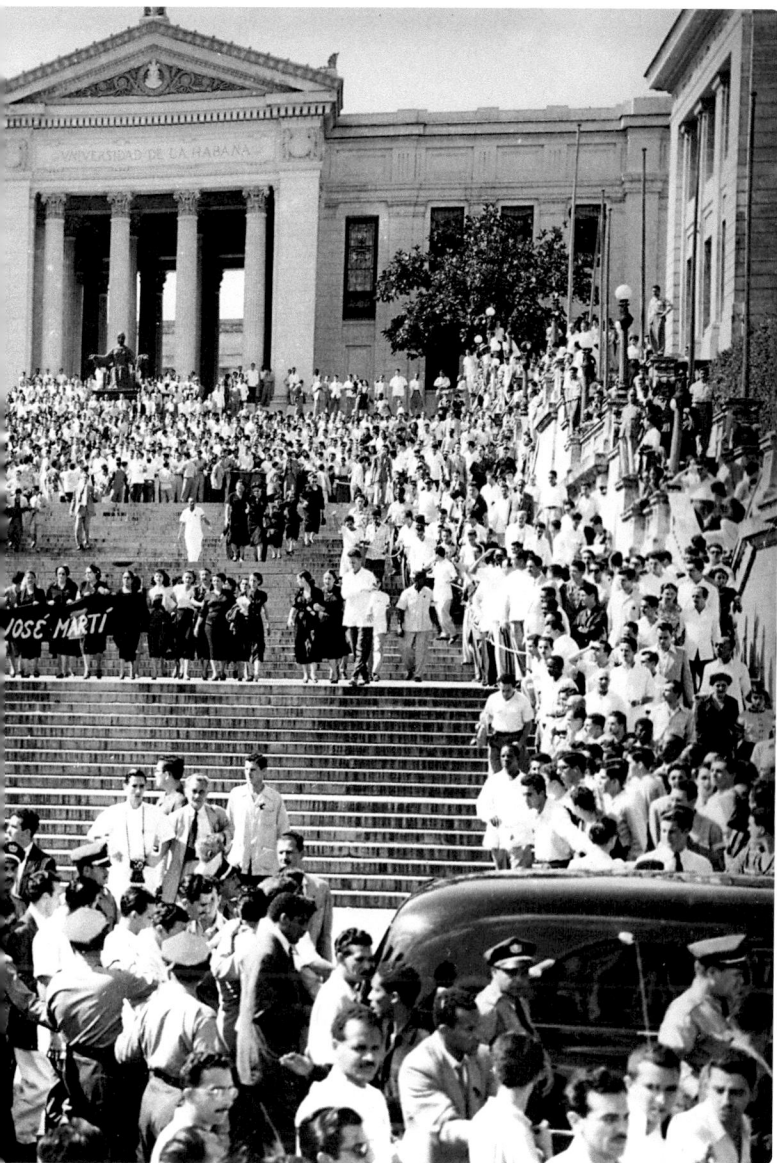

ON FEBRUARY 13, 1953, a demonstration followed the first killing of a university student, Rubén Batista. The banner reading "The Blood of the Just Is Not Shed in Vain" is held up entirely by members of the Frente Cívico de Mujeres Martianas, who always carried a banner containing José Martí's words when protesting in public.

THE FIRST MOTHERS' march in Santiago. This silent demonstration followed the murder of William Soler on December 30, 1956. William Soler was fifteen years old.

PARTICIPANTS OF THE SECOND mothers' march in Santiago.

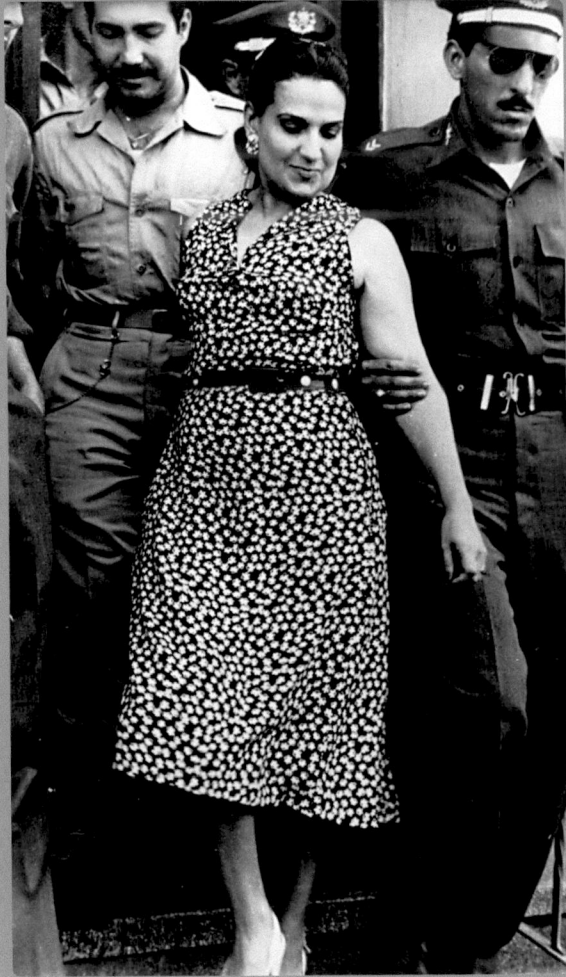

EVA JIMÉNEZ WAS ONE OF THE FOUNDERS of the Frente Cívico de Mujeres Martianas. In April 1952, a month after the coup d'état, she was part of an aborted plan headed by Rafael Bárcenas, a university professor, to attack the army headquarters at Campo Columbia. Here, she is being taken to trial for later actions.

IN THIS BOOK, ON THE LEFT PAGE, are portraits of Olga Román, Eva Jiménez, Alicia de Armas, and Mercedes Rodríguez, all Martianas, who were detained after a physical confrontation with the police who attempted to block the women marching. The righthand page portrays the Martianas in the process of dissolving the Frente Cívico de Mujeres Martianas on January 28, 1959, the birthday of José Martí, in front of Martí's tomb in Santiago. Aida Pelayo, giving what in essence was its eulogy, declared that its tasks had been accomplished.

MARTIANAS ON TRIAL IN DECEMBER 1957 after the Galiano march. From left to right are Margarita Roqueta (second from left, in a dark dress), Mercedes Rodríguez, Margot Aniceto (in dark glasses), Lolo Pérez, Dolores Nieves López, Emma Surí, and Aida Pelayo (in a white blouse).

IN FEBRUARY 1957, the trial of Nilda Ravelo, Lilia Mesa, Faustino Pérez (head of the 26th of July Movement in Havana), and Enrique Hart occurred. They had been trapped in an apartment in Vedado where armaments were stored. They met in that apartment to plan the assassination of Batista. Nilda knew where Batista would be on a certain date, and this formed the basis of the plan.

ÁNGELA ALONSO IS ACCOMPANIED INTO COURT BY her lawyers and Dora Rivas, who represented multiple arrested clandestinas. Alonso was captured as she took part in sabotage actions in one of the nascent 26th of July fronts in Pinar del Río. Imprisoned in Mantilla, she and Mirta Rodríguez Calderón undertook a hunger strike in sympathy with the hunger strike in the men's holding prison El Príncipe.

IN JULY 1957, WOMEN MARCHED in support of the prisoners on hunger strike in El Príncipe, demanding the ouster of Ugalde, who controlled the Isle of Pines prison. The march included women from a wide range of groups. It was organized and led by young girls who were members of the Frente Cívico de Mujeres Martianas with the help of Carmen Castro. It began on Galiano Street; despite being under violent attack by the police, a group of the marchers made their way to 23rd Street to the CMQ television station. As they passed by the site of the Havana Hilton, then under construction, workers pelted the police with anything at hand.

MARIÍTA TRASANCOS AND NORMA PORRAS (RIGHT),
who helped organize the 1957 march.

THE NIGHT OF ONE HUNDRED BOMBS, on November 8, 1957, was intended to wake up the residents of Havana to the existence of an insurgency to bring down Batista. The bombing was the idea of Sergio González, El Curita (on the left), who planned the action with Gerardo Abreu Fontán, the head of the 26th of July youth brigades. The material for the explosives was gathered by Mariíta Trasancos, who, with Norma Porras, Digna and Teresa Abreu, and Pilar Sa, assembled the bombs. Mariíta distributed these explosives, which were set off in Barrios throughout the city by militants in the student brigades and the Civic Resistance Movement.

ONE OF THE FREQUENT PRESS conferences in 1957 at which 26th of July Movement prisoners and their arms were on display. Each of the prisoners was dressed in neat clothes for the occasion. The press conference was presided over by Esteban Ventura, dressed in a white suit. He was officially the head of the Ninth Police Station but in fact circulated among various stations and supervised the torture of those arrested. Present as well was General Pilar García (fourth from right), the chief of the National Police. Nilda Ravelo (in the darker dress) served as a courier between Faustino Pérez, the head of the 26th of July Movement in Havana, and the heads of Action and Sabotage. Next to Nilda is Jesusa Baltar, a Spanish woman in Action and Sabotage. Her house was a meeting place for insurgent leaders.

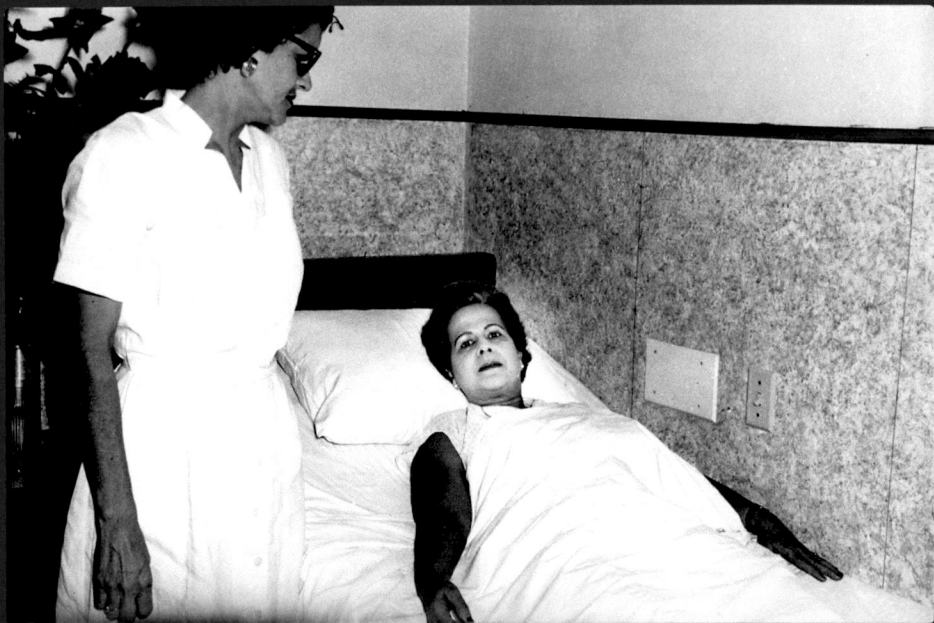

IN FEBRUARY 1958, ESTERLINA MILANÉS was taken prisoner, raped with an umbrella, and tortured. Batista had temporarily lifted censorship, and as a result her brutal treatment was widely publicized both in Cuban and international presses.

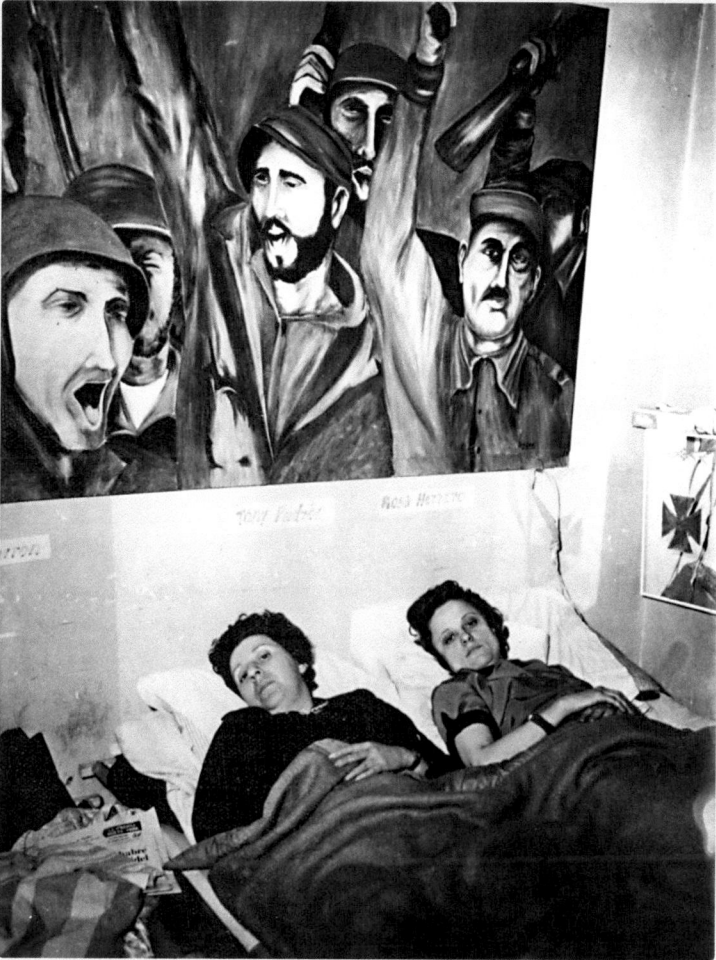

IN NEW YORK, ON MARCH 31, 1958, five members of the Ortodoxo Party, affiliated with the Civic Resistance Movement, began a hunger strike to protest the detention of thirty-six Cubanos in Brownsville, Texas.

THIS ARMBAND WAS WORN BY WOMEN in one of the two groups organized directly after the revolution took power to mobilize women in various ways to actively support it. Both were called into being by the 26th of July Movement leadership and both were headed by women who had been in the clandestine movement. The Women's Section of the 26th of July Movement in Havana was organized by Mirta Rodríguez Calderón and worked around the port area among poor women. The second, the Women's Revolutionary Brigade, was organized by Gladys Marel García and, among other things, demonstrated publicly in support of policies being enacted by the revolution. When the 26th of July Movement dissolved in 1962 to form the Integrated Revolutionary Organizations (ORI), which also encompassed the Partido Socialista Popular and the Directorio Revolucionario, both women's groups were dissolved with it. Neither played a role of any significance in the formation and institutionalization of what would become the Federation of Cuban Women, the formal women's organization in Cuba.

GLADYS MAREL GARCÍA is at the head of a demonstration in 1959 by the Women's Revolutionary Brigade to protest against those opposing the execution of men who had killed and tortured under Batista.

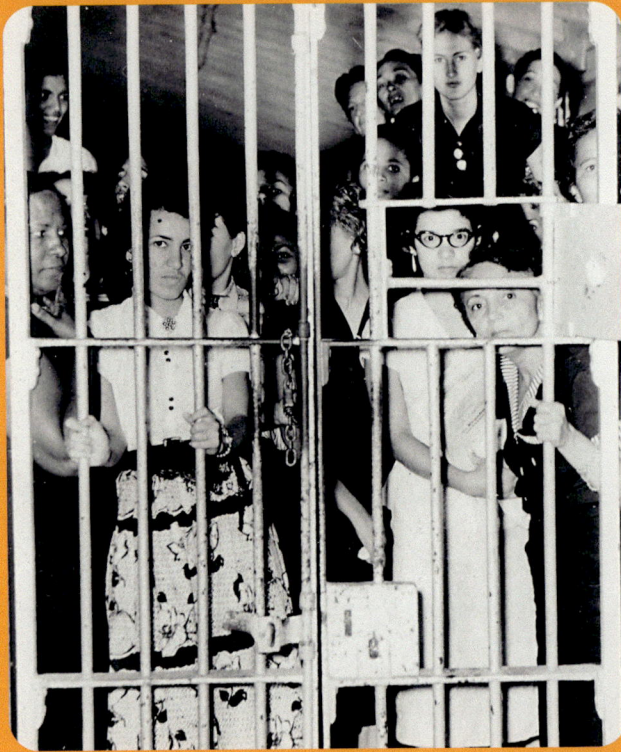

Nilda Ravelo recluida en
el Vivac de Mantilla.

THESE IMAGES SHOW WOMEN in detention. Nilda Ravelo
points to herself in a photograph that remains on display
at the Cárcel de Mantilla.

NILDA RAVELO is looking at the clothes that she wore when she arrived at the Cárcel de Mantilla.

THIS HOUSE WAS THE LOCATION in which Digna Abreu, her sister Teresa, Pilar Sa, and two male insurgent leaders were caught in a police raid. The weapons stored in the house were destined for 26th of July fronts in Pinar del Rio.

AT EL PRÍNCIPE, THE MEN'S HOLDING PRISON, women, mainly mothers and sisters, had lined up daily to visit prisoners. Men, whether brothers or fathers, would have raised suspicions had they been visitors. Mixed with family members were girls like Sonnia Moro, related to the 26th of July Movement or

the Directorio, carrying messages to the prisoners. These visits were one of the major channels through which girls became more deeply involved in the insurgent movements.

THIS IMAGE DEPICTS JULIO DÁMASO'S OFFICE at Casa de los Combatientes of Havana in January 2023. Casa de los Combatientes is one of the disparate sites at which material dealing with the 1950s insurrection are housed. The Office of the Asociación de Combatientes de la Revolución Cubana is carefully watched over by Dámaso, who was himself a clandestino and captain of Action and Sabotage in a Havana municipality. Assembled in this office is a wealth of writings of the clandestine movement in Havana, including old

newspapers, pamphlets, unpublished documents, and largely unavailable books. While materials related to clandestinas are among the collection in this office, the balance of what is there and what is therefore made available overwhelmingly concerns the men who fought in the underground movement.

NOTES

1   The terms *sierra* and *Sierra* mean two different things throughout the text: *sierra* refers to the *guerrilla* fighters led by Fidel Castro, who established a base and fought the Batista regime in the eastern mountains of Cuba; *Sierra* always means the Sierra Maestra mountains themselves. *Llano*, which literally means "valley," or "plain," was used to describe the urban insurgency.

       Although this is far from clear, *sierra* and *llano* were probably terms that came into general use following the triumph of the revolution (interview with Juan Valdés Paz, May 2014). Magali Jacobo, who fought in the clandestine movement in Guantánamo and later in the sierra, gives perhaps the most logical explanation of the origin of the term. She recalls from her time in the sierra that *llano* was a general term used by campesinos in the region to describe the cities (personal correspondence, April 2018).

2   Ross, *May '68 and Its Afterlives.*

3   Provided by the Club Martiano de Herencia Rebelde. This chart of faces of the heroes is reproduced in this book's visual essay.

4   Interview with Juan Valdés Paz, Havana, May 2012.

5   Pérez, *The Structure of Cuban History*, 160, 157.

6   Carlos Manuel de Céspedes, who served from 1869 to 1873 as the first president of the Cuban Republic in Arms, issued the call that initiated the 1868–78 War of Independence (the Ten Years' War). He was killed by the Spanish in 1874. Antonio Maceo and Máximo Gómez fought in each of the wars of independence. Gómez was commander-in-chief of the Cuban rebel army in the 1895–98 war and Maceo was major general, or second in command. Maceo died in battle in 1896. José Martí, the brilliant poet and writer, organized the Cuban Party of Independence that initiated the 1895–98 war. He died in battle in 1895.

7   Ferrer, *Insurgent Cuba*, 2. Ferrer notes the dramatic differences in the geography of slavery across the island, largely a direct result of the concentration of sugar production. Thus, in 1862 in the eastern city of Bayamo, slaves and free people of color accounted for 12.6 percent of the population. In Cárdenas, in Matanzas Province, a hub of sugar production in 1862, slaves made up 48.7 percent of the population.

8 Africanos de nación were slaves who had been born in Africa. Peninsulares were Spaniards living on the island.

9 Sommer, *Foundational Fictions*.

10 Ferrer, *Insurgent Cuba*, 122.

11 Ferrer, *Insurgent Cuba*, 126 (brackets in Ferrer's text).

12 Ferrer, *Insurgent Cuba*, 126.

13 See Kutzinski, *Sugar's Secrets*, 163–98. The feminist literary scholar Eve Kosofsky Sedgwick, in her foundational study, *Between Men*, gives perhaps the clearest account of the idea and congruent implications of male homosocial construction. Discussing her book's subtitle and its theme, *English Literature and Male Homosocial Desire*, Sedgwick writes that homosocial desire "is a kind of oxymoron. 'Homosocial' is a word occasionally used in history and the social sciences, where it describes social bonding between persons of the same sex; it is a neologism, obviously formed by analogy with 'homosexual' and just as obviously meant to be distinguished from 'homosexual.' . . . I do not mean to discuss genital homosexual desire as 'at the root of' other forms of male homosociality—but rather a strategy for making generalizations about and marking historical differences in the structure of men's relations with other men" (1–2).

14 Ferrer, *Insurgent Cuba*, 127.

15 See Pérez, *To Die in Cuba*; Bustamante, *Cuban Memory Wars*, 25–63.

16 *Granma* was a broken-down former yacht in which Fidel and eighty-two rebels returned to Cuba from Mexico. Bustamante, *Cuban Memory Wars*, 33.

17 Sarabia, *Ana Betancourt Agramonte*, 59.

18 Cited in Hernández Alonso, "Ana Betancourt."

19 Cento, *Nadie puede ser indiferente*.

20 Cento, *Nadie puede ser indiferente*, 114, 131. The treatment of the women who were combatants in the 1895–98 war illustrated what happens when the borders of the male construct are threatened. Lynn Stoner, in the prelude to her study of the women's movement in twentieth-century Cuba, *From the House to the Streets*, writes that in this second war of independence, "mambisas moved into the masculine sphere of military affairs and won men's respect for their efforts." While this assertion is in itself problematic more problematic still was the treatment of these women in the aftermath of the war. The Camagueyan historian Elda Cento relates the story of Adela Ascuy Labrador, who during the war and by its end had fought on the front lines in some forty-nine combats. But at its conclusion she was denied the pay given to the troops during their demobilization on the grounds that her "condition as a woman"

rendered improbable any military actions by her. The Settlement Commission ruled: "Because of her sex the plaintiff could not have been able to render services in the army; therefore, her request is hereby rejected."

21   The stories about women in the narrative of the Ten Years' War are concerned virtually exclusively on the wives of the white mambí leadership. Thus for instance the story of Amalia Simoni and by contrast the brief mentions of her sister Matilde. Amalia Simoni is portrayed in the literature as eternally selfless, eternally pure, faithful even in the face of the death of her husband Ignacio Agramonte, and through this to the nation. She serves as a stereotype, forever frozen in time. As the eternally faithful wife, she is positioned as secondary in the insurrection; her life is entirely focused on unending support for him and later to his memory. Her sexual abstinence, that is, her desexualization, thus serves to naturalize and reinforce the male construction of the nation. Biographers write of her that "she was characterized fundamentally by her stoic resistance, her discretion, her fidelity to her husband and her determined commitment to the patria, and her unbreakable belief in its independence. She did not seek the role of a protagonist: hers was to support, to give strength and to hope" (Méndez and Pérez Pino, *Amalia Simoni*, 85). By definition, then, the abnegada viuda must never remarry. Remarriage would mean in effect a betrayal of her dead mambí husband and thereby of the national project. The implication of sexual activity represented a potential incursion into the male construct, with consequences not only for the women but even for her dead husband. Yet this is exactly what Matilde Simoni, Amalia's sister and the wife of Eduardo Agramonte (Ignacio Agramonte's cousin) did. She remarried six months after she learned of Eduardo's death in battle. In doing this, Matilde had abandoned her dead husband, and, in remarrying and presumably renewing sexual relations, she had violated the demands of purity that were a measure of her loyalty to the war effort and thereby her position in the project of the nation. In the scant mentions of her in accounts of the Ten Years' War she is portrayed almost always in comparison to her sister as having "a more shallow and ordinary personality" and in exile unable to fend for herself (141).

A century later in the 1950s insurrection there was, of course, no question about the nationality of women in the underground insurrection. Nor was their relation to the battle to overthrow the dictatorship mediated through men. Nonetheless, a violation of sexual abstinence was understood as a betrayal of the project of the nation-to-be-reborn, as a deviation from the commitment to the struggle to realize that nation. The narrative of desexualized relationships in the clandestinidad as requisite proof of devotion to the nation purified would surface once again, particularly in the stories of the men and women who lived together. Pilar Sa lived with a captain in the Havana underground as his fictive wife. In due course a romantic attachment developed between them but was never acted upon. As Pilar said, that would have been an irremediable violation of the insurrection's very purpose, a deviation from the sole aim of bringing down the dictatorship. The two slept every night on the floor of the apartment in which they lived, separated by a barrier of newspapers that served as a pillow and was never crossed (interview with Pilar Sa, Havana, May 2014). Chase notes that male rebels were free to engage in sexual activity with women who were not in the underground (Chase, *Revolution Within the Revolution*, 103). But in fact sex with a woman in the movement had no consequences for these men either. The abiding male construct of the insurrection and its purpose dictated that virtually by definition men were subject to no form of policing of their sexual engagements, nor did they suffer any diminution of position or power.

22   See Pilar Sa's story in chapter 4.

23   Chase, *Revolution Within the Revolution*, 6, 19–44. Bayard de Volo calls these actions by women to deny Batista legitimacy "winning hearts and minds," a phrase that circulated widely in the United States during the war in Vietnam (*Women and the Cuban Insurrection*, 65–73).

24   Chase, *Revolution Within the Revolution*, 92–97; Chase, "Women's Organizations and the Politics of Gender in Cuba's Urban Insurrection 1952–1958."

25   See Kruijt, *Cuba and Revolutionary Latin America*, 31.

26   The Partido Socialista Popular and its youth branch, given their opposition to the strategy of armed struggle, explicitly threatened ejection from the Party any members who also worked with the 26th of July Movement or the Directorio. The girl I mention here was thirteen when she joined the Juventud and appears to have been only loosely connected to it. (See the account given by Consuelo Elba in chapter 4.)

27   See, for example, Rodríguez Calderón, *Semillas de fuego*; Castro Porta et al., *La lección del Maestro*; Bell Lara et al., *Cuba: La generación revolucionaria: 1952–1961*; Bell Lara et al., *Cuba: Las mujeres en la insurrección 1952–1961*; Bell Lara et al., *Combatientes*; Meyer, *El futuro era nuestro*; Nieves, *Rogelio*; and Consuelo Elba's 2017 film *Mujeres de la clandestinidad*. Studies in English that draw on

interviews to varying degrees include Klouzal, *Women and Rebel Communities*; Shayne, *The Revolution Question*; Maloof, *Voices of Resistance*; Bayard de Volo, *Women and the Cuban Insurrection*; and Chase, *Revolution Within the Revolution*.

28 Jelin, "Citizenship and Identity," 8.

29 Portelli, *The Death of Luigi Trastulli and Other Stories*, 52.

30 Ross, *May '68 and Its Afterlives*, 1.

31 Ross, *May '68 and Its Afterlives*, 17.

32 Chase, *Revolution Within the Revolution*, 72–73.

33 Ross, *May '68 and Its Afterlives*.

34 The Caravan of Liberty comprised the trucks and jeeps and whatever was on four wheels that came across the island from Santiago de Cuba to Havana, and it was headed by Fidel and the columns of guerrilla fighters. It arrived in Havana on January 8, 1959.

35 For instance, a published testimony from one clandestina remembered her arrest along with a second clandestina and that clandestina's mother. Caught in a police trap, she relates word for word the dialogue between the mother and the policemen holding them that, she said, managed to get them released from prison. But in fact, when she read it, the other clandestina laughed: Her mother had carried on no such conversation. See Bell Lara et al., *Combatientes*; interview with Mirta Rodríguez Calderón, Havana, March 2015.

36 Frank País, "Carta a América," from the collection of Dianita Ramonín Domitro, unpublished.

37 For "heroic city," the Cuban Academy of Language repeatedly criticized the telling grammatical error in the phrase "la ciudad héroe." In Spanish, the noun *ciudad* is feminine; therefore by the rules of Spanish grammar the attached adjective must be feminine as well. That is, Santiago should be described as the ciudad heróica. We can suppose that implicit in this silence in the face of criticism is the notion that the heroic must always be male.

38 Rosabal García, "El movimiento revolucionario 26 de julio," 30–32.

39 The 1930 revolution, for Cubans writing about it, refers to the protests at the end of the 1920s and continuing into the 1930s, both against Machado, who was overthrown in 1933, and then the regime that took over in 1934, with Batista in de facto control. Sweig, *Inside the Cuban Revolution*, 2–4.

40 See more recently the works of Fernando Martínez Heredia, Ana Cairo, and Julio César Guanche.

41 García Pérez, "Mujer y revolución."

42 Bayard de Volo, *Women and the Cuban Insurrection*, 145–64. Bayard de Volo's focus on these female veterans is intended to support

her argument that the portrayal of the 1950s revolution as the work of young people must be questioned.

43 Eqbal Ahmad provides a concise and sharp critique of this theory of revolution in his article "Radical but Wrong."

44 Bayard de Volo, *Women and the Cuban Insurrection*; Chase, *Revolution Within the Revolution*.

1. BATISTA'S QUEST FOR LEGITIMACY

1 Chase, *Revolution Within the Revolution*, 22.

2 Bayard de Volo, *Women and the Cuban Insurrection*, 65–78.

3 Chase, *Revolution Within the Revolution*, 20.

4 Pérez, *On Becoming Cuban*, chapter 3.

5 Eduardo Ardura, "Raíces de la crisis cubana," cited in Pérez, *The Structure of Cuban History*, 185.

6 Pre-universities were upper secondary schools consisting of grades 10–12. Interview with Elvira Díaz Vallina, Havana, January 2012.

7 Julio Antonio Mella was probably the most radical and most important person in the protests against Machado both in and out of the University of Havana. In 1922 he was one of the founders of the Federation of University Students, and in 1925, a founder of the Cuban Communist Party (from which he was in short order expelled for lack of discipline for staging a hunger strike while in prison against Party orders). He went to Mexico and was assassinated there on orders of the then Cuban dictator, Machado. He was twenty-five when he was killed.

8 Castro Porta et al., *La lección del maestro*, 69–74.

9 Eduardo Chibás was founder and head of the Ortodoxo Party. For his impact on the people who would form the insurgent movements, see chapter 4. See also Lillian Guerra's discussion of Chibás in *Heroes, Martyrs and Political Messiahs*.

10 Interview with Sonnia Moro, Havana, January 2012.

11 Chase, *Revolution Within the Revolution*, 25–39.

12 See chapter 2 for a discussion of women and protest marches in Havana.

13 The assassination of Frank País, beloved in Santiago and on an equal plane with Fidel Castro in the 26th of July Movement hierarchy, brought virtually all of Santiago, six thousand people, to walk behind his coffin (Bayard de Volo, *Women and the Cuban Insurrection*, 153). This procession was led by Frank's mother and the mother of América Domitro. See the epilogue for elaboration of the relationship of América and Frank.

14 Chase, *Revolution Within the Revolution*, 79–80.

15   A second prong of Batista's strategy was in line with the populist
      policies that were in vogue in these years among dictators else-
      where in Latin America—his model, in particular, was Vargas in
      Brazil. Batista enacted a series of public works projects like the
      construction of the Malecón tunnel, which provided jobs for a mass
      of unemployed men. But at the same time these projects became
      enmeshed in the web of corruption so historically endemic on the
      island. The third prong was violence and targeted assassination.

16   Interview with Sonnia Moro, Havana, January 2012.

17   Interview with Graziella Pogolotti, Havana, September 2015.

18   Interview with Margarita Mateo, Havana, September 2015.

19   Batista's 1933 coup itself had effectively eliminated whatever there
      was of the leadership of the military. And this by a lowly sergeant
      and, to top everything off, a mulato, who would quickly have the
      full backing of the United States. The 1933 Sergeants' Revolt that
      brought Batista to de facto power served to eliminate the officer
      class in the standing Cuban army. But his accession to military and
      political power did not erase awareness of his lowly status upon his
      entry into the military, his class origins, the fact that he was mulato,
      or his pre-colonels' revolt ranking in the Cuban army. All this, com-
      bined with his de facto selection by the United States during its inter-
      vention into the 1930 revolution as its man in Havana (El Hombre, as
      he came to be called) did nothing for his reputation among Cubans.

20   For example, Carlos Cantillo, who would play the key role in the
      repression of the insurrectionary movement in Santiago; Rafael
      Salas Cañizares, who was killed in the 1956 military attack on the
      Directorio rebels who had taken refuge in the Haitian embassy
      after assassinating the head of the Military Intelligence Service;
      and, as I will discuss in chapter 6, Pilar García, who Batista ap-
      pointed head of police in Havana in 1958, and his son Irenaldo,
      appointed at the same time head of the Naval Intelligence Service
      in Havana. Batista's appointment and promotion of officers whose
      only qualifications were their past personal and political loyalty to
      him produced discontent, resentment, disaffection, and eventually
      division among young officers in the military academies. García
      Pérez concludes: "With this coup d'état, Batista initiated the process
      of decomposition of the armed forces. By taking power in his hands
      for his followers . . . Batista frustrated the positions of young officers
      in the army and in the navy who later would organize themselves to
      act against the regime." This took the form, notes García Pérez, of a
      series of military conspiracies that plagued the regime: the "conspi-
      ración de los puros" in April 1956, the aborted attack by officers in
      the navy in Cienfuegos in September 1957. As the revolution gained

strength, an escalating number of officers changed their allegiances to the rebels' side. Herein lay the roots of the seemingly easy defeat of the large army Batista sent to the sierra in June and May 1958 in the faulty belief that he could now wipe out the significantly less numerous guerrilla forces. See García Pérez, *Insurrección y revolución*; and Pérez, *Army Politics in Cuba*, 33–40.

21 Pérez, *Army Politics in Cuba*.

22 Guerra, *Heroes, Martyrs and Political Messiahs*, 184.

23 Guanche, *La libertad como destino*, 122.

2. DISRUPTING THE NARRATIVE

1 Cubans made up the greatest percentage of foreign fighters in this Spanish Civil War.

2 Among the women in the Salón de los Mártires were Aida Pelayo, Carmen Castro, Olga Román, Pastorita Núñez, Marta Frayde, María Catalina Corina Leyva, Rosa Roque González, Alicia de Armas Menéndez, Eva Jiménez, Mercedes Rodríguez, María Teresa León, Maruja Iglesias, and Rosa Mier. At the formal constitution of the group, in November 1952, the Martianas, as they came to be known, took the name Frente Cívico de Mujeres del Centenario Martiano, to mark the hundredth anniversary of the birth of José Martí. After the centennial year had passed, they altered the name of their organization. See Castro Porta et al., *La lección del Maestro*, 40.

The Frente Cívico de Mujeres del Centenario Martianas was one of the two women's organizations that actively supported the armed insurgency. The second was the Mujeres Oposicionistas Unidas (MOU). Michelle Chase attempts heroically to differentiate between the two (*Revolution Within the Revolution*, 95; see also Bayard de Volo, *Women and the Cuban Insurrection*, 37–38), but there was very little difference between them in practice. They shared the same goals (the overthrow of the Batista regime) and the same means for achieving this. Chase notes one very substantive difference: Membership in the MOU required an invitation. The fact that you could not simply join the MOU on your own but had to be invited implied that the MOU, in limiting its membership, perhaps contemplated more violent actions as an organization. The only evidence of this might be Natalia Bolivar's participation in the explosion at the Seventeenth Police Station late in 1958. The Directorio is portrayed as responsible for the explosion, and Natalia of course was a militant in the Directorio. But she was also a founder of the MOU. There were also differences in numbers of adherents (the MOU had forty-six members; the FCMM claimed six hundred to seven hundred, as formal members and thousands of others spread through different provinces [see Bayard de Volo, *Women and the Cuban Insurrection,* 35]), and the FCMM had the greater presence and impact during the insurrection. I focus in this chapter entirely on the FCMM.

In 1956 Frayde, one of the four women who first had the idea of creating what became the FCMM, split from it to organize the MOU. The few accounts that attempt to elucidate Frayde's reasons for creating a second women's organization provide rather questionable explanations. Julio César González Pagés (*En busca de un espacio*) and other investigators suggest that Frayde was close to the Partido Socialista. But the evidence is not very convincing. First, like Frayde, various of the older generation of the Frente had over the years circulated on the edges of the Cuban political world and thereby had personal relationships with various political organizations, including no doubt the PSP, or the Communist Party as it was known before 1944. And they without qualms drew on these relationships whenever it benefited their ends. Second, Natalia Bolívar and Zoila Lapique, both DR insurgents, were founding members of the MOU and there were hardly warm and fuzzy feelings between the Partido Socialista and the Directorio. Third, the FCMM itself had no formal affiliation with any movement or party and we can therefore surmise that Partido Socialista women were among its members. Fourth, several of the women I interviewed understood themselves as members of both women's organizations. There is in all probability a much less political explanation for Frayde's decision to create a separate organization. Those well acquainted with her surmise that it was entirely a matter of personalities. Frayde liked to direct, to be in charge. The FCMM's collective structure of decision-making, to say nothing of the strong characters of its key members, Aida Pelayo and Carmen Castro, left little room for her to exercise the kind of leadership role to which she was accustomed (interview with Zoila Lapique, May 2016; interview with Graziella Pogolotti, February 2016). Following January 1, 1959, Frayde, a doctor, was charged by her friend Fidel to head the National Hospital and the Nursing School of Havana. Following this she was appointed as the Cuban ambassador to UNESCO. In 1976, after her return to Havana, she was arrested and tried for working with oppositional groups and sentenced to a term of twenty-nine years. She was released after serving three-plus years of her sentence and went into exile in Spain.

3   Kruijt, *Cuba and Revolutionary Latin America,* 31.

4   Bayard de Volo, *Women and the Cuban Insurrection,* 33–38; Chase, "Women's Organizations"; and Chase, *Revolution Within the Revolution,* 92–97.

5   Rodríguez Calderón, "Pastorita Núñez," 35–37.

6   Castro Porta et al., *La lección del Maestro*, 63, 39.

7   Maloof, *Voices of Resistance*, 57.

8   Castro Porta et al., *La lección del Maestro*.

9   Acción Armada Auténtica, or "Triple A," favoring armed struggle, split off from the Auténtico Party and was founded after the 1952 coup.

10   Castro Porta et al., *La lección del Maestro*, 48.

11   García Bárcena was head of the short-lived MNR, the Movimiento Nacional Revolucionario (National Revolutionary Movement). Pablo de la Torriente Brau, a writer, journalist, and soldier, fought for the Spanish Republic and died in combat in 1936.

12   Ramón Grau San Martín was also president of Cuba during the One Hundred Days government in 1933–34.

13   Castro Porta et al., *La lección del Maestro*, 53.

14   Castro Porta et al., *La lección del Maestro*, 56.

15   Castro Porta et al., *La lección del Maestro*, 103.

16   Castro Porta et al., *La lección del Maestro*, 103–4.

17   In the 1940s to early 1950s, Acción Revolucionaria Guiteras was a clandestine movement that favored armed struggle. It was named for Antonio Guiteras, the 1930s student leader who had served as the radical home minister in the 1933–34 One Hundred Days government, and after its collapse he founded Joven Cuba. He was murdered by Batista's forces in 1935, as he tried to escape to Mexico to organize an armed invasion of Cuba. (Note here once more the way in which Cubans "wrapped themselves in their history." Fidel Castro would seek to follow this same path in 1955.)

18   Castro Porta et al., *La lección del Maestro*, 61. The Frente did try at critical junctures to serve as the space within which the leadership of various insurgent groups could coalesce. Thus, for instance, in expectation of the return of the Fidelistas from Mexico in late 1956, Havana-based leaders of the Directorio, the 26th of July Movement, and the Organización Auténtica (OA) assembled in urgent meetings in one of the FCMM's clandestine apartments. The issue was whether and how to support the landing, which in the plans of the 26th of July Movement was to be the clarion call for a nationwide strike to bring down the regime. Carmen recalls that the FCMM served as a liaison: Both she and Aida were present at the meetings, and both talked with the DR and the OA separately. In the end, the effort to forge a unified strategy failed.

19   Bayard de Volo cites its formal membership as between six hundred and seven hundred. *Women and the Cuban Insurrection*, 34.

20   Bayard de Volo, *Women and the Cuban Insurrection*, 96.

21   Bayard de Volo, *Women and the Cuban Insurrection*, 100.

22 Faustino Pérez, in private correspondence with Mirta Rodríguez Calderón, March 1991.

23 Armando Hart Dávalos and Faustino Pérez were 26th of July Movement leaders in the llano. Pérez was head of the 26th of July Movement in Havana until May 1958. See chapter 3 for details about his tenure in Havana.

24 Interviews with Carlos Enrique Pelayo and Nilda Ravelo, Havana, May 2016.

25 Interview with Rosa Mier, Havana, July 2014.

26 In 2012, Cuban television presented a documentary on Aida. The story of why this documentary was made adds further texture to the mystery around Fidel's message to Carmen. Carlos Enrique Pelayo, Aida's son, relates that, drawing on the generally held belief that the ARG had become in the end nothing more than a criminal organization, Reinaldo Taladrid, a major Cuban TV personality, did a show on mafiosas in Cuba, explicitly naming Aida Pelayo and Olga Román (both had been militants in the Acción Revolucionaria Gutiérrez). Carlos Enrique laughingly remembers that "the show caused such an uproar at the Cuban Television and Radio Institute with lots of people phoning the institute, that Taladrid came here [to my house] to apologize for what he had said on the air: 'I was wrong, I am going to do another show and I will say that I made a mistake.' So, the following Sunday he said on TV: 'I was wrong. One of my sources erroneously told me that Aida was a gangster.' So, he apologized, and, afterwards, the director of the Cuban Television and Radio Institute sent me a formal letter of regret. As a result of that incident, they made a documentary about my mother" (interview, Havana, July 2014).

27 Interview with Nilda Ravelo, Havana, June 2016.

28 Interview with Carlos Enrique Pelayo, Havana, May 2016.

29 Interview with Nilda Ravelo, Havana, June 2016.

30 Cited in Maloof, *Voices of Resistance*, 58.

31 Castro Porta et al., *La lección del Maestro*, 41.

32 Castro Porta et al., *La lección del Maestro*, 41.

33 See Chase, *Revolution Within the Revolution*, 77–97.

34 Castro Porta et al., *La lección del Maestro*, 311.

35 Castro Porta et al., *La lección del Maestro*, 104–9. Preceding quotes within the description of the demonstration are from the narrative in this source.

36 A bicho 'e buey is the popular name for the powerful lash made out of the penis skins of bulls, dried and knotted into a ball at its end, for use on oxen. It was employed by Cuban slave owners to beat their slaves and by esbirros on captured insurgents in the 1930 revolution.

37   Castro Porta et al., *La lección del Maestro*, 144.

38   Castro Porta et al., *La lección del Maestro*.

39   Interview with Mirta Rodríguez Calderón, Havana, February 2014.

40   Orieta Cordeiro, *Mujeres en Mantilla*, Radio Progreso program, March 2016.

41   Castro Porta et al., *La lección del Maestro*, 83.

42   The white rose refers to a poem by José Martí, popularly known as "Cultivo una rosa blanca" (verse XXXIX, which appears in *Versos Sencillos*, a collection of his poems).

43   Castro Porta et al., *La lección del Maestro*, 109–11.

44   Esperón, "Entrevista a Aida Pelayo."

45   In a 1992 interview with an American researcher, Aida declared, "I decided I wanted to have a baby. So, I got pregnant and had a son. My marriage lasted for only one day because we never really understood each other" (Maloof, *Voices of Resistance*, 57). This comment was picked up subsequently in other accounts of her life (for instance, González Pagés, *En busca de un espacio*). But in fact it was not true: It amuses and slightly bewilders both her son and the women still living who knew her, who assume Aida, as she was wont to do, probably threw it into the interview for shock value.

46   Interview with Carlos Enrique Pelayo, Havana, May 2016.

47   Interview with Carlos Enrique Pelayo, Havana, May 2016. Colón at the time was a red-light district.

48   Interview with Rosa Mier, Havana, February 2016.

49   Ala Izquierda Estudiantil differences with the Student Directorate had to do with its view that the Student Directorate was "too reformist and not sufficiently anti-imperialist" (Whitney, *State and Revolution in Cuba*, 73–80). Whitney notes that Ala Izquierda Estudiantil was the only group in the 1930s political spectrum other than the Communist Party to raise questions about race.

50   Esperón, "Entrevista a Aida Pelayo."

51   In terms of percentages, more Cubans fought the Republican side in the Spanish Civil War than individuals from any other country.

52   Maloof, *Voices of Resistance*, 56.

53   Esperón, "Entrevista a Aida Pelayo."

54   Esperón, "Entrevista a Aida Pelayo."

55   Interview with Nilda Ravelo, Havana, July 2014. Agostini, an Olympics champion and anti-Batistiano killed in 1955, was the husband of Emma Surí, one of the founders of the Frente.

56   That is, the years of the Machado dictatorship. Rodríguez Calderón, "De estrellas en la frente," 51.

57   Interview with Rosa Mier, Havana, July 2016.

58 Rodríguez Calderón et al., "Carmen Castro," 12.

59 Westbrook was a leader in the Directorio, murdered in the aftermath of the failed attack by the Directorio on the Presidential Palace in 1957. He was twenty years old.

60 Interview with Carlos Enrique Pelayo, Havana, May 2016.

61 Castro Porta et al., *La lección del Maestro*, 250–51. Bernardo Juan Borrell, a 26th of July Movement insurgent, was killed when he was twenty. Armando Pérez Pintó and Tirso Urdanivia were militants in the DR. Mario Reguera (Reguerita) was a militant in the DR, killed in April 1958 at the age of twenty-two.

62 Rodríguez Calderón et al., "Carmen Castro," 9.

63 Castro Porta, "Recuerdos de mis prisiones," FCMM ARCHIVES, courtesy of Rosa Mier. Carmen frequently wrote commentaries for her friends, some humorous and sarcastic and most apparently now lost. The one that seems to be most fondly remembered was her "Diez mandamientos de las mujeres" (Ten commandments of women), which Mariíta Trasancos describes as "locos [crazy] but funny." In these commandments, among other things, Carmen decrees the right of women to "scratch ourselves wherever we want to and any time we want to, a 'right' which men already freely exercise." Interview with María (Mariíta) Trasancos, Havana, May 2016. An ergastulum was a Roman building where slaves were punished or where more dangerous slaves were held in chains.

64 Rodríguez Calderón et al., "Carmen Castro."

65 Rodríguez Calderón et al., "Carmen Castro," 58.

66 Esperón, "Entrevista a Aida Pelayo."

67 Interview with Carlos Enrique Pelayo, Havana, May 2016.

68 Castro Porta et al., *La lección del Maestro*, 91–92.

69 Castro Porta et al., *La lección del Maestro*, 92.

70 Rodríguez Calderón, "Pastorita Núñez."

71 Interview with Pilar Sa, Havana, May 2016.

72 Interview with María (Mariíta) Trasancos, Havana, May 2016.

73 The tribunales de urgencia were first established in 1934 with the specific purpose of hearing cases dealing with "terrorism."

74 Rodríguez Calderón, "De estrellas en el frente," 58.

75 Thus, the gunning down of Machaco Almajeiras, at this point (November 1958), the 26th of July Movement head of Action and Sabotage in Havana, whose story is told in Fernando Pérez's film *Clandestinos*. Margot had gotten word from one of her sources that the apartment in which Machaco and two others were hiding was about to be raided, and she warned them: They failed to heed this warning soon enough, with tragic consequences. Interview with Pilar Sa, Havana, January 2019.

76 Interview with Pilar Sa, Havana, February 2017. Pilar recalls that once, driving by Margot's partner's house along with Morúa, Margot suggested quite casually that they drop in to see her.

77 The Giralt sisters were two 26th of July Movement clandestinas killed in Havana in 1958. See chapter 6.

78 Castro Porta et al., *La lección del Maestro*, 262.

3. MALE BONDING

1 Interview with Alberto Morales, Havana, March 2012.

2 Casteñeda, *Compañero*, 101–2.

3 Franqui, *Cuba, la revolución*, 165. Figures on the numbers who arrived in the mountains vary enormously. Carlos Franqui's *The Twelve* gives the number a religious tint. Most recently Lillian Guerra puts the figure of arrivals at twenty-two, and these are just a few variations on a theme (*Heroes, Martyrs, and Political Messiahs*).

4 Sippial, *Celia Sánchez Maduley*, 53.

5 Interview with Consuelo Elba, Havana, February 2019. See as well Bayard de Volo, *Women and the Cuban Insurrection*, 175. Bayard de Volo tells the story of Zobeida Rodríguez (Mimi), a clandestina quemada, who in 1958 fled to the sierra and joined her husband, Israel Chavez, in the Ciro Redondo guerrilla column. Bayard de Volo notes that Mimi sought to perform her identity as a "mother," that is, to desexualize her presence among the men with whom she was living, in order to dispel the sexual tension her presence evoked. And that she "refrained from sleeping near her husband 'to avoid any temptation'" (214–15). With a twinkle in her eyes, Mimi continued her tale in my interview with her. After she arrived in Havana with the triumphant Caravan of Liberty, Che, who had an errand for her, sent someone on a futile search to find her. Mimi and her husband were well ensconced in the first hotel room they could grab (interview, Havana, March 2014).

6 See Consuelo Elba's film *Mujeres de la guerrilla* (2006). Consuelo herself, quemada in Havana, spent the last years of the insurrection in the sierra.

7 Celia became a permanent resident in the sierra as chief assistant to Fidel. Haydée was put in charge coordinating from abroad the acquisition of critically needed arms and the funds to buy them. Vilma, after carrying out remarkable feats in the clandestine movement in Santiago, joined Raúl Castro's front in the sierra. With the exception of the Mariana Grajales brigade, no woman's name comes up. The brigade was organized in September 1958 over the

resistance of men who objected to wasting scarce weapons on women. In the story, Fidel made the final decision and reportedly was planning a second women's brigade.

8   See Guevara, *Episodes of the Revolutionary War.*

9   Guevara, *Guerrilla Warfare*, 111.

10   Guevara, *Guerrilla Warfare*, 111–12.

11   Faustino Pérez fell out of that circle in 1960, when he disagreed with the decision to arrest Huber Matos. Matos was a comandante in the rebel army and in October 1959, he renounced his position as head of the rebel army in Camaguey in protest against the direction in which the revolution was moving. He was arrested, convicted of treason, and spent twenty years in prison. But in reaction to the Bay of Pigs invasion, Pérez reemerged as an active revolutionary leader, if not as a member of the deep inner circle.

12   Sweig, *Inside the Cuban Revolution*, 126.

13   Sweig, *Inside the Cuban Revolution*, 9.

14   Sweig, *Inside the Cuban Revolution*, 9. The meeting at Altos de Mompié in May 1958 in the wake of the failure of the April 9th national strike resulted in the restructuring of the 26th of July Movement, putting Fidel as commander-in-chief of the entire 26th of July Movement insurgency.

15   Oltuski, *Vida Clandestina*, xix.

16   Interview with Graciela Aguiar, Havana, March 2014.

17   Interview with Consuelo Elba, Havana, January 2014.

18   Interview with Natalia Bolívar, Havana, February 2012.

19   Quoted in Prado, *La secretaria de la república.*

20   Interview with Margarita Mateo, Havana, September 2015.

21   Interview with Mirta Rodríguez Calderón, Amherst, November 2012.

22   The Movement of Civic Resistance (MRC) was established in February 1957 as an organization parallel to the 26th of July Movement. Formally, its purpose was to provide a venue in which professionals sympathetic to the insurrection could support it in various manners. Under the umbrella of the MRC, insurgent groups joined or carried out action against the regime.

23   Interview with Elvira Díaz Vallina, Havana, January 2012.

24   Interview with Nilda Ravelo, Havana, February 2012.

25   The Cuban Communist Party changed its name to the Partido Socialista Popular in 1944.

26   Sweig, *Inside the Cuban Revolution*, 129.

27   Sweig, *Inside the Cuban Revolution*, 111; Guanche, *La libertad como destino*, 120.

28   In her discussions of the period of the insurgency and beyond, Michelle Chase uses the label the "Marxist left" to describe the PSP

and its women members. But "Marxist left" seems both confusing and jarring. The adherence of both the PSP and the Democratic Federation of Cuban Women (the Party's women's front) to the orthodox Soviet version of "socialism" in their structure and determination of actions to be taken and those to oppose makes it impossible to describe their members and the positions they took during the insurrection as either Marxist or leftist.

29 Interviews with Pilar Sa and María (Mariíta) Trasancos, Havana, May 2016.

30 Steve Cushion, in *A Hidden History of the Cuban Revolution*, his study of the working class and the Cuban revolution, meticulously details incidences of cooperation at the factory level between PSP and 26th of July Movement insurgents, beginning in the early years of the Batista regime and comprising short work stoppages lasting from ten minutes to several hours. He demonstrates that this cooperation was strongest in the eastern provinces where the national-level bureaucracy of the trade unions was least present and therefore less able to exercise control. And most interesting for this study, he understands these joint actions were in part possible because of long-term relationships between workers both in their workplaces and in the adjacent neighborhoods in which they lived. The degree of participation by women in these actions was surely circumscribed by the fact that even in 1959 only 17 percent of women were in the paid labor force. Pérez-Stable, "Cuban Women and the Struggle for 'Conciencia,'" 53–54.

31 The Moncada Program, written three days before the attack on the fortress, previewed much the same ideas that Fidel would reiterate in "History Will Absolve Me." Interview with Juan Valdés Paz, Havana, March 2012.

32 Interview with Pilar Sa, Havana, May 2016.

33 Interviews with Pilar Sa and Mirta Rodríguez Calderón, Havana, May 2016.

34 Interviews with Hidelisa Esperón, Havana, March 2016.

35 Bonos were coupons that sympathizers with the insurgency could buy. They were basically donations, each usually ranging from 5 to 25 pesos. Natalia Bolívar, in Consuelo Elba, *Mujeres de la clandestinidad* (film), 2016.

36 Interview with Pilar Sa, Havana, May 2016.

37 Interview with Nilda Ravelo, Havana, March 2012.

38 Guanche, *La libertad como destino*, 126.

39 This meant that, because it was entirely men who left Havana to organize an armed invasion, all the female Directorio insurgents were left on the island and presumably faced this extreme repres-

sion that followed the attack (interview with Juan Valdés Paz, Havana, March 2014).

40 Héctor Terry Molinart, in Bell Lara et al., *Combatientes*, 363.

41 Bell Lara et al., *Combatientes*, 363.

42 Interview with Mariíta Trasancos, Havana, January 2023.

43 Bell Lara et al., *Cuba: Las mujeres en la insurrección 1952–1961*, 13–15.

44 Interview with Magaly Martínez, Havana, March 2018.

45 Interview with Guillermo Jiménez, Havana, March 2018.

46 Laura Fernández Rueda, in Bell Lara et al., *Combatientes*, 153.

47 Bell Lara et al., *Cuba: Las mujeres en la insurrección 1952–1961*, 44–45.

48 Sweig, *Inside the Cuban Revolution*, 120–21.

49 Interview with Sonnia Moro, Havana, February 2012.

50 Sweig, *Inside the Cuban Revolution*, 120.

51 There is another, although clearly a minority, school of thought put forth by some who were key figures in the llano and in the strike, which challenges the idea of its failure, understanding it instead as a critical victory in the struggle to bring down the dictatorship. Julio César Rosabal García, in his PhD thesis, captures this argument: "The Moncada was the conception of a new creature and April 9th was like the breaking of water that precedes labor" ("El movimiento revolucionario 26 de julio"). He argues this by elaborating the widespread actions of the insurgents across the island in anticipation of April 9th, on the day itself, and in its immediate aftermath: "At various points across the island, organized groups representing the people rose in arms or improvised weapons against the power of the dictatorship. . . . The April uprising was the spark that triggered the end of the dictatorship." Most critically, Rosabal García argues, first, that the strike "brought home to the general population the ongoing and widespread nature and unflinching determination of the opposition to Batista, and the need for armed insurrection to defeat it. Second, in its wake other opposition groups could no longer dispute the leadership of the 26th Movement. And third, in putting down the strike and its aftermath, the regime was forced to use all its resources, thereby delaying its offensive in the sierra and giving the rebel army time to regroup and fortify itself. Its failure had little to do with questions of timing or weapons delivery, or indeed anything that the llano leadership did or didn't do. Rather, it came before its time. Without accompaniment by a full-scale armed attack launched and carried out by the sierra, it was doomed to failure" (144). Héctor Ravelo, who had been the head of the 26th of July Movement in Havana Campo and a key informant for Rosabal García, laid out much the same argument (interview with Héctor Ravelo, Havana, March 2014).

Michelle Chase relates that in May 1959, a few short months after the revolution took power, the PSP directed its members not to take part, because, as Rosabal García would also later argue, the PSP "rued" its conduct in the strikes that the llano attempted to carry out and, most importantly, the April 1958 strike. Chase cites the conclusions of the Pleno Comité del Nacional del Partido Socialista Popular, which declared that even failed strikes had a notable impact: "The constant threat of the strike kept a large part of the repressive forces and the military . . . in the cities, impeding their concentration in the zones of armed struggle." In this revised assessment then, the strikes that the PSP had formerly condemned had in fact served a purpose: They had facilitated the guerrilla struggle in the sierra and thus its victory. Chase adds that few insurgents saw it that way (*Revolution Within the Revolution*, 69). One can argue that the PSP, in throwing the llano insurgents a bone, conveniently aligned itself with the already gelling narrative that the llano's role was always subservient to the sierra.

52 Quoted in Sweig, *Inside the Cuban Revolution*, 149.

53 Interview with Pilar Sa, Havana, May 2016.

54 Interview with Juan Valdés Paz, Havana, May 2016.

55 Interview with Sonnia Moro, Havana, March 2012.

56 Thelma Bernot, in Consuelo Elba, *Mujeres en la clandestinidad* (film), 2016.

57 Rodríguez Calderón, *Semillas de fuego*, 1:132.

58 Sweig, *Inside the Cuban Revolution*, 104.

59 Nieves Rivera, *Rogito*, 73.

60 Of those killed in the aftermath of the strike, twenty-seven were disappeared. The assassinations reached a crescendo in December 1958, despite the fact that it was by then clear that the Batista regime was doomed: Twenty-four clandestinos were killed that month. Interview with Julio Dámaso, head of the Fondo Documental de los Combatientes, Havana, March 2018.

61 Castro Porta et al., *La lección del Maestro*, 235.

62 Interview with Sonnia Moro, Havana, February 2012.

63 Interview with María (Mariíta) Trasancos, Havana, April 2016.

64 Rosabal García, "El movimiento revolucionario 26 de julio," 148.

65 Leyva Pagan, *Historia de una gesta libertadora*, prologue.

4. THE CLANDESTINAS

1 In these chapters I draw as well on lengthy discussions with family members and close friends about Ángela Alonso (26th of July Movement; twenty-seven when she joined the insurgency) and América Domitro (26th of July Movement and prior to this the ARO), both

of whom were insurgents in the underground in Havana as well as Santiago but had passed away before I began my fieldwork.

2   Chase, *Revolution Within the Revolution*. Chase gives the number of women involved in the underground movement nationwide as three thousand.

3   A pre-university is the same as an upper secondary school.

4   Mirta Rodríguez Calderón, private correspondence with the author, August 2012.

5   Meyer, *El futuro era nuestro*, 541.

6   Pérez, *The Structure of Cuban History*, 173.

7   Interview with María (Mariíta)Trasancos, Havana, August 2014.

8   Juan José Sicre sculpted the statue of José Martí in the Plaza de la Revolución.

9   Interview with Sonnia Moro, Havana, May 2016.

10 Interview with Sonnia Moro, Havana, May 2016.

11 Interview with Magaly Martínez, Havana, March 2018.

12 Bell Lara et al., *Combatientes*.

13 Interview with Mirta Rodríguez Calderón, Amherst, November 2015.

14 Elvira Díaz Vallina, a 26th of July Movement militant, was the president of the Faculty of Education at the moment of the coup. In 1957, she was chosen president of FEU in a secret election.

15 Bell Lara et al., *Combatientes*, 359.

16 Meyer, *El futuro era nuestro*, 518–19.

17 Interview with Nilda Ravelo, Havana, May 2016.

18 Rodríguez and Rodríguez, *Vilma*, n.p.

19 Pérez, *The Structure of Cuban History*, 173.

20 Consuelo Elba, interview with Nélida Álvarez, in *Mujeres de la clandestinidad* (film), 2016.

21 Consuelo Elba, interview with Nélida Álvarez, in *Mujeres de la clandestinidad* (film), 2016.

22 Julio Lobo, popularly called Cuba's "sugar king," was a powerful sugar trader and financier. From the late 1930s to 1960, when he left Cuba to go into exile, Lobo was considered the single most powerful sugar broker in the world.

23 Interview with María (Mariíta) Trasancos, Havana, May 2016.

24 Interview with María (Mariíta) Trasancos, Havana, May 2016.

25 Bell Lara et al., *Cuba: La generación revolucionaria 1952–1961*, 56.

26 Interview with María (Mariíta) Trasancos, Havana, May 2016.

27 Interview with María (Mariíta) Trasancos, Havana, July 2016.

28 Interview with Pilar Sa, Havana, January 2012.

29 Interview with Pilar Sa, Havana, January 2012.

30 Interview with Pilar Sa, Havana, January 2012.

31 Michelle Chase notes that telephone operators, generally women, served as major communications conduits during the insurrection (*Revolution Within the Revolution*, 99).

32 Pilar García was chief of the national police. For a fuller description, see chapter 6.

33 In the eighteenth and nineteenth centuries, the Abreu family owned huge swathes of land in Santa Clara that were mainly involved in sugar production, and they used slaves to work the plantations. Slaves were regularly given their masters' names and these names were passed down through generations.

34 Interview with Digna Abreu, Havana, June 2016.

35 Interview with Selma Díaz, Havana, February 2012.

36 Interview with Selma Díaz, Havana, February 2012.

37 A solar is a house that, over time, was subdivided to lodge poor people in miserable conditions. Families usually lived in one room, and they shared bathrooms and kitchens with multiple other families.

38 Interview with Consuelo Elba in Kruijt, *Cuba and the Revolutionary Latin America*, 51.

39 Interview with Consuelo Elba, Havana, March 2012.

40 Spence Benson, *Antiracism in Cuba*, 39.

41 Spence Benson, *Antiracism in Cuba*, 41.

42 Díaz Vallina et al., "La mujer revolucionaria en Cuba," 24–32.

43 Interview with Consuelo Elba, Mirta Rodríguez Calderón, and Sonnia Moro, Havana, January 2013.

44 Interview with Digna Abreu, Havana, January 2018.

45 Interview with Digna Abreu, Havana, March 2014.

46 The Partido Independiente Color (PIC; Independent Party of Color) was formed principally by black men who had been leading figures during the war of independence: Its membership was largely veterans of the war. Its program rotated around the economic and social inequities suffered by Cuban blacks. But the massacre was indiscriminate in whom it targeted among the black and mulato populations, particularly from eastern provinces of Cuba. Until recently, its very occurrence had literally been expunged from Cuban history. For excellent recent accounts of the PIC and the massacre and its lasting aftermath, see Helg, *Our Rightful Share*.

47 See Gloria Rolando's three-part film, *Breaking the Silence*.

48 Interview with Digna Abreu, Havana, March 2014. For an account of Digna's imprisonment, see chapter 6.

49 Spence Benson, *Antiracism in Cuba*, 39–40.

50 See Whitney, *State and Revolution in Cuba*, 76–79. In the 1930s the Ala Izquierda Estudiantil (Student Left Wing) along with other non-Stalinist Marxist groups carried on a polemic about race with the Communist

Party, arguing that the Party's simplistic and superficial application of a Stalinist model to Cuban realities kept it from taking account of the unique problems facing black workers. It is hardly surprising that Aida Pelayo was one of the founders of Ala Izquierda Estudiantil.

51 Spence Benson, *Antiracism in Cuba*, 32.

52 Spence Benson, *Antiracism in Cuba*, 32.

53 Interview with Digna Abreu, Havana, May 2016.

54 Spence Benson, *Antiracism in Cuba*, 41.

55 Interview with Pilar Sa, Havana, January 2012.

56 Interview with Aimée de los Ángeles Afón and Guillermo Jiménez, Havana, May 2018.

57 Interview with Ercilia Gutiérrez, Havana, May 2018.

58 Interview with Magaly Martínez, Havana, 2018.

59 Interview with Xiomara Blanco, Havana, 2014.

60 Interview with Niurka Lipiz, Havana, March 2012.

61 Interview with Sonnia Moro, Havana, April 2016.

62 Interview with Sonnia Moro, Havana, April 2016. After January 1959, Sonnia's mother became a fervent Fidelista, not so much out of any political commitment but because she knew the insurgency was over and her daughter was now safe.

63 Interview with Pilar Sa, Havana, May 2016.

64 Castro Porta et al., *La lección del Maestro*, 150.

65 Interview with Mariíta Trasancos, Havana, May 2016.

66 Interview with Natalia Bolívar, Havana, February 2012.

67 See chapter 6.

68 This marriage between Hidelisa and Tony Fernández, one of the men in the safe house in which she had lived, was an important factor in the suspicion that others in the clandestinidad had about him. It was certainly the only such marriage ceremony to occur between insurgents in El Príncipe.

69 Interview with Hidelisa Esperón, Havana, April 2014.

70 The term *novia* as it was used in the underground movement seems to have meant a "special friendship" with generally no implications beyond this. Interestingly, however, the term is almost never used in reverse. A male clandestino's name is never joined to that of his "novia."

71 Hamilton, *Sexual Revolutions in Cuba*, 83. Hamilton notes that prohibitions communicated by parents or older female family members concerning sexuality hung on in some cases according to interviews she did decades into the revolution. She cites the case of one young woman whose aunt counseled her: "Well, Lily if you have a boyfriend you can have a little kiss. If they put their hand on your waist there's no problem. But if they put their hand on your hip they'll make you señora. . . . You'll never get married again" (87).

72   Interview with Mirta Rodríguez Calderón, Havana, February 2018.

73   Interview with Mirta Rodríguez Calderón, Havana, June 2014. Ángela, although involved in a sexual relationship with Orlando Nodarse, had been previously married and had a child: In this sense she was not bound by the constraint of unmarried clandestinas.

74   Hamilton, *Sexual Revolutions in Cuba.*

75   Interview with Pilar Sa, Havana, May 2012.

76   Chase, *Revolution Within the Revolution*, 102–3.

77   Interview with Hidelisa Esperón, Havana, January 2016.

78   Interview with Hidelisa Esperón, Havana, January 2016.

79   Chase, *Revolution Within the Revolution*, 103.

80   Interview with Fernando Pérez, Havana, January 2017.

81   Interview with Mirta Rodríguez Calderón and Sonnia Moro, Havana, January. Whatever resentment still existed about Porras, at least until her death in October 2021, was largely tied to her portrayal as the representative of the clandestinas. That is, she was named. This, of course, is not entirely her fault, although she clearly enjoyed the notoriety. Her relationship with Machaco and Pérez's movie certainly underscores this attention. Not for nothing, when Marta Jiménez (the wife of Fructuoso Rodríguez) passed away, *Granma*, the Cuban newspaper, celebrated Norma along with Marta as the two heroines of the clandestinidad.

82   Conversations with Julio Dámaso (January 2024) and Gladys Marel García (February 2023).

5. CLANDESTINAS IN HAVANA

1   Mouffe, *Return of the Political.*

2   Chase, *Revolution Within a Revolution*, 25.

3   Interview with Elvira Díaz Vallina, Havana, January 2012.

4   Interview with Pilar Sa, Havana, June 2016.

5   Interview with Pilar Sa, Havana, June 2016.

6   The rest of the cell structure, at least on paper, situated two individuals, always men, as second in command first under El Curita and, after El Curita was murdered, Machaco. At the next level down there were seventeen captains, one for each barrio in Havana. Each captain had several groups under his command, depending on the size of the barrio operating under his command (interview with Julio Dámaso, Havana, February 2023).

7   Interview with Pilar Sa, Havana, October 2015.

8   Consuelo Elba, interview with Nélida Álvarez, in *Mujeres en la clandestinidad* (film), 2016.

9   Interview with Juan Valdés Paz, Havana, February 2016.
10 Interview with Juan Valdés Paz, Havana, May 2016.
11 Interview with Sonnia Moro, Havana, April 2011.
12 Meyer, *El futuro era nuestro*, 546.
13 There are two notable exceptions: Lidia Doce and Clodomira Acosta. I deal with them more extensively in chapter 6.
14 Interview with Sonnia Moro, Havana, March 2014.
15 Interview with Sonnia Moro, Havana, March 2014.
16 Interview with Hidelisa Esperón, September 2015.
17 Interview with Magaly Olivero, Havana, January 2013.
18 A petardo is a small bomb consisting of two sticks of dynamite tied together and a wick.
19 Interview with Hidelisa Esperón, Havana, March 2014.
20 Interview with Hidelisa Esperón, Havana, March 2014.
21 Klouzal, *Women and Rebel Communities*, 260.
22 In that year Batista, a sergeant at Campo Columbia, the army base, organized and led the Sergeants' Revolt, which in effect brought down the dictatorship of Gerardo Machado.
23 Orieta Cordeiro, *Mujeres en Mantilla*, Radio Progreso program, March 2016.
24 See chapter 6 for a fuller discussion of Ventura.
25 Interview with Nilda Ravelo, Havana, June 2016.
26 A fósforo vivo consisted of a paste of dynamite powder or any other type of explosive. Twenty minutes after this paste was combined with a capsule of acid, it produced an explosion. This action was a forerunner of the much bigger 03C campaign (Cero Cabaret, Cero Cine, Cero Compra [Zero Cabaret, Zero Cinema, Zero Shopping]), launched in a most ingenious fashion around Christmas of the following year. For a fuller discussion, see Chase, *Revolution Within the Revolution*, 37–38; and Guede, *Cuba*, 184–218. Emilio Guede, an advertising executive, had the idea for the 03C campaign. The campaign itself is fictionalized in Fernando Pérez's film *Clandestinos*.
27 Interview with Mirta Rodríguez Calderón, Amherst, April 2012.
28 Interviews with Digna Abreu, January 2019 and February 2023; interview with Julio Dámaso, January 2023.
29 Nieves, *Rogito*, 62.
30 Loaches was a leader in the Directorio Revolucionario.
31 Interview with Ercilia Gutiérrez and family, Havana, June 2016.
32 Interview with Guillermo Jiménez, Havana, June 2016.
33 Interview with Guillermo Jiménez, Havana, June 2016.
34 Interview with Ercilia Gutiérrez and family, Havana, June 2016.
35 The cañonazo is the firing of the old cannon in Old Havana, a tradition since colonial times. "Bombs" may be a euphemism here. In

fact, according to Enio Leyva, who worked with the youth brigades together with Abreu Fontán, what exploded that night was mainly petardos. Insurgents claimed never to have used actual bombs in these actions out of concern that they would harm civilians. Moreover, in those areas in different municipalities to which explosives had not arrived in time, Leyva says, anything that made the greatest noise was employed (interview with Enio Leyva, Havana, February 2019). See also Guede, *Cuba*.

36 Interview with Fernando Pérez, Havana, February 2019.

37 Rodríguez Calderón, *Semillas de fuego*, 1:27–29.

38 Guerra, *Heroes, Martyrs and Political Messiahs*, 233.

39 For Mariíta Trasancos's account of El Curita's escape from El Príncipe along with seven or eight others, see Bell Lara et al., *Combatientes*, 376–77.

40 Bell Lara et al., *Combatientes*, 377; interview with María (Mariíta) Trasancos, Havana, May 2016.

41 Interview with María (Mariíta) Trasancos, Havana, May 2016.

42 Interview with María (Mariíta) Trasancos, Havana, May 2016. See chapter 6 for an account of what happened to Mariíta when she was arrested.

43 Bell Lara et al., *Combatientes*, 379.

44 See Sweig, *Inside the Cuban Revolution*, 104–13.

45 In the end Batista gave up on this. The election was held in November 1958.

46 For a first-person account of the fire at the Esso plant, see Rodríguez Calderón, *Semillas de fuego*, 1:36–37. The attack was planned and organized by El Curita, who had been as well the planner and organizer of the Night of One Hundred Bombs.

47 For a first-person account of the attack on the bank, see Rodríguez Calderón, *Semillas de fuego*.

48 For a brief account of the student strike, see Rodríguez Calderón, *Semillas de fuego*, 59–60; and Sweig, *Inside the Cuban Revolution*, 105–6.

49 Sweig, *Inside the Cuban Revolution*, 105.

50 The three women were popularly referred to then and now as the "norteñas" or even as the "americanas" because they lived on Calle Norte in Nuevo Vedado.

51 Interview with Ángel Fernández Vila (Horacio), Havana, June 2018. When Fangio returned to Havana some years after the revolution took power, he remembered Fernández Vila: "a young man, maybe twenty years old, with a mustache and a really bad driver" (interview with Ángel Fernández Vila [Horacio], Havana, June 2018). In an interview with *Bohemia* sixty years later, Fernández Vila

confessed that at the time he drove the getaway car, he did not have a driver's license (interview with Rafael Pérez Valdés, Havana 2018).

52 By coincidence, the Argentine ambassador was Che Guevara's cousin.

53 Rodríguez Calderón, *Semillas de fuego*, 1:51.

54 Camin, "Por un momento pensé." Camin was permitted to interview Fangio during the time he was sequestered.

55 Rodríguez Calderón, *Semillas de fuego*, 1:51.

56 Quoted in Sweig, *Inside the Cuban Revolution*, 105.

57 Interview with Agnes de los Ángeles Afón, Havana, June 2018.

58 A. Rodríguez, *Operación Fangio*, 5–6.

59 Fernández Vila said that some of these cars had Florida license plates, implying by this that the United States was involved in the actual search. Patricia Calvo González, in an article examining coverage of the insurrection by reporters in 1957–58, reports that there were hundreds of patrol (or other) cars circulating in Havana searching for Fangio and his kidnappers ("Percepciones de la Sierra Maestra").

60 Álvarez Estévez, "De la Operación Fangio."

6. THE USES OF TORTURE

1 Bengelsdorf, *The Problem of Democracy in Cuba*, 70.

2 Interview with Sonnia Moro, Havana, February 2012.

3 Pérez, *To Die in Cuba*.

4 Rodríguez Calderón, *Semillas de fuego*. Michelle Chase observes that female martyrdom fits uncomfortably into this conflation of hero/martyr. Throughout Cuban history, male heroes/martyrs had been wrapped in a mantle of military glory. Female martyrs, on the other hand, enter into this history in terms of sexual victimization and pathos. See Chase, *Revolution Within the Revolution*, 55–59.

5 This was the reason given to me at a meeting of the members (all female) of the Club Martiano de Herencia Rebelde, Havana, June 2014.

6 Quoted in Chase, *Revolution Within the Revolution*, 59.

7 There were two distinct police forces in prerevolutionary Cuba. The first, the policía azul (named as such for the color of their uniforms), operated under the aegis of the National Police and in Havana worked out of the nineteen police stations. The policía amarilla, named likewise for the color of their uniforms, were the rural guard, a military force, or, as Juan Valdés Paz called them, the armed enforcers for latifundia owners (interview with Juan Valdés Paz, February 2020).

8 The Tigres de Masferrer was a paramilitary body organized by Rolando Masferrer, which operated mainly in Oriente Province but

had tentacles elsewhere on the island. Eusebio Mujal was head of the National Trade Union and an ally of Batista. Julio César Rosabal, "El movimiento revolucionario 26 de Julio," 131.

9   Ventura died in his bed at the age of eighty-two in Miami, Florida. He fled Cuba the night of December 31, 1958. When he learned that Batista had fled, he rushed to the airport with a machine gun and demanded a spot on the second and last helicopter that was about to depart. He was given asylum in the United States. Frequent requests for his extradition by the Cuban government were ignored.

10   Orieta Cordeiro, *Mujeres en Mantilla*, Radio Progreso program, March 2016.

11   The "33.33" refers to the salary that a chivato received.

12   Consuelo Elba, interview with Pilar Sa, in *Mujeres en la clandestinidad* (film), 2016. During the centuries of slavery in Cuba "echar un palo" was used in popular jargon to refer to the places on slave plantations where firewood was stacked, which served as well for liaisons for male and female slaves. Various instruments of torture used in the era of slavery—for example, the bicho 'e buey made from the penis of the bull, dried and twisted to be used as a whip—continued to be used through the 1950s insurrection.

13   Interview with Mirta Rodríguez Calderón, Havana, March 2014.

14   Consuelo Elba, interview with Pilar Sa, in *Mujeres en la clandestinidad* (film), 2016. José Ángel Rosell was an insurgent in the 26th of July Movement working in Action and Sabotage. He was thirty when he was assassinated.

15   Interview with Pilar Sa, Havana, December 2011.

16   Interview with Digna Abreu, Havana, March 2018.

17   Interview with Digna Abreu, Havana, March 2018.

18   Consuelo Elba, interview with Nélida Álvarez, in *Mujeres de la clandestinidad* (film), 2016.

19   Castro Porta et al., *La lección del Maestro*.

20   Interview with Xiomara Blanco, Havana, April 2016.

21   Interview with Mirta Rodríguez Calderón, Havana, June 2014.

22   Interview with Mirta Rodríguez Calderón, Havana, June 2014.

23   Interview with Hidelisa Esperón, Havana, March 2016.

24   Interview with Mirta Rodríguez Calderón, Havana, June 2014.

25   Quoted in Bayard de Volo, *Women and the Cuban Insurrection*, 130.

26   Calviño, one of the regime's most brutal torturers, was actually a former 26th of July Movement member. Released from prison after his first arrest, he began his career as a torturer and assassin. He returned to Cuba with the Bay of Pigs invaders, was captured, tried before a televised audience, and executed.

27   Bayard de Volo, *Women and the Cuban Insurrection*, 99–101.

28 Interview with Hidelisa Esperón, Havana, March 2016.

29 Interview with Hidelisa Esperón, Havana, March 2016.

30 Interview with Hidelisa Esperón, Havana, March 2016.

31 Chase, *Revolution Within the Revolution*, 103.

32 Interview with Hidelisa Esperón, Havana, March 2016.

33 Meyer, *El futuro era nuestro*, 21–33.

34 *Aquella larga noche*, a film made by Enrique Pineda Barnet in 1979, is a fictionalized account of the last day in the lives of Lidia and Clodorima. Interview with Enrique Pineda Barnet, Havana, February 2019.

35 Bayard de Volo, *Women and the Cuban Insurrection*, 120–30.

36 Interview with Mirta Rodríguez Calderón, Havana, January 2014.

37 Female insurgents supposedly did not carry out armed actions. Such actions were the domain of men.

38 Franco, *Critical Passions*, 23.

39 Bell Lara et al., *Combatientes*, 279–80; interview with María (Mariíta) Trasancos, Havana, May 2016.

40 Three prisoners in El Príncipe had been shot and killed that day. See Graña Eirez, *Clandestinos en prisión*, 313–32.

41 Graña Eirez, *Clandestinos en prisión*, 381–82.

42 Graña Eirez, *Clandestinos en prisión*, 382.

43 El Laguito is an isolated area in the exclusive country club district of Havana.

44 Consuelo Elba, interview with Natalia Bolívar, in *Mujeres de la clandestinidad* (film), 2016.

45 Interview with Natalia Bolívar, Havana, February 2012.

46 Interview with Natalia Bolívar, Havana, February 2012.

47 Interview with Carlos Pino, Havana, March 2012; interview with Verena Pino, Havana, July 2014.

48 Forcing people to drink castor oil was a regularly employed police technique during the student protests in the 1920s and 1930s. *Prensa Libre*, February 6, 1956, 1–2.

49 Interview with Mirta Rodríguez Calderón, Havana, May 2014.

50 See Meyer, *El futuro era nuestro*.

51 Guede, *Cuba*, 175.

52 Interview with Mirta Rodríguez Calderón, Havana, May 2014.

53 Rodríguez Calderón, *Semillas del fuego*, 129; interview with Mirta Rodríguez Calderón, Amherst, November 2015.

54 Interview with Pilar Sa and Sonnia Moro, Havana, January 2013.

55 Consuelo Elba, interview with Nélida Álvarez, in *Mujeres de la clandestinidad* (film), 2016.

56 Interview with Pilar Sa, Havana, June 2014.

57 Consuelo Elba, interview with Nélida Álvarez, in *Mujeres de la clandestinidad* (film), 2016.

58   Consuelo Elba, interview with Nélida Álvarez, in *Mujeres de la clandestinidad* (film), 2016.

59   Interview with Pilar Sa, Havana, May 2014.

60   Interview with Mirta Rodríguez Calderón, Havana, June 2016.

61   Orieta Cordeiro, *Mujeres en Mantilla*, Radio Progreso program, March 2016.

7. AFTERMATHS

1   Chase, *Revolution Within the Revolution*, 10.

2   Chase, *Revolution Within the Revolution*.

3   Interview with Mariíta Trasancos, Havana, February 2016.

4   Interview with Mirta Rodríguez Calderón, Havana, February 2015.

5   Interview with Selma Díaz, Havana, February 2012.

6   Interview with Mirta Rodríguez Calderón, Havana, February 2018; group interview with Mariíta Trasancos, Pilar Sa, and Mirta Rodríguez Calderón, Havana, January 2019.

7   Interview with Hidelisa Esperón, Havana, March 2014.

8   Interview with Nilda Ravelo, Havana, January 2013.

9   Interview with Ercilia Gutiérrez and her family and Guillermo Jiménez, Havana, June 2016.

10   Guillermo Jiménez, "Despedida de duelo de Marta Jiménez," Havana, March 3, 2016.

11   Interview with Juan Valdés Paz and Aurelio Alonso, Havana, March 2014. Rosario Alfonso Parodi, a young historian and filmmaker, has made two superb videos, one on the trial of Marquitos (*Los amagos*) and one on Humboldt 7 and the murders of the four DR leaders (*38 días*), thereby recovering for history the events following the DR's failed attack on the Presidential Palace.

12   Interview with Marta Jiménez, Havana, May 2014. The photograph of the boy is reproduced in this book's visual essay.

13   Interview with Xiomara Blanco, Havana, March 2014.

14   Interview with José (Pepito) Robustillo, Havana, March 2014.

15   Rodríguez Calderón, "Pastorita Núñez," 35.

16   Interview with Loren González, Havana, May 2014.

17   Pastorita's closest friends give a different explanation of what happened to INAV. In 1962 Pastorita received a call from a leading figure in the old PSP (specifically, Lázaro Peña), telling her that INAV "would cease to exist." It was to be dissolved into the Ministry of Construction. There was, as mentioned in chapter 3, no love lost between Pastorita and the PSP during the insurrection, and Pastorita was not the type to forget things easily and neither was the PSP leadership. The Ministry of Construction was headed by Osmany

Cienfuegos, before the revolution a member of the Juventud of the PSP. She called Fidel and through Celia Sánchez was told that INAV would indeed be no more (interview with Nilda Ravelo, Havana, March 2012).

18   Rodríguez Calderón, "Pastorita Nuñez."

19   Interview with José (Pepito) Robustillo, Havana, March 2014.

20   Interview with Mirta Rodríguez Calderón, Havana, January 2016.

21   Chase, *Revolution Within the Revolution*, 117.

22   See Chase, *Revolution Within the Revolution*, 115–33, for a more detailed discussion of the two groups and the issues around the formation of the FMC.

23   See Scott, *Gender and the Politics of History.*

24   Interview with Georgina Herrera, Havana, January 2018.

25   Interview with Pilar Sa, Sonnia Moro, and Mirta Rodríguez Calderón, Havana, January 2013. In 1996 the Cubans shot down two planes of Brothers to the Rescue, an organization whose stated purpose was to rescue Cubans leaving the island by sea. The Cuban government claimed that the planes were flying illegally in the country's airspace. The incident produced yet another confrontation between the United States and Cuba. In the wake of this confrontation, the Cuban government seemed to be clamping down on organizations within Cuba that it determined had close relations with Western and in particular US intellectuals. The deactivation of MAGIN received virtually no attention as compared to the focus on the Cuban government's attack on the Center for the Studies of the Americas (CEA), which was itself a party organization.

    Two decades after its dissolution, women who were in the collective put together a book of testimonies in which various of its members speak to the impact MAGIN had on their lives, and particularly on them as women. See Rubiera and Moro, *MAGIN.* For a further discussion of MAGIN, see Fernández, "Transnationalism and Feminist Activism."

26   Interview with Sor Alicia at Asilo Santovenia, Havana, March 2016.

27   Interview with Graziella Pogolotti, Havana, April 2016.

8. CHILDREN

1   Interview with Mariíta Trasancos, Havana, August 2014.

2   Interview with Consuelo Elba, Amherst, November 2015.

3   Sonnia herself had not been imprisoned during the insurgency.

4   Interview with Sonnia Moro, Havana, January 2012. Sonnia included the interview she did with her granddaughter as the conclusion of her autobiography.

5   Interview with Mariana Pita Rodríguez, Havana, January 2012.

6   Alegría de Pío was the site of the first encounter with Batista's army after the rebels reached the Sierra Maestra mountains on December 5, 1956. The Second Front was established on March 1958 under the leadership of Raúl Castro in the Sierra Cristal mountains in the eastern province of Holguín. The rebel column headed by Che arrived in Santa Clara at the end of December 1958. The battle that ensued, resulting in Che's seizure of the city, is seen as the critical final blow to the dictatorship. Batista would flee Cuba on December 31, 1958.

7   Interview with Alina González, Havana, January 2012.

8   Mónica Alfonso, during a meeting of the Club Martiano de Herencia Rebelde, Havana, March 2014.

9   Interview with José (Pepito) Robustillo, Havana, March 2014.

10 Interview with Iya Meznarova, Havana, January 2012.

11 Interview with Renata Meznarova, Havana, January 2012.

12 Interview with Odalys Villafranca, Havana, April 2014.

13 I interviewed Nilda Ravelo multiple times in addition to extensive conversations over the course of my work on this project. As far as I know, there are no other recordings of her.

14 Interview with Odalys Villafranca, Havana, March 2014.

15 Mónica Alfonso, at a meeting of the Club Martiano de Herencia Rebelde, Havana, March 2016.

16 Interview with Alina González, Havana, January 2012.

17 The *Granma* was to land on November 30, but it veered off course and landed December 2 at the wrong place.

18 Interviews with Carlos Pino, Havana, April 2011 and March 2012.

19 Interview with Natalia Bolívar, Havana, March 2014.

20 Interview with Mirta Rodríguez Calderón, Amherst, April 2012.

21 Interview with Mariana Pita Rodríguez, Havana, January 2012.

22 Interview with Mirta Rodríguez Calderón, Amherst, April 2012.

23 Two weeks earlier, Renata, Iya, and I had stopped at the Fifth Police Station (now a school) and spoken to its administrator. A day or two later, we told Pilar about our visit. She then decided that, accompanied by the three of us, she would go back to the station for the first time since she had been imprisoned there. She never uttered a word about this visit after it was over.

EPILOGUE

1   This story was told to me by Graciela Aguiar, América's closest friend, who was with her on that shopping trip and heard, with her, the bullets that killed Frank País.

2   Interview with Dianita Ramonín Domitro, Havana, January 2013.

BIBLIOGRAPHY

Abreu Cardet, José. *Las fronteras de la guerra: Mujeres, soldados y regionalismo en el 68.* Santiago de Cuba: Editorial Oriente, 2007.

Abreu Cardet, José. *Los senderos de la pasión.* Holguín: Ediciones Holguín, 2010.

Abreu Cardet, José. "Sexo y resistencia en la Guerra del 68 en Cuba." *Gaceta* 6 (November/December 2010): 51–53.

Ahmad, Eqbal. "Radical but Wrong." In *The Selected Writings of Eqbal Ahmad*, edited by Carolee Bengelsdorf, Margaret Cerullo, and Yogesh Chandrani. New York: Columbia University Press, 2006.

Alfonso Parodi, Rosario. "Entrevista a Alba Molina." Unpublished manuscript.

Alfonso Parodi, Rosario. "Entrevista a Zaida Trimino." Unpublished manuscript.

Alfonso Parodi, Rosario. "Las mujeres en el Directorio Revolucionario: Marta Jiménez Martínez." Unpublished manuscript.

Álvarez Estévez, Rolando. "De la Operación Fangio: Acción revolucionaria a recordar." Radio Cubana. https://www.radiocubana.cu.

Álvarez Estévez, Rolando. *Un día en abril de 1958.* Havana: Letras Cubanas, 2008.

Anderson, John Lee. *Che Guevara: A Revolutionary Life.* New York: Grove, 1997.

Angulo, Walfredo. "'Soy solo un sobreviviente': Entrevista a Julio García Oliveras." *Temas* (October–December 2008).

Anillo, René. *Que nuestra sangre señale el camino.* Havana: Casa Editora Abril, 2011.

Aresti Esteban, Nerea. "A la nación por la masculinidad: Una mirada de género a la crisis del 98." In *Feminidades y masculinidades: Arquetipos y prácticas de género*, edited by Mary Nash. Madrid: Alianza Editorial, 2014.

Arguelles Almenares, Oraima Bárbara. "Momentos de la imagen pictórica de Mariana Grajales Cuello." In *Mariana Grajales Cuello: Doscientos años en la historia y la memoria*, edited by Damaris Torres Elers and Israel Escalona. Santiago de Cuba: Ediciones Santiago, 2015.

Barcia, María del Carmen. *Capas populares y modernidad en Cuba 1878–1930.* Havana: Ediciones de Ciencias Sociales, 2009.

Barcia, María del Carmen. *Mujeres al margen de la historia.* Havana: Editorial de Ciencias Sociales, 2009.

Bayard de Volo, Lorraine. *Mothers of Heroes and Martyrs: Gender Identity Politics in Nicaragua 1979–1999*. Baltimore, MD: Johns Hopkins University Press, 2001.

Bayard de Volo, Lorraine. *Women and the Cuban Insurrection: How Gender Shaped Castro's Victory*. Cambridge: Cambridge University Press, 2018.

Bell Lara, José, Tania Caram, Dirk Kruijt, and Delia López. *Combatientes*. Havana: Editorial Ciencias Sociales, 2014.

Bell Lara, José, Tania Caram, Dirk Kruijt, and Delia López. *Cuba: La generación revolucionaria 1952–1961*. Havana: Editorial Félix Varela, 2012.

Bell Lara, José, Tania Caram, Dirk Kruijt, and Delia López. *Cuba: Las mujeres en la insurrección, 1952–61*. Havana: Ediciones Félix Varela, 2002.

Bell Lara, José, Tania Caram, Dirk Kruijt, and Delia López. *Fase insurreccional de la revolución cubana*. Havana: Editorial Ciencias Sociales, 2007.

Bengelsdorf, Carollee. *The Problem of Democracy in Cuba: Between Vision and Reality*. New York: Oxford University Press, 1994.

Benson, Devyn Spence. *Antiracism in Cuba: The Unfinished Revolution*. Chapel Hill: University of North Carolina Press, 2016.

Blancomer, León Rosabal. *La voz del mambí: Imagen y mito*. Havana: Editorial de Ciencias Sociales, 1997.

Bolívar, Natalia. "De bellas (y malas) artes." *Revista UNION*, no. 82 (2004): 34–49.

Bolívar, Natalia, and Natalia del Río Bolívar. *La muerte es principio, no fin: Quintín Banderas*. Panama City: Editorial Mercie Ediciones S.A., 2004.

Bonachea, Ramón, and Marta San Martín. *The Cuban Insurrection 1952–1959*. New Brunswick, NJ: Transaction Books, 1974.

Bonachea, Ramón, Marta San Martín, and Nelson Valdes, eds. *Revolutionary Struggle 1947–1958*. Cambridge, MA: MIT Press, 1972.

Bouvard, Marguerite. *Revolutionary Motherhood: The Mothers of the Plaza de Mayo*. Wilmington, DE: Scholarly Resources, 1994.

Bustamante, Michael J. *Cuban Memory Wars*. Chapel Hill: University of North Carolina Press, 2021.

Butler, Judith. *Bodies That Matter: On the Discursive Limits of Sex*. London: Routledge, 1993.

Caballero, Armando. *La mujer en el 68*. Havana: Editorial Gente Nueva, 1978.

Caballero, Armando. *La mujer en el 95*. Havana: Editorial Gente Nueva, 1982.

Cairo, Ana. "Emilia Casanova y la dignidad de la mujer cubana." In *Mujeres latinoamericanas: Historia y cultura*, edited by Luisa Campuzano. Havana: Casa de las Américas/UAM, 1997.

Calvo González, Patricia. "Percepciones de la Sierra Maestra, la visión de la insurrección cubana 1957–58 a través de los periodistas latinoamericanos." *Revista Internacional de Historia de la Comunicación*, no. 7 (2016): 92–115.

Camin, Manuel. "Por un momento pensé que los secuestradores querían llevarme para la Sierra." *Excelsior* (Mexico), February 24, 1958.

Caplan, Caren, Norma Alarcón, and Minoo Moallen, eds. *Between Woman and Nation*. Durham, NC: Duke University Press, 1999.

Casa de las América. *La sierra y el llano*. Havana: Casa de las Américas, 1969.

Castañeda, Jorge. *Compañero: The Life and Death of Che Guevara*. New York: Alfred A. Knopf, 1977.

Castro Porta, Carmen, et al. "Carta a Olga Roman." March 1956. Unpublished manuscript. Archivo Rosa Mier.

Castro Porta, Carmen, et al. "Carta a su hermana Raquel, Nueva Gerona." June 12, 1932. Unpublished manuscript. Archivo Rosa Mier.

Castro Porta, Carmen, et al. *La lección del Maestro*. Havana: Oficina de Publicaciones del Consejo del Estado, 2010.

Castro Porta, Carmen, et al. "Recuerdos de mis prisiones." Isla de Pinos, 1932, Machadato, Prisión Nueva Gerona. Unpublished manuscript. Archivo de Rosa Mier.

Cento, Elda. *Nadie puede ser indiferente: Miradas a las guerras de 1868–1898*. Santiago de Cuba: Ediciones Oriente, 2013.

Cento, Elda, and José Abreu Cardet. *Matar al mambí: Documentos de la ofensiva española en el Camagüey (1870)*. Camagüey: Editorial Ácana, 2015.

Chase, Michelle. *Revolution Within the Revolution: Women and Gender Politics in Cuba 1952–1962*. Chapel Hill: University of North Carolina Press, 2015.

Chase, Michelle. "Women's Organizations and the Politics of Gender in Cuba's Urban Insurrection 1952–1958." *Latin American Research Bulletin* 29, no. 4 (October 2010): 440–58.

Confino, Alón. "Collective Memory and Cultural History: Problems of Method." *American Historical Review* 102 (December 1997).

Connell, R. W., and J. W. Messerschmidt. "Hegemonic Masculinity: Rethinking the Concept." *Gender and Society* 19, no. 6 (2005): 829–59.

Cooke, Miriam, and Angela Woollacott, eds. *Gendering War Talk*. Princeton, NJ: Princeton University Press, 1993.

Cuesta Braniella, José María. *La resistencia cívica en la guerra de la liberación de Cuba*. Havana: Editorial Ciencias Sociales, 1997.

Cushion, Steve. *The Hidden History of the Cuban Revolution: How the Working Class Shaped the Guerrilla Victory*. New York: Monthly Review Press, 2016.

Dávila, Rolando. *Los días y los años*. Havana: Ediciones UNION, 1983.

Dávila, Rolando. *Lucharemos hasta el final: Cronología 1955*. Havana: Oficina de Publicaciones del Consejo de Estado, 2011.

Dávila, Rolando. *Lucharemos hasta el final: Cronología 1956*. Havana: Oficina de Publicaciones del Consejo de Estado, 2012.

Dávila, Rolando. *Lucharemos hasta el final: Cronología 1957*. Havana: Oficina de Publicaciones del Consejo de Estado, 2013.

Deere, Carmen Diana, and Magdalena León. "Empowering Women: Land and Property Rights in Latin America." Pittsburgh: University of Pittsburgh Research Library Digital Editions, 2009.

de la Fuente, Alejandro. *A Nation for All: Race, Inequality, and Politics in Twentieth-Century Cuba*. Chapel Hill: University of North Carolina Press, 2001.

de la Osa, Enrique. *En Cuba: Tercer tiempo 1955–1958*. Havana: Editorial Ciencias Sociales, 2009.

Díaz Vallina, Elvira, and Julio César González Pagés. "The Self Emancipation of Women." In *Cuban Transitions in the Millennium*, edited by Eloise Linger and John Cotman. Largo, MD: International Development Options, 2000.

Díaz Vallina, Elvira, Olga Dotre Romay, and Caridad Dacosta Pérez. "La mujer revolucionaria en Cuba durante el período insurreccional 1952–1958." *Ciencias Sociales* (Puerto Rico), June 1997, 24–32.

Dore, Elizabeth, ed. *Gender Politics in Latin America: Debates in Theory and Practice*. New York: Monthly Review Press, 1997.

Esperón, Hidelisa. "Entrevista a Aida Pelayo, dirigente del FCMM." 1994. Unpublished manuscript.

Esperón, Hidelisa. "Entrevista a la compañera Mercedes Castro Carluch, compañera de luchas de Machaco Ameijeiras and José Antonio Fernández." August 1993. Unpublished manuscript.

Farber, Samuel. *The Cuban Revolution Reconsidered*. Chapel Hill: University of North Carolina Press, 2006.

Farber, Samuel. *Revolution and Reaction in Cuba, 1933–1960: A Political Sociology from Machado to Castro*. Middletown, CT: Wesleyan University Press, 1976.

Fernández, Sujatha. "Transnationalism and Feminist Activism: The Case of MAGIN." *Politics and Gender* 1, no. 3 (September 2005): 431–52.

Fernández Soneira, Teresa. *Mujeres de la patria: Contribución de la mujer a la independencia de Cuba*. Vol. 1. Miami: Ediciones Universal, 2014.

Ferrer, Ada. *Freedom's Mirror: Cuba and Haiti in the Age of Revolution*. New York: Cambridge University Press, 2014.

Ferrer, Ada. *Insurgent Cuba: Race, Nation, and Revolution, 1868–1898*. Chapel Hill: University of North Carolina Press, 1999.

Ferrer, Ada. "Raza, religión y género en la Cuba rebelde: Quintín Banderas y la cuestión del liderazgo político." In *Espacios, silencios y los sentidos de la libertad: Cuba entre 1878 y 1912*, edited by Fernando

Martínez Heredia, Rebecca Scott, and Orlando García Martínez. Havana: Ediciones UNION, 2001.

Finch, Aisha. *Rethinking Slave Rebellion in Cuba: La Escalera and the Insurgencies of 1841–1844*. Chapel Hill: University of North Carolina Press, 2015.

Fischer, Sybille. *Modernity Disavowed*. Durham, NC: Duke University Press, 2004.

Flint, Grover. *Marchando con Gómez*. Havana: Editorial Ciencias Sociales, 1983.

Fondo Documental ICRC Provincia de Havana. "Síntesis biográfica de asesinados por la tiranía en el año 1958 vinculados a la capital." Havana: Marzo, 2013.

Franco, Jean. *Critical Passions: Selected Essays*. Durham, NC: Duke University Press, 1999.

Franco, Jean. *Cruel Modernity*. Durham, NC: Duke University Press, 2013.

Franco, Jean. *Trapped in Bad Scripts: The Mothers of the Plaza de Mayo*. Durham, NC: Duke University Press, 1997.

Franqui, Carlos. *Cuba, la revolución: ¿Mito o realidad? Memorias de un fantasma socialista*. Barcelona: Ediciones Península, 2006.

Franqui, Carlos. *Diario de la revolución cubana*. Barcelona: Ediciones R. Torres, 1976.

Franqui, Carlos. *Family Portrait with Fidel*. New York: Vintage, 1985.

Franqui, Carlos. *The Twelve*. New York: Lyle Stuart, 1968.

Frayde, Marta. "Cuba vive un momento de parálisis política total: Interview with Wilfredo Cancio Isla." *El Nuevo Herald* (Spain), January 5, 2009.

Gálvez, William. *Frank entre el sol y la montaña*. Havana: Ediciones UNION, 1991.

García Olivera, Julio. *José Antonio Echeverría: La lucha estudiantil contra Batista*. Havana: Editora Política, 1980.

García Pérez, Gladys Marel. "Cuba siglo XX. Historia de vida y familia: Eva Jiménez." *Revista Brasileira do Caribe*. Centro de Estudios de Caribe no Brasil, Universidad de Federal de Goias, Goiania, 2008.

García Pérez, Gladys Marel. *Insurrección y revolución 1952–1959*. Havana: Ediciones UNION, 2006.

García Pérez, Gladys Marel. "Memoria e identidad: Un estudio específico 1952–1958, ensayo." Havana: Editorial Ciencias Sociales, 1996.

García Pérez, Gladys Marel. "Mujer y revolución: Una perspectiva desde la insurgencia (1952–1959)." 2009. Unpublished manuscript.

Gómez de Avellaneda, Gertrudis. *Sab and Autobiography*. Translated by Nina Scott. Austin: University of Texas Press, 1993.

González Barrios, René. *Apuntes autobiográficos de la vida de Ricardo Batrell Oviedo*. Havana: Editorial Ciencias Sociales, 2014.

González Pagés, Julio César. *En busca de un espacio: Historia de mujeres en Cuba.* Havana: Editorial de Ciencias Sociales, 2005.

Graña Eirez, Manuel. *Clandestinos en prisión.* Havana: Editorial de Ciencias Sociales, 2008.

Guanche, Julio César. *La libertad como destino: Valores, proyectos y tradición en el siglo XX cubano.* Havana: Ediciones UNION, 2013.

Guede, Emilio. *Cuba: La revolución que no fue.* N.p.: Original Books, 2012.

Guerra, Lillian. *Heroes, Martyrs and Political Messiahs in Revolutionary Cuba, 1946–1958.* New Haven, CT: Yale University Press, 2018.

Guerra, Lillian. "Searching for the Messiah." In *The Revolution from Within: Cuba 1959–1980,* edited by Michael Bustamente and Jennifer Lambe. Durham, NC: Duke University Press, 2019.

Guerra, Lillian. *Visions of Power in Cuba: Revolution, Redemption and Resistance, 1959–1971.* Chapel Hill: University of North Carolina Press, 2012.

Guevara, Ernesto. *Episodes of the Revolutionary War.* New York: International Publishers, 1963.

Guevara, Ernesto. *Guerrilla Warfare.* 3rd ed. With introduction and case studies by Brian Loveman and Thomas M. Davies Jr. Lanham, MD: SR Books, 1997.

Hamilton, Carrie. *Sexual Revolutions in Cuba.* Chapel Hill: University of North Carolina Press, 2009.

Hansen, Jonathan M. *Young Castro: The Making of a Revolutionary.* New York: Simon and Schuster, 2019.

Hart Dávalos, Armando. *Aldabonazo.* Havana: Editorial Ciencias Sociales, 2006.

Helg, Aline. *Our Rightful Share: The Afro-Cuban Struggle for Equality, 1886–1902.* Chapel Hill: University of North Carolina Press, 1995.

Hernández Alonso, Indira. "Ana Betancourt: Encasillada en la historia." http://islalsur.blogia.com/2017/042704-ana-betancourt-encasillada-en-la-historia.php.

Herrera, Georgina. *Penúltimo sueño de Mariana.* Havana: Editorial Letras Cubanas, 2005.

Ibarra, Jorge. *Prologue to Revolution: Cuba, 1898–1958.* Boulder, CO: Lynne Rienner, 1998.

Jelin, Elizabeth. "Citizenship and Identity." In *Women and Social Change in Latin America,* edited by Elizabeth Jelin. Atlantic Heights, NJ: Zed Books, 1990.

Jiménez, Guillermo. "Despedida de duelo de Marta Jiménez." March 3, 2016.

Johnson, Sherry. *The Social Transformation of Eighteenth Century Cuba.* Gainesville: University of Florida Press, 2001.

Kampwirth, Karen. *Feminism and the Legacy of Revolution: Nicaragua, El Salvador, Chiapas.* Athens: Ohio University Press, 2004.

Kampwirth, Karen. *Women in Guerrilla Movements: Nicaragua, El Salvador, Chiapas, Cuba*. University Park: Pennsylvania State University Press, 2002.

Kampwirth, Karen, A. Mufti, and Ella Shohat, eds. *Dangerous Liaisons: Gender, Race, and Postcolonial Perspectives*. Minneapolis: University of Minnesota Press.

Kaplan, Leslie. *Depuis maintenant: Miss Nobody Knows*. Paris: P.O.L., 1996.

Karol, K. S. *Guerrillas in Power: The Course of the Cuban Revolution*. New York: Hill and Wang, 1970.

Klouzal, Linda. *Women and Rebel Communities in the Cuban Insurgent Movement, 1952–1959*. Amherst, NY: Cambria, 2008.

Kruijt, Dirk. *Cuba and Revolutionary Latin America: An Oral History*. London: Zed, 2017.

Kutzinski, Vera. *Sugar's Secrets: Race and the Erotics of Cuban Nationalism*. Charlottesville: University of Virginia Press, 1993.

Leyva Pagan, Georgina. *Historia de una gesta libertadora 1952–1959*. Havana: Editorial Ciencias Sociales, 2014.

Loveman, Brian, and Thomas M. Davies Jr. "Introduction: *Guerrilla Warfare*, Revolutionary Theory, and Revolutionary Movements in Latin America." In *Guerrilla Warfare*, by Che Guevara, 3rd ed. Lanham, MD: SR Books, 1997.

Loynaz del Castillo, Enrique. "La mujer cubana: María Cabrales de Maceo." In *Epistolario de héroes*, edited by Gonzalo Cabrales. Havana: Editorial Ciencias Sociales, 1996.

Maloof, Judy. *Voices of Resistance: Testimonies of Cuban and Chilean Women*. Lexington: University Press of Kentucky, 1999.

Mangini, Shirley. *Memories of Resistance: Women's Voices in the Spanish Civil War*. New Haven, CT: Yale University Press, 1995.

Martí, José. *Obras completas, tomo IV*. 2nd ed. Havana: Editorial Ciencias Sociales, 1991.

Martínez Heredia, Fernando. *La revolución cubana del 30: Ensayos*. Havana: Editorial Ciencias Sociales, 2007.

Matthews, Herbert. *The Cuban Story*. New York: George Brazillier, 1961.

Mazola, Geraldo. "La noche de las cien bombas." *Bohemia*, November 15, 2012.

McClintock, Anne. *Imperial Leather: Race, Gender, and Sexuality in the Colonial Contest*. Minneapolis: University of Minnesota Press, 1995.

Méndez, Roberto, and Ana María Pérez Pino. *Amalia Simoni: Una vida oculta*. Havana: Editorial Ciencias Sociales, 2001.

Meyer, Eugenia. *El futuro era nuestro: Ocho cubanas narran sus historias de vida*. Mexico City: Fondo de Cultura Económica, 2007.

"Modesto homenaje a Faustino." *Dedeté* 21/12/27 (1992).

Montejo, Carmen. "Minerva: A Magazine for Women (and Men) of Color." In *Between Race and Nation*, edited by Lis Brock and Digna Castaneda. Philadelphia: Temple University Press, 1998.

Montenegro, Emma. "Como fue secuestrado Fangio." *Bohemia*, January 18–25, 1959, 76–78.

Montero Sánchez, Susana. *La cara oculta de la identidad nacional*. Santiago de Cuba: Editorial Oriente.

Montero Sánchez, Susana. *Los huecos negros del discurso patriarcal*. Havana: Editorial Ciencias Sociales, 2007.

Moran Arce, Lucas. *La revolución cubana, 1953–1959: Una versión rebelde*. Ponce, Puerto Rico: Imprenta Universitaria, 1980.

Moro, Sonnia. *Nostalgias de una niña habanera de ciudad*. Havana: Ediciones La Memoria, Centro Cultural Pablo de la Torriente Brau, 2006.

Mouffe, Chantal. "Hegemony and New Political Subjects: Towards a New Concept of Democracy." In *Marxism and the Interpretation of Culture*, edited by Cary Nelson and Lawrence Grossberg. Urbana: University of Illinois Press, 1988.

Mouffe, Chantal. *The Return of the Political*. London: Verso, 1993.

Nagel, J. "Masculinity and Nationalism: Gender and Sexuality in the Making of Nations." *Ethnicity and Racial Studies* 2, no. 21 (1998).

Nieves Rivera, Dolores. *Rogito*. Havana: Editora Política, 1981.

Nora, Pierre. "Between Memory and History Les Lieux de Memoire." *Representations* 26 (Spring 1989): 7–24.

Nuiry Sánchez, Juan. *Tradición y combate: Una década en la memoria*. Havana: Editorial Imagen Contemporánea, 2007.

Núñez Pichardo, Hortensia. "Mariana Grajales y Antonio Maceo: Notas sobre una relación ejemplar." *Mariana* (Santiago), 2015.

Oltuski, Enrique. *Gente del llano*. Havana: Ediciones Imagen Contemporánea, 2000.

Oltuski, Enrique. *Vida Clandestina: My Life in the Cuban Revolution*. New York: Wiley and Sons, 2002.

Oltuski, Enrique, Héctor Rodríguez Llompart, and Eduardo Torres Cuevas. *Memorias de la revolución*. Havana: Ediciones Imagen Contemporánea, 2007.

O'Reilly, James. *The Mambi-land or Adventures of a Herald Correspondent in Cuba*. Philadelphia: Lippincott, 1874.

Padrón, Abelardo. *Mambisadas*. Havana: Editorial Gente Nueva, 1985.

Padrón, Abelardo, and Héctor Terry. "Desnutridos y victoriosos." Unpublished manuscript.

Paterson, Thomas. *Contesting Castro: The United States and the Triumph of the Cuban Revolution*. New York: Oxford University Press, 1994.

Pérez, Louis, Jr. *Army Politics in Cuba, 1898–1958*. Pittsburgh: University of Pittsburgh Press, 1976.

Pérez, Louis, Jr. *Cuba in the American Imagination*. Chapel Hill: University of North Carolina Press, 2008.

Pérez, Louis, Jr. "In the Service of the Revolution: Two Decades of Cuban Historiography 1959–1979." *Hispanic American Review* 60, no. 1 (February 1980): 79–89.

Pérez, Louis, Jr. *Intimations of Modernity: Civil Culture in Nineteenth Century Cuba*. Chapel Hill: University of North Carolina Press, 2017.

Pérez, Louis, Jr. *On Becoming Cuban*. Chapel Hill: University of North Carolina Press, 1999.

Pérez, Louis, Jr. *The Structure of Cuban History*. Chapel Hill: University of North Carolina Press, 2013.

Pérez, Louis, Jr. *To Die in Cuba: Suicide and Society*. Chapel Hill: University of North Carolina Press, 2005.

Pérez, Louis, Jr. "Women in the Cuban Revolutionary War, 1953–1958: A Bibliography." *Science and Society* 39, no. 1 (Spring 1975): 104–8.

Pérez-Stable, Marifeli. *The Cuban Revolution: Origins, Course and Legacy*. New York: Oxford University Press, 1993.

Pérez-Stable, Marifeli. "Cuban Women and the Struggle for 'Conciencia.'" *Cuban Studies* 17 (1987): 51–72.

Pérez Valdés, Rafael. "Yo le manejé a Fangio aquella noche." *Bohemia*, February 23, 2018.

Portelli, Alessandro. *The Death of Luigi Trastulli and Other Stories: Form and Meaning in Oral History*. Albany: State University of New York Press, 1991.

Prado, Pedro. *La secretaria de la república*. Havana: Editorial Ciencias Sociales, 2001.

Prados-Torreira, Teresa. *Mambisas: Rebel Women in Nineteenth Century Cuba*. Gainesville: University of Florida Press, 2006.

Pratt, Mary Louise. "Género y ciudadanía: Las mujeres en el diálogo con la nación." In *Esplendores y miserias del siglo XIX: Cultura y sociedad en América Latina*, edited by Beatriz González, Javier Lasarte, Graciela Montaldo, and María Julia Daroqui. Venezuela: Monte Ávila Editores Latinoamericana–Universidad Simón Bolívar, 1995.

Ramírez Chicharro, Manuel. "Desde la clandestinidad: Una historia oral de las mujeres cubanas que lucharon contra Batista." *Ibero-Americana Pragensia*, Supp. 44 (2016): 283–89. https://www.researchgate.net/publication/319193138.

Rhode, Deborah. "The Politics of Paradigms: Gender Difference and Gender Disadvantage." In *Feminism and Politics*, edited by Anne Phillips. Oxford: Oxford University Press, 1998.

Rodríguez, Arnol. *Operación Fangio*. Havana: Editorial Ciencias Sociales, 2005.

Rodríguez, Juan Carlos, and Marilyn Maira Rodríguez, eds. *Vilma: Una vida extraordinaria*. Havana: Editorial Capitán San Luis, 2013.

Rodríguez, Rolando. *Bajo la piel de la manigua*. Havana: Editorial Ciencias Sociales, 2015.

Rodríguez Acosta, Olga. "Carmen Castro." *El Mundo*, August 1932. Archivo Rosa Mier.

Rodríguez Astiazaraín, Nicolás. *Episodios de la lucha clandestina en La Habana 1955–1958*. Havana: Editorial Ciencias Sociales, 2009.

Rodríguez Calderón, Mirta. "Apuntes para la memoria necesaria: Torturados." In *Semillas de fuego*. Havana: Editorial Ciencias Sociales, 1989.

Rodríguez Calderón, Mirta, et al. "Carmen Castro: Una mujer des tres dictadura." Unpublished manuscript.

Rodríguez Calderón, Mirta. "De estrellas en las frentes." In *Semillas de fuego*. Havana: Editorial Ciencias Sociales, 1989.

Rodríguez Calderón, Mirta. "El hombre que salvó a los muertos." In *Semillas de fuego*. Havana: Editorial Ciencias Sociales, 1989.

Rodríguez Calderón, Mirta. "La huelga de hambre de los presos políticos." February 1958. Unpublished manuscript.

Rodríguez Calderón, Mirta. "Muchachas en el clandestinaje: Una mirada a los heroísmos de las más jóvenes." Unpublished manuscript.

Rodríguez Calderón, Mirta. "No permitir que nadie escriba otro final." Speech at Hampshire College, April 17, 2015.

Rodríguez Calderón, Mirta. "Pastorita Núñez: Pupila frente a pupila." *Bohemia*, February 10, 1989, 34–41.

Rodríguez Calderón, Mirta. "Un reves que se convirtio en victoria: Entrevista al Dr. Faustino Perez." In *Semillas de fuego*, vol. 2. Havana: Editorial Ciencias Sociales, 1990.

Rodríguez Llompart, Héctor, and Enrique Hart Dávalos. *Vitalidad inquieta y desbordante*. Havana: Oficina de Publicaciones del Consejo de Estado, 2015.

Rosabal García, Julio César. "El movimiento revolucionario 26 de julio desde las zonas urbanas durante la guerra de liberación nacional." PhD diss., University of Havana, 2013.

Ross, Kristin. *May '68 and Its Afterlives*. Chicago: University of Chicago Press, 2002.

Roy, Arundhati. "Come September." Lannan Foundation lecture, Lensic Performing Arts Center, Santa Fe, NM, September 18, 2002.

Rubiera, Daisy. "El discurso femenino negro de reivindicación (1888–1958)." In *Emergiendo del Silencio: Mujeres negras en la historia de Cuba*, edited by Oilda Hevia Lanier and Daisy Rubiera. Havana: Editorial Ciencias Sociales, 2016.

Rubiera, Daisy, and Sonnia Moro. *MAGIN: Tiempo para contar esta historia*. Havana: Ediciones Magín, 2015.

Rubin, Gayle. "The Traffic in Women: Notes Toward a 'Political Economy' of Sex." In *Woman, Culture, and Society*, edited by Michelle Zimbalist Rosaldo and Louise Lamphere. Stanford, CA: Stanford University Press, 1974.

Sánchez Fusjishiro, Lidia, and Lídice Duany Destrade. "Mariana Grajales Cuello, ¿mujer de su época?" In *Mariana Grajales Cuello: Doscientos años en la historia y la memoria*, edited by Torres Elers and Israel Escalona. Santiago de Cuba: Ediciones Santiago, 2015.

Sarabia, Nydia. *Ana Betancourt Agramonte*. Havana: Editorial Ciencias Sociales, 1970.

Sarabia, Nydia. *Historia de una familia mambisa: Mariana Grajales*. Havana: Instituto Cubano del Libro, 1975.

Sarabia, Nydia. *La patriota del silencio*. Havana: Editorial Ciencias Sociales, 1990.

Sarabia, Nydia. *Tras la huella de los héroes*. Havana: Editorial Gente Nueva, 1980.

Sarmiento Ramírez, Ismael. *El ingenio del mambí, tomos I y II*. Santiago de Cuba: Editorial Oriente, 2008.

Saward, Joe. "How Fidel Kidnapped the World's Greatest Racer." *Jalopnik*, February 25, 2011.

Scott, Joan. *Gender and the Politics of History*. New York: Columbia University Press, 1988.

Sedgwick, Eve Kosofsky. *Between Men: English Literature and Male Homosocial Desire*. New York: Columbia University Press, 1985.

Semillas de fuego: Compilación sobre la lucha clandestina en la capital, tomos I and II. Havana: Editorial de Ciencias Sociales, 1989.

Shayne, Julie. *The Revolution Question*. New Brunswick, NJ: Rutgers University Press, 2004.

Sierra Madero, Abel. *Del otro lado del espejo: La sexualidad en la construcción de la naciócubana*. Havana: Fondo Cultural Casa de las Américas, 2006.

Sierra Madero, Abel. *La nación sexuada: Relaciones de género y sexo durante la primera mitad de siglo XIX en Cuba*. Havana: Editorial Ciencias Sociales, 2001.

Sippial, Tiffany A. *Celia Sánchez Manduley: The Life and Legacy of a Cuban Revolutionary*. Chapel Hill: University of North Carolina Press, 2020.

Smith, Lois, and Alfred Padula. *Sex and Revolution: Women in Socialist Cuba*. New York: Oxford University Press, 1996.

Sommer, Doris. *Foundational Fictions: The National Romances of Latin America*. Berkeley: University of California Press, 1991.

Sonora Soto, Ivette. "Feminismo y género: El debate historiográfico en Cuba." *Anuario de Hojas de Warmi*, no. 16 (2011). https://raco.cat/index.php/HojasWarmi/article/view/252945.

Spence Benson, Devyn. *Antiracism in Cuba: The Unfinished Revolution*. Chapel Hill: University of North Carolina Press, 2016.

Stoler, Laura. *Carnal Knowledge and Imperial Power: Race and the Intimate in Colonial Rule*. Berkeley: University of California Press, 2002.

Stoler, Laura. *Imperial Debris: On Ruin and Ruination*. Durham, NC: Duke University Press, 2013.

Stoner, K. Lynn. *From the House to the Streets: The Cuban Women's Movement for Legal Reform, 1898–1940*. Durham, NC: Duke University Press, 1991.

Stoner, K. Lynn. "Militant Heroines and the Consecration of the Patriarchal State: The Glorification of Loyalty, Combat and National Suicide in the Making of Cuban National Identity." *Cuban Studies* 34 (2003): 71–96.

Stubbs, Jean. "En busca de Mariana: Raza y género en la nación." In *Mariana Grajales Cuello: Doscientos años en la historia y la memoria*, edited by Damaris Torres Elers and Israel Escalona. Santiago de Cuba: Ediciones Santiago, 2015.

Stubbs, Jean. "Social and Political Motherhood in Cuba: Mariana Grajales Cuello." In *Engendering History*, edited by Verena Shepherd, Bridget Bereton, and Barbara Bailey. New York: St. Martin's, 1995.

Stubbs, Jean, and Pedro Pérez Sarduy. *Afro-Cuba: An Anthology of Cuban Writing on Race, Politics and Culture*. Melbourne: Ocean Press, 2002.

Suárez, Reinaldo. *Dejando jirones de sí mismo*. Havana: Ediciones UNION, 2011.

Suárez, Reinaldo, and Oscar Puig. *La complejidad de la rebeldía*. Havana: Ediciones la Memoria, Centro Cultural Pablo de la Torriente Brau, 2010.

Suarez León, Carmen. "Mariana, rostro de maravilla." In *Mariana Grajales Cuello: Doscientos años en la historia y la memoria*, edited by Damaris Torres Elers and Israel Escalona. Santiago de Cuba: Ediciones Santiago, 2015.

Sweig, Julia. *Inside the Cuban Revolution: Fidel Castro and the Urban Underground*. Cambridge, MA: Harvard University Press, 2002.

Taylor, Diana. "Performing Gender: Las Madres de la Plaza de Mayo." In *Negotiating Performance: Gender, Sexuality, and Theatricality in Latin America*, edited by Diana Taylor and Juan Villegas. Durham, NC: Duke University Press, 1994.

Thomas-Woodard, Tiffany. "'Toward the Gates of Eternity': Celia Sánchez Manduley and the Creation of Cuba's New Woman." *Cuban Studies* 34 (2003).

Torres Elers, Damaris. "Mariana Grajales Cuello: Paradigma de patriotismo y resistencia." In *Mariana Grajales Cuello: Doscientos años en la*

historia y la memoria, edited by Damaris Torres Elers and Israel
Escalona. Santiago de Cuba: Ediciones Santiago, 2015.

Torres Elers, Damaris. "Mujeres en las guerras de independencia: Siempre a
las órdenes de la querida patria." In *Emergiendo del silencio: Mujeres
negras en la historia de Cuba*, edited by Oilda Hevia Lanier and
Daisy Rubeira. Havana: Editorial Ciencias Sociales, 2016.

Valdés Estrella, Mercedes. *Aurelia Castillo: Ética y feminismo*. Havana: Centro Félix Varela, 2008.

Vinant, Raquel. *Las cubanas en la postguerra (1898–1902): Acercamiento a
la reconstrucción de una etapa olvidada*. Havana: Editora Política,
2001.

Wade, Peter. *Race and Sex in Latin America*. London: Pluto, 2009.

Waggoner, Ann Marie. "The Role of Women in the Cuban Wars of
Independence 1868–1898." Master's thesis, Arizona State University,
1988.

Whitney, Robert. *State and Revolution in Cuba: Mass Mobilization and
Political Change, 1920–1940*. Chapel Hill: University of North Carolina Press, 2002.

INDEX

Note: Page locators in italics refer to images in "Clandestinas: A Visual Essay."

194; daughter and, 173; DR and, 64, 69, 77, 142, 144–45, 173, 194; impact of older generations on, 99–100; on the llano, 64; motivation for involvement, 64, 99–100; MOU and, 238n2. *See also* Revolutionary Directorate (DR)

bombing campaigns: 03C campaign, 253n26; cañonazo and, 119, 253n35; Night of One Hundred Bombs, 83, 106–7, 119–21, 141, *216*, 254n46

bonos, 69, 72, 110, 145, 246n35

Bornot, Thelma, 75–76, 81. *See also* 26th of July Movement

BRAC (Bureau for the Repression of Communist Activities), 44–45, 131, 132, 134, 139, 144, 145, 147

Brazil, 147, 237n15

Brothers to the Rescue, 259n25

Bureau for the Repression of Communist Activities (BRAC), 44–45, 131, 132, 134, 139, 144, 145, 147. *See also* Club Martiano de Herencia Rebelde

Bustamante, Michael J., 7

Calviño, Ramón, 138, 169, 256n26

Calvo González, Patricia, 255n59

Cantillo, Carlos, 240n17

Caravan of Liberty, 14, 21, 60–61, 152–53, 235n34, 244n5

Casa de los Combatientes archive, *202–5*, *228–29*

Castro, Fidel: Caravan of Liberty and, 14, 21, 60–61, 152–53, 235n34, 244n5; Carmen Castro and, 34–37, 199, 241n26; *Granma* and, 78–79, 232n16; hero/martyr narratives and, 1–2, 7, 14, 21–22, 57–62, 69, 72, 167; "History Will Absolve Me," 22, 26, 39, 68–69, 89–90, 97, 246n31; the Martianas and, 34–37, 69–70, 90, 161, 164–65, 199, 200, 201, 240n18, 241n26; José Martí and, 78; Moncada attack (1953)

and, 21–22, 35–36, 57–58, 89–90, 163, 246n31; Pastorita Núñez and, 37, 161, 164–65, 168–69, 200, 201; Ortodoxo Party and, 37, 89; Aida Pelayo and, 37, 197, 199; race and, 97; role of women and, 7, 156, 244n7; sierra vs. the llano and, 17, 57–62, 64, 76, 78–79, 127, 231n1; 26th of July Movement and, 67, 72, 73–74, 171, 236n13, 245n14. *See also* Moncada attack (1953)

Castro, Raúl, 59–60, 62, 63–64, 73, 244n7, 260n6

Castro Porta, Carmen (Neneína), *199*; AAA and, 31; armed insurgency and, 33–34, 92; arrests and imprisonment of, 50–51, 135–36, 165, 199; Fidel Castro and, 34–37, 199, 241n26; DR and, 71–72; Galiano protests and, 40–41, 201; on Ramón Grau San Martín, 32–33; humor of, 243n63; impact of older generations on, 33–35, 49, 99; insurgent actions and, 77, 214; Moncada attack (1953) and, 50–51, 199; motivation for involvement, 31, 33–34, 49; organization and strategies of the FCMM and, 30–37, 40–44, 48–49, 71–72, 199, 201, 238n2, 240n18; Ortodoxo Party and, 31; Aida Pelayo and, 46–48, 51, 161–62, 165, 238n2, 240n18, 241n26; godson Carlos Enrique Pelayo and, 45, 241n26; post-revolution life, 45–48, 154, 161–62, 165; torture of, 135; María (Mariíta) Trasancos and, 243n63; on the US, 38–39. *See also* José Martí Women's Civic Front (FCMM)

Cecilia Valdés (Villaverde), 5

Cento, Elda, 8, 232n20

Cero Cabaret, Cero Cine, Cero Compra (OCCC), 253n26

Céspedes, Carlos Manuel de, 4, 87, 231n6

de los Ángeles Afón, Agnes, 123–24, 126, 127. *See also* 26th of July Movement

de los Ángeles Afón, Aimeé, 82, 123. *See also* 26th of July Movement

de los Ángeles Afón, María, 98. *See also* 26th of July Movement

Democratic Federation of Cuban Women (FDMC), 68, 163, 245n28; women's front and, 68

Depuis Maintenant (Kaplan), 152–53

DEU (Directorate of University Students), 11, 242n49, 246n39, 258n11

Díaz, Selma, 82, 94, 155, 172. *See also* Juventud Socialista; Popular Socialist Party (PSP)

Díaz Vallina, Elvira, 65, 82, 95–96, 107–8, 110, 249n14. *See also* Civic Resistance Movement (MCR); Federation of University Students (FEU); 26th of July Movement

Directorate of University Students (DEU), 11, 242n49, 246n39, 258n11

Directorio Revolucionario (DR). *See* Revolutionary Directorate (DR)

Doce, Lidia, 140–41, 257n34

Domitro, América, 16, 62, 177–78, 236n1, 248n1

DR (Directorio Revolucionario). *See* Revolutionary Directorate (DR)

Echeverría, José Antonio, 28–29, 33, 72, 88

Elba, Consuelo, xiv, 82, 155, 166–67, 234n26, 244n6. *See also* Popular Socialist Party (PSP); 26th of July Movement

El Curita (Sergio González), 108, 120–21, 141, *216*, 252n6, 254n39, 254n46

El Príncipe (prison), *226*; clandestina prison visits and, 39, 43, 84–85, 91–93, 102–3, 106, 110–11, 120; hunger strikes, 42–43, 122, 146–47, 150, 213, 214; marriage ceremony

in, 251n68; message passing and, 110–11, 147–51; PSP members and, 69

Episodes of the Revolutionary War (Guevara), 58–60

esbirro, use of term, 16

Esperón, Hidelisa, *190*; arms distribution and, 112–13; arrests and imprisonment, 100, 136–39, 190; clandestina work, 82, 100, 102–3, 109, 112–13; collective trauma and, 158–59; daughter Mónica, 168, 172; entry into movement, 109; impact of older generations on, 100, 103; on Juventud members, 69; Mantilla holding prison and, 150; marriages of, 158–60, 251n68; motivation for involvement, 109; rape and torture of, 100, 137–39; safe house and, 102–3, 109, 138, 158–60, 190, 251n68. *See also* José Martí Women's Civic Front (FCMM); 26th of July Movement

Espín, Vilma, 59–60, 62, 66, 90, 156, 162–63, 244n7

Esso Standard fire, 122, 254n46

Fangio, Juan Manuel, 83, 98, 106–7, 122–27, 254n51, 255n59

Farabundo Martí National Liberation Front (FMLN), 86

FCMM. *See* José Martí Women's Civic Front

FDMC (Democratic Federation of Cuban Women), 68, 163, 245n28

Federación de Estudiantil Universitaria (FEU), 24, 28–29, 33, 49, 146–47, 236n7

Federación Democrática de Mujeres Cubanas (FDMC), 68, 163, 245n28

Federation of Cuban Women (FMC), 162–64, 181, 259n22

Federation of University Students (FEU), 24, 28–29, 33, 49, 146–47, 236n7

and, 21–22, 35–36, 57–58, 89–90,
163, 246n31; communist ideology
and, 67–69; hero/martyr narratives and, 21–22, 57–58, 89–90, 167;
1953 trial, 35, 197; Aida Pelayo and,
35–36, 44–45, 197; Haydée Santamaría and, 19

Morán, Silvina, 123–24, 125. *See also*
26th of July Movement

Moro, Sonnia, *186–87*; April 9 general
strike (1958), 111; on Batista repression, 69, 77; daughter Alina, 167–68,
172; impact of older generations on,
24, 86–87, 88–89, 251n62; MAGIN
and, 164; on José Martí, 86–87, 102;
MNR membership, 84–85; motivation for involvement, 84–85, 88;
post-revolution life, 155; prison
visits by, 111, 226–27; youth/student
activism of, 24, 75, 81, 85, 99, 110,
172. *See also* 26th of July Movement

Morúa (Fernando Alfonso Torices),
33, 74, 92–94, 99, 101–2, 133, 244n76

motherhood: collaborators and,
116–18; FCMM's use of motherhood trope, 38–41, 43–44, 244n5;
mother's marches, 24–25, 206, 207;
torture and, 140, 146–47

MOU (Opposition Women United),
238n2

Movimiento Cívico de Resistencia
(MCR), 65, 71, 84, 107, 219, 245n22

Movimiento Nacional Revolucianario
(MNR), 240n11

Mujeres de la clandestinidad (2016),
xiv, 244n6

Mujeres Oposicionistas Unidas (Opposition Women United), 238n2

National Institute of Savings and
Housing (INAV), 162, 258n17

National Revolutionary Action
(ANR), 28

National Revolutionary Movement
(MNR), 240n11

national strike (1958), 16, 62, 91, 108,
111, 127–29, 200, 247n51

National Students' Front (FEN), 75, 186

National Workers Front (FON), 67, 107

Naval Intelligence Service (SIN), 114,
131, 237n20

Nibot, Mercedes, 138

Nieves, Dolores, 76–77, 104, 116–17,
211

Night of One Hundred Bombs, 83,
106–7, 119–21, 141, *216*, 254n46

Ninth Police Station, 99–100, 115, 121,
134–38, 140–43, 158, 190, 217

Niubo, Blanca, 126

Núñez, Pastorita, *200, 201*; April 9
general strike (1958) and, 75, 168,
200; armed insurgency and, 53,
75, 200, 201; arrests and imprisonment, 41–42, 136; Fidel Castro
and, 37, 161, 164–65, 168–69, 200,
201; Eduardo Chibás and, 53, 201;
Comando Femenino and, 75, 200;
Galiano Street protest, 41–42; impact of older generations on, 31–32;
INAV and, 258n17; Mantilla holding
prison and, 150; motivation for
involvement, 52–53; organization
and strategies of the FCMM and,
30–37, 48–49, 52–53, 71–72, 199,
201, 238n2; Ortodoxo Party and,
31, 53, 201; godson Pepito, 53, 162,
167, 168–69; post-revolution life,
161–62, 164–65; prison visits and,
150–51; PSP and, 69–70, 258n17;
Mirta Rodríguez Calderón and,
30, 136–37. *See also* José Martí
Women's Civic Front (FCMM)

OA (Authentic Organization), 66,
240n18

Olivera, Magaly, 82, 112. *See also*
26th of July Movement

Oltuski, Enrique, 63

One Hundred Days government, 46,
51, 240n12

Operation Fangio, 83, 98, 106–7, 122–27, 254n51, 255n59
Operation Fangio (1987), 125–27
Opposition Women United (MOU), 238n2
Ordoqui, Joaquín, 160, 258n11
Organización Auténtica (OA), 66, 240n18
Organización Revolucionaria Integrada (ORI), 163, 220
Organization of Solidarity with the Peoples of Asia, Africa and Latin America (OSPAAL), 156
ORI (Integrated Revolutionary Organization), 163, 220
Orient Revolutionary Action (ARO), 28
Ortodoxo Party: Carmen Castro and, 31; Fidel Castro and, 37, 89; Eduardo Chibás and, 31, 47, 89, *201*, 236n9; hunger strike and, *219*; internal splits of, 25, 53; Pastorita Núñez and, 31, 53, 201; Women's Front of, 31
OSPAAL (Organization of Solidarity with the Peoples of Asia, Africa and Latin America), 156

País, Frank, 15–16, 28, 62, 73, 177–78, 236n7, 236n13, 260n1
Partido Independiente Color (Independent Party of Color), 250n46
Partido Socialista Popular (PSP). *See* Popular Socialist Party (PSP)
Pelayo, Aida, *196, 197, 211*; Ala Izquierda Estudiantil and, 250n50; arrests and imprisonment, 45, 135, 197, *211*; Carmen Castro and, 46–48, 51, 161–62, 165, 238n2, 240n18, 241n26; Fidel Castro and, 37, 197, 199; documentary on, 241n26; on electoral politics, 47; Moncada attack and, 35–36, 44–45, 197; motivation for involvement, 45–47, 92, 209; organization of José Martí

Women's Civic Front and, 30–38, 44–47, 71–72, 196, 199, 201, 238n2; Plaza de los Desamparados speech, 33; post-revolution life, 46–47, 161–62; as powerful speaker, 36, 44–45, 199, 212; pregnancy and, 242n45; son Carlos Enrique, 36, 45, 48, 52, 165, 241n26; tactics of, 45–48, 52, 115–16, 197; torture of, 135. *See also* José Martí Women's Civic Front (FCMM)
Pelayo, Carlos Enrique, 36, 45, 48, 52, 165, 241n26
Peña, Lázaro, 258n17
Perea Suárez, Rogelio, 76–77
Pérez, Faustino, *35*, 78–79, 108, 141, 148, 154, 212, *217*, 241n23, 245n11. *See also* 26th of July Movement
Pérez, Lolo, *211*
Pérez, Louis, Jr., 3, 28, 90
petardo, use of term, 253n18
PIC (Independent Party of Color), 250n46
Pineda Barnet, Enrique, 257n37
Pino, Carlos, 172–73. *See also* Díaz, Selma
Pino, Quintín, 145, 172
Pino, Verena, 72, 82, 141–42, 145
Pita Rodríguez, Mariana, 167, 174–75
Pita Rodríguez, Turcio, 175–76
Popular Socialist Party (PSP): *Carta Semanal*, 67–68, 69, 144; DR and, 70–71; FDMC and, 163; female insurgents and, 67–72, 94–95, 163, 238n2; the llano and, 66–70; as Marxist left, 47, 69, 245n28; national strike (1958) and, 247n51; 1944 change of name from Cuban Communist Party, 236n7, 245n25; ORI and, 163; Pleno Comité del Nacional del Partido Socialista Popular, 247n51; 26th of July Movement and, 66–70, 246n30; women's front and, 68, 163, 245n28; youth branch, 11, 67–69, 94–95, 172, 234n26, 258n17

Porras, Norma, 9–10, 103–4, 120–21, *215*, 216, 252n 81
Portelli, Alessandro, 13
Presidential Palace attack: DR and, 11, 29, 70–81, 142, 173, 192, 243n59; Humboldt 7 assassination and, 160–61, 192, 258n11; post-attack state repression, 64, 70–71, 91, 98, 128, 258n11; safe houses and, 98, 117–18, 192
PSP. *See* Popular Socialist Party

quemada, use of term, 200

race: Digna Abreu and, 94, 96–97, 134–35, 188; Ana Betancourt on, 7–8; Fidel Castro and, 97; clandestinas and, 95–97, 134–35, 150, 250n46; the llano and, 4–7; PIC and, 250n46; prisons and, 150; race unity and, 4, 6–7, 96–97, 209, 250n50; torture and, 96–97, 134–35
Ramonín Domitro, Dianita, 177–78
rape, 100, 133, 137–40, 256n12
Ravelo, Héctor, 154, 247n51
Ravelo, Nilda, *189, 217, 222, 223*; armed insurgency and, 89, 113–15, 141–42, 212, 217; arrests and imprisonment, 65, 113–15, 149–50, 151, 171–72, 189, 222, *223*; collective trauma and, 158–59; cousin Orieta, 114; impact of older generations on, 89, 171; mother Fela, 114, 171; motivation for involvement, 65, 89, 113–14, 189; niece Odalys, 171–72; Aida Pelayo and, 47–48; post-revolution life, 155, 159, 171–72; prison visits and, 85; student/youth brigades and, 85, 189; as targeted for death, 141. *See also* José Martí Women's Civic Front (FCMM); 26th of July Movement
Revolutionary Directorate (DR): armed insurgency and, 10–11, 28–29, 70–72, 246n39; Natalia Bolívar and, 64, 69, 77, 142, 144–45, 173, 194; Carmen Castro and, 71–72; clandestinas and, 72; Humboldt 7 and, 160–61, 192, 258n11; Guillermo Jiménez, and, 71–72, 98, 118, 159–60; male domination of, 10–11; 1955 pact between José Antonio Echeverría and Fidel Castro, 28–29; ORI and, 163; Presidential Palace attack and, 11, 29, 70–81, 142, 173, 192, 243n59; PSP and, 70–71
Rivas, Dora, 189, 213
Roa, Raúl, 146
Robustillo, Ibia, 53, 162, 165, 168–69
Robustillo, José (Pepito/Pepe), 53, 162, 168–69
Rodríguez, Fructuoso, 88, 160–61, 192, 252n81
Rodríguez, Josefina (Fifi), 82. *See also* José Martí Women's Civic Front (FCMM); 26th of July Movement
Rodríguez, Marcos (Marquitos), 160, 258n11
Rodríguez, Mercedes, *209, 211*, 238n2. *See also* José Martí Women's Civic Front (FCMM)
Rodríguez, Zobeida (Mimi), 82, 244n5. *See also* 26th of July Movement
Rodríguez Calderón, Mirta, *184, 185*; armed insurgency and, 91–93, 115–16, 185; arrests and imprisonment, 43, 50, 116, 136–37, 148, 150, 185, 213; Carmen Castro and, 50; children Mariana and Turcio, 167, 174–76; collective trauma and, 158; Comedores Populares y Escolares, 154; exile of, 64–65, 185; impact of older generations on, 87–88, 136–37; MAGIN and, 164; Sonnia Moro and, 84, 186; motivation for involvement, 84–85, 184, 186; "Muchachas en el clandestinaje," 1; Núñez and, 30, 136–37; organizing of women and, 162–63, 164, 220;

llano leadership and, 17–18; llano vs., 17–18, 63–66, 72–80, 121–22, 127; use of terms, 16–17, 232n1

SIM (Military Intelligence Service), 44–45, 114, 131, 237n20

Simoni, Amalia, 233n21

Simoni, Matilde, 233n21

SIN (Naval Intelligence Service), 114, 131, 237n20

slavery, 4–7, 231n7, 250n33, 256n12

Soler, William, 206

Sommer, Doris, 5

Spanish Civil War, 30, 46, 51, 238n1, 242n51

Stoner, K. Lynn, 232n20

strikes: hunger strikes, 42–43, 49, 122, 146–47, 150, 154, 213, *214, 219,* 236n7; PSP and, 246n30; 26th of July Movement and, 246n30; university strikes, 146. *See also* April 9 general strike (1958)

Student Left Wing (Ala Izquierda Estudiantil), 250n50

Surí, Emma, *211,* 242n55. *See also* José Martí Women's Civic Front (FCMM)

Sweig, Julia, 17, 62, 67, 73, 76, 121

Ten Years' War (War of Independence, 1868–78), 6–7, 9, 231n6, 233n21

Tigres de Masferrer, 131, 255n8

Torices, Fernando Alfonso (Morúa), 33, 74, 92–94, 99, 101–2, 133, 244n76

torture: Batista dictatorship and, 26–28, 76–77, 128–30, 243n61; clandestinas and, 128–31, 140–45; as counterproductive, 146–47; Cuban civil society and, 145–47; logical rationalization of, 130–31, 145–47; purveyors of, 131–33; race and, 96–97, 134–35; random infliction of pain on women, 130–31; rape and, 100, 133, 137–40, 256n12;

sites of, 131, 133–38; use of family informants, 135–36. *See also* El Príncipe (prison); Mantilla holding prison

Trasancos, María (Mariíta), *195, 215;* armed insurgency and, 92–93, 120–21, 142, 216; arrests of, 71, 77, 99, 121, 142, 195; on Carmen Castro, 243n63; children of, 166; El Curita and, 120–21, 140–41, 254n39; impact of older generations on, 85–86, 91, 99, 154; José Martí and, 85–86; motivation for involvement, 85–86, 91–93, 154, 195; Night of One Hundred Bombs and, 120–21, 216; post-revolution life, 154; prison visits and, 85, 91–92, 120; student/youth brigades and, 85, 92–93, 189, 195; torture of, 99, 141–44; Esteban Ventura and, 142–44. *See also* José Martí Women's Civic Front (FCMM); 26th of July Movement

Truth, Sojourner, 8

26th of July Movement: April 9 general strike (1958) and, 16, 62, 72–76, 111, 200, 245n14, 247n51; armed insurgency and, 28, 70–72, 74–75, 247n51; Batista dictatorship and, 21–22; bonos and, 69, 72, 110, 145, 246n35; Fidel Castro and, 67, 72, 73–74, 171, 236n13, 245n14; FCMM and, 10–11, 35; FMC and, 163–64; "History Will Absolve Me" and, 22, 26, 39, 68–69, 89–90, 97; male domination of, 10–11; merger with ARO, 28; Operation Fangio and, 83, 98, 106–7, 122–27, 254n51, 255n59; ORI and, 163; Frank País and, 236n7; PSP and, 66–70, 246n30; Santiago and, 24–25, 66; structure of Action and Sabotage, 107–10; women's front and, 35–36, 154, 162–64, *220;* youth and, 24–25, 195. *See also* Moncada attack (1953)